D1094381

Wyoming Summer

Wyoming Summer

MARY O'HARA

DOUBLEDAY & COMPANY, INC.
GARDEN CITY, NEW YORK

Preface

It must have been when I had lived on the ranch about ten years, keeping a journal intermittently as I always do, that it occurred to me I could weave together enough of these journal entries to make a narrative, with the theme and title of Wyoming Summer.

When I finished it I showed it to a New York publisher. He explained that the public would not be interested in an auto-biographical book by me unless I first acquired a name as an author. He suggested a novel about similar material.

When *My Friend Flicka* proved a success, I should have remembered I had this other book laid away, waiting. But in the excitement I forgot it and went on to other work. It was only a month ago, twenty years later, and by accident, that I found it among some old scripts (January 26, 1962) and began to turn the pages. . . .

When I laid it down I realized that here was the living stuff out of which *My Friend Flicka* and *Thunderhead* and *Green Grass of Wyoming* had been made. Those books had imaginary characters who, however, walked in the footsteps of real people who had lived on that ranch, and did as they had done. If there are readers who enjoyed those books and life on the Goose Bar Ranch, perhaps they may like to visit it again.

Journal entries, to be readable, must be given sequence and continuity. I have done this, condensing some episodes, adding others from other summers. And to put this tale solidly in time and space have added expository paragraphs and chapters. But it is the same ranch, same country, same scenes of epic grandeur, the same animals and their endearing and exciting companionship, the same life.

MARY O'HARA

Chapter 1

Goose Bar Ranch, Wyoming
June 194–

I have walked down to the pasture to look at the bull.

Standing there with the long chain hanging from his nose ring and dragging several feet on the ground he neither eats nor moves. The chain is the only thing that keeps him there. The abundant grass, the cool running stream, the shade trees, his beautiful Guernsey wives—he doesn't want them.

He'd rather be fighting the fences, his coat torn and snagged; rather be on the arid upland ranges walking five hot miles to a waterhole—investigating every ranch and corral in the country—driven home with blows and curses and lashes—

All around us ranchers are raising white-faced Hereford cattle for beef; Burt Langley over the saddleback to the south, Haygood and Pomroy east and west. There is nothing that infuriates a beef grower more than to find a dairy bull in his corrals. Roamer is a dairy bull.

Langley has been making threats which reach us by the country grapevine: If I find that white bull of Bergwin's on my land again, when he gets home he won't be a bull any more—

This is a typical rancher joke and we pay no attention.

All the same—now we have this long chain on Roamer.

As I walked away from him he turned to watch me go and gave a deep moan.

7

I've just come back from New York and I don't feel at home yet.

In New York, when I go there every spring to round up boys for our summer camp, I move from one apartment of my family to another—Reese's, Elma's, Bess's—or the houses and apartments of my friends. I feel like the tumbleweed that drifts across the western plains and can only come to rest when leaning against something else that has a root.

It is woeful, and I can't wait to get back, but now that I'm here it doesn't feel like home, not even inside the house. I wander through it—the house I love so well; Michael and I made it together, or rather, I sketched it and he made it and it's charming; thick stone walls made of the pink granite that is in our hills, fireplaces in every room, cement floors stained like dark oak and highly polished; everything simple and comfortable and odd. But I stand in the middle, as if I was waiting for something, look around as if I was dazed, haven't really unpacked yet—

"How are the calves?" I asked Michael. For these are the first to come from this bull I bought a year ago from the famous Golden Guernsey herd in Colorado.

"Oh, very typy," he said. "The best we've had yet. You must go down to the barn and look at them."

"Yes," I said, but felt listless. I would rather go to the piano. I've hardly touched it since I got home. I haven't dared to. If I should begin it would be hard to stop and attend to my duties.

On that hard, bare piano bench, facing the grand piano, my back to the blue Dutch door that opens out onto the terrace and the Green—that is my place.

In the big, square armchair by the radio, with curving mahogany legs, upholstered in soft blue-gray mohair—that is Michael's place. When I first bought the chair he said, planting himself in it, "I like this chair. It makes me feel pompous." And he patted the padded arms with approval.

It is a solitary chair, removed from the conviviality of the fireplace. There is a small smoking stand beside it. The arm of the chair is exactly the height to support his elbow and allow his hand to reach the pipe in his mouth. Without turning his head

8

he can stare out the door, the top half of which stands open at all times—the sort of fixed stare that proclaims, *I am not here at all . . . my spirit has gone wandering.* If he wants still more release and escape the radio is close beside him, and he has only to turn a knob.

It is usually when he is dead tired that the pompous chair takes and holds him.

I would like to sit down now with Michael and have a real talk with him; tell him all that happened in New York. In fact I'm simply bursting with news. But he is in the midst of a really exciting operation—the drilling of a well so that we shall have more water for the camp, and he can think of nothing else.

Last year, as the summer drew on, he was worried lest our spring run dry. This year he does not intend to be caught short, no matter how dry the season.

So the drillers are here—three strange men in the bunkhouse besides Riley, our regular hand, and old George. George cooks for them.

I did show Michael the list of the new boys who are coming; pulled it out of my pocket as I walked beside him when he took me up the gorge to show me where they are drilling; and I read him the names and told him the ages and what families they come from and the schools they have attended. But he was absent-minded and impatient and hardly listened. He leaves all that to me.

The boys come from the east, and so do I.

All the winters of my childhood were spent in Brooklyn Heights where my father, Reese Fell Alsop, was rector of an Episcopalian church; and all the summers at Deercreek, the Pennsylvania estate of my grandmother, Mary O'Hara Spring.

So the promotion work, the discovery and enrollment of these boys by visits to eastern preparatory schools and meetings with parents, and letters and pictures sent around—all this is for me to do.

But I have still other news. News that is so exciting to me that I wake every morning thinking, Oh what is it? What is it? There's

9

something—something awfully exciting and wonderful has happened!

And then I remember it, and I can feel my face slip in a smile; and if anyone were there I would hide it because I am as thrilled as a child, and proud and triumphant.

First: I've got this new composition I call *Joy in the Morning,* a tone poem, advanced enough, difficult enough for anyone to play in a recital; and it's really lovely; and second: I've sold four teaching pieces for children. *Papoose, When the Wind Blows, Mädchen Tanz, Schuplattle Tanz.* Schirmer will publish them.

Telling this to Michael will be like saying, So you see! After all! For Michael does not think much of my music.

He cries, "The hours and hours you spend at that piano! Or writing down music at your desk! Weeks! Months! Years! And for what? *For what?* Nothing at all!" And he looks worried, compassionate, almost heartbroken for me.

He exclaims again with a harrowed face, "The waste!"

So now I have this to tell him. I'll tell him after dinner tonight . . .

. . . but after dinner he was sitting in the pompous chair and there was a playlet on the radio. He was smoking quietly and his eyes were narrowed. I could see his thoughts were far away so I didn't try to bring him back.

Hilda, the cook I had last summer, has not returned. She is a competent Swedish woman from San Francisco who likes to come up to our altitude for her summer vacations. I must see about getting another. Meanwhile, I have the cooking to do—very hit-or-miss—

Oh, the eternal housework! I tell Michael I might have been better at it but for him—a good soldier is always a good housekeeper.

But he answers, "Not at all. I take over because you don't."

Everything he does is done with a bang. While I am taking my time, setting things in order in a leisurely fashion, no doubt committing the crime of thinking about other things as I work, even of composing music, suddenly he rushes in, there is a lot of

10

noise, great striding about, jovial and teasing shouts, and the job is done. What a great boy am I! The kitchen is tidied in the manner of an officer hurling a regiment over the top.

So this morning before he was awake I rushed at the living room and threw all the small rugs out on the terrace for George to shake. I swept and polished the floor. By the time Michael came down for breakfast the living room was shining and I was standing at the kitchen stove doing the eggs. His hand came over my shoulder, pouring in more butter—

Always such lavishness. I ask for a wheelbarrow of manure for my flower border. There arrives a team of horses drawing a wagonload. I ask for a fire. An armful of kindling is flung on the irons—

Now I am gently pushed away and the skillet is taken out of my hands—

11

Chapter 2

When I wrote my brother Reese, ten years ago, that Michael and I had bought a ranch in Wyoming and were going to raise sheep on it, he cried, How adventuresome you are!

Everyone said the same thing. To leave "the world," the life you were born into and are accustomed to, and go into the wilds —"go west"—what an adventure!

In my heart I too knew it was an adventure—not for always. More suitable, perhaps, for Michael than for me. He had never really got over those years in the war—how could any man? But I too was ready. More than ready. I had Hollywood and ten years of scenario writing to recover from.

So we came here to these great grass plains, and I saw the high tableland of this country, higher in the center, lower on the horizon, so that for the first time I not only knew but felt that the earth is round. And I looked and stared and could not get my fill of gazing at hundreds of miles of rolling upland carpeted with emerald green. It rippled with shadowy lines like watered silk and was overarched with an inverted bowl lined with a deep lapis-lazuli blue. There were masses of dazzling white high-piled clouds with intricate coils and convolutions. Their shadows on the prairie were immense and strangely dark: blue-black, purple, indigo. At first glance there seemed no motion at all. Then one noticed the almost imperceptible drift eastward—clouds and shadows ever moving, ever changing their mysterious shapes. It was a clean and empty world with a slow heartbeat.

If you are lucky with sheep you can make a fortune. But no one was lucky those years. Sheep growers *lost* fortunes. Prices went down. To save the cost of molasses cake and hay and the wages of a sheepherder we sold a couple of thousand at a price per head less than the price of a single lamb chop. Prices still fell. Then we simply turned the remainder out to fend for themselves, and were harrowed by the sight of the little band ganging up outside the corral gates, begging to be taken back and cared for; or, terrified and abandoned, tearing about the prairie, their fleeces ragged and torn—hanging in strips from the attacks of coyotes. They constantly diminished in number; at last, melted away.

So then we thought of horses.

Actually, the ranch was already stocked with horses, for when you buy a ranch in the west, certain brands go with the land. We had the IZ and the Jewish A. This means that, of the hundreds of wild horses that roam the unfenced range of Wyoming, any that bear those brands belong to us. Also the colts that are with them. Sometimes a foal, a yearling, a two-year-old and even a three- and four-year-old. So we didn't know how many horses we had. A hundred? Or two? Or three? And the romantic fact about these wild horses of the west is that they have royal blood in their veins. Descended from the Arab and the Barb, originally brought to Mexico by the Spaniards, they have drifted over the sparsely settled states of our southwest, and northward to the high tablelands where, in summer, the finest tubular grasses are found.

The stock has run down with generations of in-breeding and lack of protection from the elements, but still, the blood tells. They have the short back, the head carried so high and proudly, the nimbleness, speed, the trick of turning on a dime, the ability to endure anything and live on nothing, above all the intelligence that makes of a cow pony a partner and companion, willing and eager to share the work and the very life of his master as the original Arabian horse did—walk right into the tent and lie down beside you.

Michael and I would stand on the topmost ridge up behind the saddleback, scanning the labyrinth of hills rising to the Buckhorn Mountains of Colorado to the south, and the hundreds of miles of rolling grasslands to the west, our eyes seeking out every sign of life—*See there!* A line of ridge-runners strung out across

13

the sky. Or a group of motionless black dots at the base of a hill twenty miles away. *That's horses feeding!* And we thrilled to the possibility that among those catch colts might be a prize. A beauty. A throwback to a prince among horses. That he probably belonged to us and, someday in a round-up, we might get him into the corral and tame him!

Many a cowboy rides a horse comparable to the famous individuals of the Arabian blood lines.

To Michael, whose commission in the war was in the Remount service, the idea of breeding these horses was irresistible.

At all government remount stations they have pure-bred stallions at stud. Choose among these, get the mare into the horse trailer at the proper time—and if she's a wild mare this is quite something to do—and transport her to the station.

But the nearest remount station to our ranch was in Nebraska. Obviously, we would have to have a stallion of our own. So we acquired Blazes, and, over the years a harem of twenty half-tamed mares.

Sheep can be bred and the lamb sold, all within one year. But a horse cannot even carry a rider until he is three. Besides, he must be trained for whatever work he is to do—army, police, polo, racing, saddle, hunting, or harness; otherwise he will not bring a decent price. All this takes three, four or five years—not a very encouraging business prospect. Still, we hoped.

I had noticed that ranchers hereabout were likely to have, no matter what else they raised, a string of milch cows, and to explain it in an offhand manner (half ashamed of it) as just a little side line to carry the overhead. This seemed to me admirable insurance. While Michael struggled with the horses I could take charge of the dairy.

So I bought thirty milch cows and delivered milk in Cheyenne all one year, bringing to the creamery the cleanest milk produced anywhere around.

To feed the cows and produce this superlative milk Michael foraged for feed. Down to Colorado for sugar beets; Nebraska for corn; and (alas!) the elevator for other grains—barley, bran, oats. All these immense distances were covered in a secondhand truck that threatened to fall to pieces at every turn.

14

Winter nights I stood at the window straining my eyes to follow the ranch road northward, lost where it curves around the shoulder of the hill, then emerging again to cross the railroad tracks two miles distant and turn into the Lincoln Highway. Nine o'clock—ten—eleven—midnight—Ah! *There!* Two big headlights glaring—lost again—nothing but the black night and the wind—then the lights again and the clatter of the truck, still holding together but sounding like disaster.

After these terrible journeys Michael's face would be gray, his expression a mingling of shock and fixed amazement.

"That truck!" He sought the right word. "It's just drama—"

I was not without romantic notions about my dairy. I would call it the Mary-Dairy. On the side of the smart delivery truck would be a painting of a beautiful Guernsey cow. Underneath the painting would be the slogan, *That Yellow Cream.*

But actually, I carried the milk to the creamery myself.

The ten-gallon cans were stacked in the trailer, hitched to my car, and I drove the thirty-odd miles to town on the Lincoln Highway.

This fine road (#30) runs east and west across Wyoming close beside the Union Pacific Railroad tracks and is built on a slightly higher level with deep gulches on each side so that its surface can be kept fairly clear of snow, in winter, by the wind.

The tracks are the northern boundary of our long, three-thousand-acre ranch.

I delivered the milk in all weathers. In this altitude of nearly eight thousand feet, this means blizzards, ground blizzards, sub-zero temperatures, and winds of frightening velocity.

It felt, often, as if my car, trailer, milk and all, would be blown into the ditch.

One winter afternoon when I had done all my Cheyenne errands and was about to head for home I noticed that it was far darker than it should be at four o'clock.

Ordinarily, heading west on the Lincoln Highway near the end of the day one faces an orange glow or a blazing sunset. But today I saw a leaden sky everywhere. This means snow, but you never can tell just how soon it will come.

15

To be on the safe side I told the man at the garage to put my chains on.

The trailer was quite heavily loaded. Michael had asked for cement and lime and nails; there were some sacks of feed and the usual assorted supplies, besides the empty milk cans.

The man dug the chains out of my car. Oh, how many broken links!

"If you're not in a hurry I can put these links in for you. It won't take a minute—"

While he worked I walked around, looking east, looking west. Yes. Snow. But how soon? And from what direction? There was no wind at all. If the storm came from the east, it would help me. The wind would be behind me.

Our ranch had no telephone. Talking over these possibilities in advance with Michael, we had decided that if bad weather came up suddenly, we must just stay in Cheyenne, and the one waiting at the ranch must not worry.

But I knew he *would* worry. Besides, I didn't really have any doubt about being able to get there even with snow; it was the lack of light I minded. Hurry then—

But it took quite a long time—gas, oil, water, mending chains, getting them on. Of course the trailer had to be unhitched and moved away, then swung into place again and hitched on (two men to lift the tongue).

At last I paid the man, got in and circled out onto the highway. The heavy trailer swung into line behind me. It has big tires and rides smoothly.

I had hardly straightened out and got my foot well down on the throttle when I saw that snowflakes were falling. They were large and far apart. They hesitated. They stopped entirely. Then began again.

When I got out of Cheyenne where the road for many miles is up on a sort of ramp, I felt the car was laboring. That meant wind, and not behind but against me. I stopped the engine and listened to the low steady whine. I got out and looked all around. Not a car to be seen, ahead or behind.

It was only about thirty miles to the ranch, but one climbed a

16

thousand feet. It was so gradual one hardly noticed it, but it was there, and I had a heavy load.

Here is the occasion, I thought, that Michael and I talked about. This is the time to be wise and go back. And I felt a premonition. I began to study the position of the car and trailer and the width of the road—about wide enough for three cars to stand abreast, close to each other. And the sharpness of the drops off the shoulders, and the depth of the gullies—about fifteen feet. Yes, quite steep and quite deep. Although, with a lot of backing and filling, always calculating correctly on the contrary performance of trailers when they are hitched to cars, it might have been done, yet I saw the possibility of getting car and trailer into a position from which I could not extricate them. Nor, if I unhitched the trailer and turned the car alone, would I ever be able to lift the tongue and hitch the trailer on again.

That is when I realized there were hazards all around me, and my heart began to pound.

But there is always a push to go forward. It is difficult even to make the mind turn around and go back, to say nothing of cars and trailers.

So I got in again and buckled down to a long, hard drive.

The snow was falling steadily now, a loose curtain through which I could see. The wind blew it slantwise off the road.

I put my foot all the way down on the throttle and the car did its best. Mile by mile we mounted the big hill. It grew steadily darker, the whine of the wind got louder, the snow thicker, the grade slightly steeper.

I was not worried, merely striving with all my might to keep my bearings. This was not easy, for the ride was taking longer, the way seemed farther, and all the landmarks were coming at the wrong times.

Halfway there, the snow was wrapped around the car like a sheet. It was difficult to see.

There were certain places where the grade was much steeper, and I had to drop to second gear, then first gear. And my heart did at last come up in my throat, when, in low gear, the pace of the engine slowed, slowed, slowed, but then the grade flattened a little and we were over; and my heart went down again where

17

it belonged, and I peered and peered through the windows and curtain of snow, trying to see the landmarks. I felt we should be near the ranch. We might even have passed the road.

Finally I knew myself lost. We could have been near, just there, or past. But I told myself, No, there was still that last steepest bit, curving up, and then felt myself on it. Again, down to second gear, the slowing engine, first gear, and the engine still slowed. Desperate, I began to tack across the road, back and forth, anything to keep the engine going and car moving.

It was while I was doing this, gaining just a few feet on each tack, that I realized that perhaps the odds were now against me. This put my whole thought into a new key. All fear left me.

But that grade, too, leveled off. I was over, running straight again, hanging my head out the window, squinting for something familiar at the edge of the road which would tell me when to turn off.

Now. Here it is. Turn.

And a comforting feeling welled up in me. On the home road anyway—not lost. No more than two miles to go, and that should be easy. But by now the snow was deep.

I had several tough struggles, but got through every time and then ran into a drift and did not get through. I made the car fight. The engine died. I started it, tried again. She was buried and could not move. I must get the shovel from the trunk compartment, dig through, and then perhaps all would be clear sailing, and before too long I'd be sitting before the blazing fire telling Michael all about it—

I got out of the car and the wind knocked me down.

Very astonished, I clambered to my feet. But the moment I stepped out of the lee of the car I could not stand. The wind was ice. The whine sounded like a siren.

Clinging to the car, I examined the drift. Not just a short drift that I could dig out of, but a three-foot-deep covering that had blotted out road, rocks, fences, every landmark. The plains again —endless undulating plains, but white now, not green.

My face was encased in ice on the side where the wind hit it. I slapped it. The ice shattered and fell and immediately formed

18

again. My body was made stiff and clumsy by the cold. My hands, I knew, would never succeed in opening the catch of the lid of the trunk compartment or finding the shovel. Besides, what use?

I stood, wavering, holding on to the door of the car, and thought that perhaps all I could do was get back into the warm car and stay there till morning. I did not really entertain the thought, because I knew I would be dead by morning. I had seen the articles in the newspapers every winter. And one picture of a couple sitting clasped in each other's arms in their car, frozen stiff, the car just a hundred yards from home.

The only thing to do, then, was walk home. So, braced and ready for the onslaught of the wind this time, bent nearly double, I turned away from the car and took off.

There was an eerie, glimmering snow light, by which I saw that there were hills and dales. I floundered and plunged and often fell and struggled to my feet again. I beat the ice off my face.

There was a row of dots on the snow, about ten feet apart. When I realized that these must be the top of the fence posts, I felt better. For the fence bordered the road all the way to the ranch house. They would lead me home.

But there were rolling hills to climb. At every step I sank above my knees. More and more strength and energy I found within myself as I summoned more and more determination, and was immensely surprised when I began to realize that it wasn't going to be enough.

I remembered a story an aviator had told me when he saw smoke pouring up through his airplane and exclaimed, This is it!

I wondered about the jobs I would be leaving unfinished. And if there was anyone who would feel lost without me. I was in a place, mentally, I had never been in before, and it excited me.

Automatically, my struggles continued, and when I was down and half smothered I got up again.

In the morning the storm had blown itself out and the sun was blazing.

19

When Michael and I went out to look at the car, the inside of it, from rubber floor mat to roof, was one solid block of frozen snow.

The Mary-Dairy lasted just a year. At the end of that time, we broke even. And Michael cried, "All for nothing! What waste!"

I wondered what had made my experiment fail if other ranchers succeeded. Hindsight gave me the answer. I had bought retail and sold wholesale. If that had been reversed (not, in our location, possible) my dairy would have carried the overhead.

So now we feed the milk to the boys.

Chapter 3

When we first came to the ranch we had no cat, and the place was overrun with gophers.

Get a cat, everyone told us. Feed it nothing. It will live on the gophers.

I had never cared anything about cats. Dogs, yes. We had many of them at Deercreek. I had grown up with them, but never a cat either in country or town house. If there were any, they were in the kitchen and basement, underground creatures— close kin to the slinky shadows one saw in city alleys around garbage pails, never privileged companions of the family.

A dog, now, would give whole-souled devotion to a master. Do brave things like saving your life if you were drowning, or bringing you out of a burning house if you were a helpless baby in a cradle, or giving you a gulp of brandy out of a neat little Swiss flask if you were a traveler lost in the Alps and just about to sink into the fatal snow sleep.

But a cat—*feline*—the very word expresses something sinister.

One cold winter day, buying grain at the elevator, we saw a black mamma cat and some kittens at the skittering age. From between two sacks of grain, a tiny, wild black face peered out.

I remembered the gophers and asked the man if we could have a kitten. He said, Take any one you want. I pointed at the gollywog. He got it and came to the car, holding the little mad, fighting thing in his hand.

I knew the reason for those shrieks and writhings. It wanted the dark, not to be able to see, and to be against something warm and alive. I can well understand Freud's contention that it is natural for even human animals to long for the womb again.

I took the infant and thrust it under my corduroy jacket, which was lined with sheepskin. Instantly it was quiet and never stirred all the way home.

Arrived at the ranch and a big fire built in the living room we put it on the hearth with a saucer of warm cream. And there it was brought up.

I began to notice that it lay looking at me all the time. I would glance toward the fire and see those eyes upon me, a steadfast gaze, even while I played the piano.

I asked Michael one day, "Do you notice the way Felix watches me all the time?"

"Yes, I have noticed," he said. "He's crazy about you."

I was enormously flattered, for cats are supposed to be indifferent. How come, then, that without any particular encouragement Felix should have dared to raise his eyes to the reigning queen of the ranch and fall in love with her?

From then on *the cat* never left me. I went about my daily tasks with, as it were, a cat in the traditional attitude of the Sphinx somewhere off there in the air watching me. The deep repose, the utter stillness, as his face contemplated my face gave the impression that he had achieved the goal of existence.

I became permanently cat-conscious.

Felix found himself a wife somewhere. Cats accumulated and the gopher colony diminished in numbers.

He became and has remained the very model of all papa cats. When mother cats get tired of nursing their kittens, or the time comes to wean them, Felix takes over. He stretches on his side and allows each kitten a tiny tuft of hair to suck on. There they lie in a row, blissfully kneading his stomach. When we come to look at him he lifts his head and regards us proudly, but does not disturb the infants.

When they must learn to eat he brings them to the bowls of food near the kitchen door, eats a little himself, then stands back and encourages them to come on and have some.

To show them not to be afraid of the dogs, he walks up and smacks them on the face, then looks at the kittens as if to say, See that? Nothing to it!

22

When they are older they must learn about the very important and special thing—music.

When he hears the sound of the piano, he collects the kittens and leads them single file through the dining room to the living room, and no skittering, please! This is a privilege. Lie down on the floor as close as you can get to the piano bench and give yourself up to the most hypnotizing experience that can assail the feline nerves.

One fall there was a cat epidemic on the ranch. They diminished rapidly in number. Felix remained immune, but his wives disappeared, his children and grandchildren. At last only one sickly grandchild was left, and then he was gone.

Felix felt his solitude acutely. He went about searching. In and out every room, into corners, behind sofas, under beds, convinced that somewhere he would find that ailing grandchild.

Now and then he would give a single sharp cry.

Michael and I agreed we must get another cat.

Late one afternoon, finishing up my errands in town, I paid a visit to the veterinarian to make some arrangements about the inoculation of cows.

As I talked to him, I noticed a kitten on the back of an armchair. It climbed about, weaved in and out the bars, cast glances at me as if calculating the distance for a leap.

It was tortoise-shell with long silky hair, a very short body so that it looked like a round ball, a tail that stood out belligerently, a particularly pretty face with yellow slit eyes.

I finished my business and, leaving, said, "Don't want to get rid of a cat, do you?"

"Do you mean that?" The twist of his thumb indicated the ball of fluff on the chair.

"Yes."

He picked it up and tossed it to me. "I was just going out to buy hamburger for her. It's a female," he warned.

"I want a female."

I carried her out to the car, made a comfortable little nest of the robe on the back seat, put her in it, took my place and said, "Westward ho! Missy."

23

With one leap she landed on the back of my shoulders, then in my lap, then clawed up to my neck and hung under my chin.

I wondered how long since she had been weaned, for her little paws and mouth were nuzzling.

With one hand I tried to lift her off; she would not be lifted. Sharp claws fastened in my coat and held on. I had to stop the car, draw up at the side of the road, and do a thorough job of it, putting her back into the shawl again.

By the time I had gone through the gears, she was back in my neck.

She was lonesome of course—the back seat was too far away. I arranged her nest in the shawl on the front seat beside me, but the result was the same.

Then I tried driving with one hand, holding her firmly in her nest with the other. But on that thousand-foot climb against the wind, in the gathering darkness, one needs both hands for driving. So I gave up, and drove the thirty miles with her arms clasped around my throat, her nose under my chin, and her little hindy sitting on the V of my coat lapels.

Felix was enchanted and took complete charge of her. He shared his kills with her (Felix was a mighty hunter). He lay beside her, licking and grooming her. He took her to the piano when I was playing. He told her that milk warm and fresh from the cows was best; taught her to sit on the edge of the gutter in the barn at milking time waiting for their own special little bowl to be filled; or, if they had to wait too long, to creep to the feet of the milker, rise up on hind legs between the bucket and the milker's knees, and there, steadied by one paw on the milker's knee, to try to get a tongue between the needle-sharp stream of milk and the bucket.

When I went out to bring the cows in—and sometimes they were far away and I had an hour's hunt for them—Felix and Missy went too. More likely than not, the cats were ahead of me, lying under the cows, eyeing the full udders.

Felix and Missy have a calendar of behavior. Winters, when we are away, they live in the bunkhouse with the men. Springtime, when we return they come back to the house, the terrace, the Green.

The first spring, Missy had forgotten us. Michael and I, amused, watched her tramping back and forth unconcernedly along the little dark path in the snow between barn and bunkhouse. She saw our feet, our legs, but did not lift her eyes.

I spoke to her, but her ears were stopped. For too many months she had been ignoring human voices.

Then one day, she passed me, paused, glanced at me and I smiled.

She froze into a stillness so absolute it seemed as if she was in a state of shock. Then the past flooded back upon her; the music and the fire on the hearth and the warm kitchen when, in the mornings, I would go about getting breakfast with her sitting on my arm, her right arm hooked around my neck.

And she screamed and ran to me and stood on her hind legs, lifting her front paws, and I took her up and she wound herself around my neck, purring, stopping her purrs to murmur and talk, purring again, licking my face, trying to lick my mouth with her rough little red tongue.

She never forgot again. Other springs, when we returned, it was as if she were just waiting, sure that we would come.

I just heard Michael's car coming down behind the house from the stables. He stopped to yell, "I'm going down to the Crooked Meadow. Want to come?"

I ran to the back window, stuck my head out and called, "Oh, I've got too much to do." Then, as he started off, I shrieked, "Wait!"

I caught him before he reached the cattle guard. He grinned, leaned over to open the door for me and I climbed in.

Down in the meadow he let me out, then drove on to inspect the break in the dam where Riley is working.

I just stood there looking around. I was suddenly a blissful blank.

The late afternoon air was mild. The long oval meadow—about a half mile by a quarter—was already lush with young growing timothy and red-top. We've had plenty of rain this spring. There's a big purplish thunderhead that hangs in the sky over the ranch. It circles slowly, and at some time during the day it suddenly

25

opens, pours out rain, then closes, circles away, sometimes growling a little, until it slides over the mountains and the sun comes blazing out again. What could be better for the hay? We're sure to have a big crop. Michael gloats. The meadow is the most exquisite shade of fresh green with a faint tinge of blue, a fascinating color I often mixed on the palette of my paintbox when I was a child.

The creek comes tumbling down from the top of the Rocky Mountain Divide thirty miles west, and runs the whole length of our long, trough-shaped ranch. It is dammed up between meadows to give us a reserve of water.

Here and there Michael has built little arched bridges over it —beautifully laid stone, of course our own pink granite, and strategically placed. He is incapable of putting his hand to anything without making it into a thing of beauty.

Its name is Lone Tree Creek. It could be called creek, stream or river, depending on how much water has recently fallen out of the skies, for here on the top of the world we run the gamut from fog and mist to unseasonable hail, snow and ice storms—or flash floods.

One evening Michael and I left the ranch to go to a dance at Fort Russell Warren, north of Cheyenne. It was clear and balmy. I wore no wrap over my chiffon evening dress.

As we left the party after midnight someone called to us from another car, "Flash flood out your way!" So we were somewhat prepared when we found a strange, wide new river running through our ranch.

The road ran right into it. We stopped and stared.

Where was the little arched stone bridge with the creek running under it? Wondering if it had been torn loose, Michael took off shoes and socks, turned up his trousers, and explored. He found the bridge still there, the parapets on each side just about a foot underwater.

So we left the car on the road, I took off shoes and stockings, lifted my long skirts in my arms, and, shrieking and laughing like a couple of kids with the fun of it, we both walked the parapets to the other side and so got to our home and beds.

In the morning, the river had vanished. Lone Tree Creek was there again, running neatly through the arched bridges.

Right now, the creek is well behaved, quite swift, keeping in the twisted, crooked channel that has given that meadow its name.

I could hardly see the water for the snaky line of alders and willows that bent over it on either side.

Far away, I could hear Michael shouting to Riley.

Over all, and low above me, was a pale blue sky, calm and benign. On it, thin, flat sheets of cloud, with indeterminate, melting edges, floated so slowly, so indifferently, so serenely that they made me feel slow, indifferent and serene too. A balmy breeze blew steadily down the meadow and lifted my hair and held it streaming.

I put my hands in the pockets of my gray flannel slacks and stood there for half an hour.

Chapter 4

Of all the crops we have raised—sheep, milk, horses, boys—only the boy crop has carried itself. It has done better than that. It has grown. It is organic. And we have been asked by parents and schoolmasters if we could not extend the work to the winter months; a small tutoring school for boys who for one reason or another have dropped out of their classes in preparatory schools —a place where Michael could put them on their feet again.

It could not be here in Wyoming; the winters are too confining. We would need a good-size country house in New England. And this has been offered us. My old schoolmate, Betty Bedford (her son Alan comes regularly to our summer camp) has two country places but seldom uses either—she goes to Europe. She has offered us the one in northern Connecticut, rent free.

Having the ranch at all is like having a bear by the tail. It is valuable and must be cared for and operated. But a part-time operation (the summer camp) means part-time earnings, too. The winters eat up the summers. Long, lonely, expensive winters.

To move east, establish the school and carry it till it gets going would require a few thousand dollars. It is not impossible that a small ranch—the size of ours—should clear that much in one lucky year, by a good sale of horses or cows, or our fine mountain hay.

This is what we are hoping and waiting for. Several times we have thought we would bring it off, but something has always happened to swallow those few thousand and we've had to settle down to wait another year.

Michael is so busy with the well crew he won't sit down to eat.

I had finished my lunch and was sitting at the piano playing *Joy in the Morning* when I heard him in the kitchen, and presently he came in through the dining room and stood beside me. He had a slab of Ry-Krisp plus Swiss cheese plus more Ry-Krisp in one hand and a can of beer in the other.

"What's that you're playing? It must be new. You didn't play it last summer."

"Yes, it's new. Do you like it?"

"Yes. It's prettier than most of your things. Simpler."

He went out to rejoin the men and I went on playing.

I was immoderately pleased and felt I could compose anything! And I thought of Rachmaninoff's prescription for composers: They need just three things. Praise. More praise. And still more praise.

I simply love this piece.

I woke up in New York one morning with the melody going full tilt in my head. So, apparently, it was composed by my subconscious mind while I was asleep.

I don't know what woke me but I sat up with a start, wondering where I was. I didn't recognize the room and could remember nothing. This is a strange feeling.

I looked around. One square window looked out on a gray brick wall with a bit of blank gray sky above it. That told me nothing.

I looked at my bed. A very neat and shining four-poster, single size, covered with a satin puff that had half slipped to the floor.

I remembered. I was in the spare room of my brother Reese's apartment in New York.

I piled the pillows behind me, sat up against them, straightened and pulled up the covers and took my notebook and pencil from the table beside the bed. I was in a fever to get enough written down so that I would not forget it.

I sketched the periods, wrote down each theme, indicated the harmonies and in no time at all was offering it to Schirmer who said, "This is a beautiful piece. We will publish it and give you royalties."

The musical ideas crowded and I recognized its spirit of early morning and joyousness. I scrawled the title, *Joy in the Morning*.

. . . the way children positively burst out of bed, out of the night into the day and into life!

. . . and the way, at the ranch, all the little animals are so chipper and so glad to be alive!

. . . sunshine and sunshine and more sunshine! Beams of light with motes drifting and sliding and dancing, not bacchanal dancing, which belongs at night, but the innocent dancing of mindless things—bees and meadow grass, thistledown and tree-tops!

In the early morning I myself am ready to be new and find the whole world new. I can't *wait* to get going. And the people that sleep and sleep and can't get up! I know they must be considered, and breakfast at a reasonable hour, but I would like breakfast not later than five-thirty or six, and to have a small piano beside my bed, and a warm comfortable room, so that I could compose in the mornings without an empty feeling and a slight headache, or a room so cold my hands freeze, sitting up in bed with pencil and paper.

I always want to rush into Michael's room and wake him—fling myself on the bed. Sometimes I do.

He sits up in bed, looking at me, bewildered; furious, really, at being waked up, but telling himself that he must bear with me, and that if I've waked him, well, I've waked him, and that's that. And he just manages to be silent and not scold me. Rubs his head with one hand and reaches for a cigarette with the other; and by that time, I'm scared at what I've done, and fly out of the room.

All this is in *Morning*.

And last winter when, in zero weather, I was the milker. Two cows to milk and no man to milk them. I had to run and shout to keep warm.

I wore my blue denim jodhpurs and a heavy sweater.

Michael said, "Will I never see the end of those pants?"

I would burst out of the kitchen door into the bitter cold, the blinding sunshine, the cobalt sky; and there, waiting for me, the animals.

How *they* love the morning. How do they always know at exactly what moment those rattling milk pails will come through the door on my arm? Michael thinks they watch the house and see the curl of smoke come from the chimney. For of course, before I go out to milk, I have made the fire in the kitchen range.

There they are; Bunny, the brown cocker, always so adoring, sitting watching the door, turning into a perpetual motion of wags and jumps when I appear.

The ducks. Papa and Mama, seven children as large as their parents but perfectly knowing their place in line, and waddling in exact order Indian file, behind me down to the barn.

The cats and kittens. Felix, the dignified paterfamilias; big, solid, with a shining black coat, one white spat and a white shirtfront, an air of authority. Missy, little tortoise-shell Angora devil with topaz eyes.

And the young sorrel stallion, Rheingold, who knows it's *lèse majesté* to foregather at the kitchen door with small assorted animals but just can't resist the attraction and always gives a great start and clatters away when the rattling pails appear, but then turns and follows meekly behind the ducks.

A knock at my door—and with another jolt I returned from the ranch to Reese's apartment.

"Come in!" I called, shoving notebook and pencil under the silk puff. Early coffee or tea is routine in Reese's home.

Maud entered and we exchanged good-mornings. She placed the little tray with my steaming coffee on my knees (how good it smells!) closed the window and left the room.

As I drank the coffee and ate the one thin crisp piece of buttered toast, the work went on in my mind.

Mingling with my excitement was a sense of guilt. I knew the piece would take possession of me and consume all my time. What about the little teaching pieces of the first, second, third grade I was supposed to be writing? This thing, I knew, was all over the piano. Was it the sort of thing Vernon Spencer would declare *much ado about nothing*? Too difficult for immature students, yet not deep enough, not important enough either in conception or development to interest a mature artist? I did not think so. This time—at last—he was really going to be impressed.

31

I finished the toast, set the tray on the table, pulled out my notebook and pencil and went on writing.

If Schirmer didn't want it, then it could be added to the pile of manuscripts in the file marked *For the Musical*. And I had plenty of ideas for teaching pieces besides.

I longed, I ached, for breakfast to be over and Reese gone away to his law office and Jerome, his young stepson, out of the way somewhere, so I could get to the piano in the living room and hear this lovely thing with my physical ears.

But after breakfast it was Jerome, not I, who sat down at the piano.

It is, after all, *his* piano. It is an old war horse of a Chickering concert grand left to him by Eloise, his mother, who died a year ago.

Jerome, at his Chickering grand piano—at any piano—uses hands and body passionately, puffing and panting, expressing vast emotions. Streams of notes pour forth. Niagara Falls of notes! Anywhere in the apartment one is drenched with the spray.

Such a drenching would be very bad for *Joy in the Morning*, so I put a mental capsule around my new composition and turned my mind to other things.

As I was not yet dressed I could do my face. I like to meet every fresh day with a fresh face, wiped clean of yesterday. I do this with peach kernel oil—substitute for the more expensive almond oil—and a five- or ten-minute massage.

I promised Michael I would do this every day—have not been doing it.

Eugenie telephoned me. "I spent the night in town."

"In your apartment?"

"Yes. All alone. Can you imagine it?"

I cannot. She is always surrounded by family, friends, servants.

She continued, "I enjoyed every minute of lunch with you yesterday."

She had lunched here, and afterward we talked; and I looked at her sitting in the big chair, slim legs crossed, perfect hose and pumps on her tiny feet, smart spring print dress cut with the formality that is part of her personality and imparts something of authority, even of pomp; her lovely smooth blond face framed in perfectly done (by Michael-of-the-Waldorf) golden hair; her smart white and blue beret. And I thought how French she looked.

"Ed arrived from Washington this morning; and we had breakfast in a garden."

"A garden? In New York? How come?"

"Yes. With some friends who live near us and have a garden."

I felt it to be an adventure. To sleep all alone in the city apartment in the summertime, among the shrouded furniture; to hear husband's key in the door in the morning; to welcome him without any of the usual ceremony of servants, breakfast trays, children—I imagined Ed and Eugenie in a happy and youthful embrace, then going off to the garden of a friend for breakfast.

"Eugenie! I think it is an adventure!"

"Yes. It was. We decided that when we can, we will spend the whole summer comfortably in New York when all our friends have gone to Long Island, and have a real change and rest. Mary, I think Jeannie and I will come to the ranch in August."

"Of course you will. I'm counting on it."

"You mustn't count on it. Ed doesn't know we're even thinking of such a thing when we've just taken the big house on Long Island for the summer. And we're spending much more money than we should."

"Still, I feel sure you'll come."

Not till Sunday morning did I finally get a chance to play *Joy in the Morning* on Jerome's piano.

It was a hot day. Reese and Jerome went off in the car to spend the morning at Jones Beach. I gathered up my notes and sketches of *Joy in the Morning* and went to the living room and arranged them on the rack of the Chickering.

I sat down to play and for the first time heard that music with my physical ears. I played it over and over, my eyes drifting around the room, hardly seeing. I played, entranced, like a sleep walker.

I became aware, at last, of pictures on the wall. I was looking at them as I played and some part of my mind was thinking

33

about them. Several nude female figures like the line drawings made by sculptors, one of them coiled intricately on herself like a foetus. Reese likes such drawings because of his carving. When we were young together in the Brooklyn house, he would sit in the evenings with the top of a cigar box and a sharp carving tool, and carve Greek gods and goddesses on the soft wood.

Here was another picture with coiling lines. A dog. He looked like the convolutions of a brain.

Here was an extraordinary oil painting by Jerome. A graveyard with a misty blue background and a vague floating white shape above one of the graves.

Then there were all the pictures of Eloise, Jerome's mother. They looked back at me from the walls, the mantel, every corner of the room—so sad, so awfully sad.

We had all thought she did not know until the very end that she was going to die. But now, with surprise, I saw by her face that she had known all along.

She died last summer when Jerome was at the ranch with us, and when the telegram came it was I who had to tell him.

Elma stopped in to have lunch with me and afterward I played her the piece. My fingers had become very fluent in it.

"What verve!" she exclaimed. "Play it over again right away!"

I played it over and over to her.

"What gaiety! What charm! What dash!"

And I heard the jubilation in her voice as of one who witnesses something newborn and cries, "It's a boy!"

Whenever the room was empty I played it.

I played it day after day until the time was near for my return to the ranch.

One evening, playing in the half-dark living room, I hardly noticed that Maud had brought in a baggage man to carry away the big packed trunk that stood in the middle of the floor. Jerome was going away on a visit. Maud went back to her kitchen.

The big fellow in his leather apron looked exhausted—that sweating, gray pallor of the hot-weather New York face.

He closed the trunk and then there was no movement in the room. I played on, oblivious, then heard, "Gee, that's pretty."

I glanced up. He stood leaning on the upended trunk, ab-

34

sorbed, watching me, listening. Then he swung the trunk up on to his back. My fingers rippled on—by this time they played of themselves.

He bent, gave a little jounce, settling the great hump between his shoulders. I played on, waiting for him to go, but he did not move. After a while he said again, "Awful pretty."

I again gave him a brief glance, wondering if he knew he had a trunk on his back, a trunk that, no doubt, contained a moving picture camera and other cameras, piles of music and books, boxes of games, paintboxes and palettes, innumerable pairs of shoes and boots, size eleven.

I wished he would go. I couldn't bear the weight of that trunk another minute on that tired young face.

But he didn't go until I had come to the end and dropped my hands in my lap. Then, turning, bent nearly double, he sidled out of the room muttering again, "Awful pretty."

I had heard it through his ears and thought it was good.

Playing it now at the ranch on my Mason and Hamlin grand piano, I still think it is good. It has a gay ripple. And Michael has said it is pretty.

I have at last unpacked, put away, gone over the linen.

Chapter 5

I have just been down to look at the calves. Very high-bred and typy and more white than tan. One of the young mothers, just a two-year-old heifer, promises to be a heavy producer.

Much as I love the house I love the barn better. It is sunk deep into the earth, and the red roof hoods it so closely there is only a strip of white-washed wall to be seen above ground.

It forms the lower boundary of the Green.

This Green is the very heart of the ranch.

When first we came here it was the dump and trash heap. Now it is smooth and covered with grass. Three horses are grazing on it, keeping the grass cut.

It covers about an acre and is, roughly, square. It slopes from the ranch buildings on the right—bunkhouse, spring house, tool house, ice house—to the barn down below on the left. In the middle of it is a stone basin from which all the animals drink. The water, piped down from the spring house, is cold and delicious.

On the opposite side, across from our house, is the tall nearly perpendicular cliff, thickly planted with jack pines and ferns and wild flowers. It is a veritable rock garden with tiny paths across which our sure-footed horses daintily pick their way.

The barn opens eastward into corrals that, in turn, open into a one-half-mile pasture that we call the Calf Pasture. This slopes down (north) to Lone Tree Creek. The cows wander through the corrals and pasture to drink and stand in the shade of the big cottonwood trees along its bank.

I don't know how long the barn has been there. Certainly

since the ranch was first homesteaded, and that was long ago. It seems, indeed, part of the earth.

Inside, it is big as a small city block. Cool and dark as a church.

Here are rows of stanchions for cows. Pens for maternity cases. Stalls for work teams and a few saddle horses. Compartments for calves, bull, and junior bull. Bins for grain. Partitioned sections for the storage of crates and trunks. And still the greater half—a vast half—left for hay.

It could hold a hundred and fifty or two hundred tons if the hay were baled, but as we have no baler, nor need go to the expense of baling when the hay is to be fed out to our own stock, we put it into the barn loose from an opening in the roof, and it holds twenty or thirty tons.

The remainder of the hay crop is stacked in a long lozenge outside parallel to the barn, and in a square peaked tower at the extreme end of the cowshed which forms an L with the barn. This L encloses two corrals in its elbow and makes an outdoor feeding rack, and a cosy shelter for the cows in winter.

I stood in the barn, enjoying the smell of the hay, the old wood, the hard earth floor. Looking up, I saw far above me the long peaked roof braced by pitch pine poles. They were smooth, perfectly matched, and a beautiful shade of warm, weathered, golden brown.

These poles came originally from Pole Mountain, so named because of this growth of straight pitch pine which furnishes roof poles for all the ranchers hereabouts.

One day Michael said, standing in the barn and looking up into the cool dark roof, braced so neatly with the poles of pine, "I am glad we took the extra furniture out of here; the crates; your mother's mirror; the portraits."

He says the barn is a tinder box because of the pitch in the pines. He says the first thing he looks for when he comes back from town and rounds the shoulder of the hill is the barn. Is it still there? He does not allow the men to smoke in it.

But they do, all the same.

He does, himself.

37

I heard that deep moan of the Roamer and went to the side door of the barn and looked out into the corral. I saw him standing beyond the corral fence in the pasture. He is mostly white, but inside he's the true Guernsey color. Before I bought him I parted the white hairs on his shoulder and saw the hide—you would have thought it orange peel. And the base of his horns is yellow, and the edges of his eyelids, and his hoofs and inside his nostrils and there are a few of the characteristic Guernsey yellow-tan splotches on his body.

The long dragging chain, I saw, was gone. I had spoken of it to Michael and had touched off one of his quick shouting rages.

"He's going down in flesh! He's starving himself! I won't treat animals that way!"

"But what's the matter with him, Michael?"

"Nothing! He's just a nervous, restless, wandering brute—like all of them."

Now I saw, hanging from the nose ring a short chain that just cleared the ground. Just long enough, I supposed, to keep him from going through or over fences.

I went out into the corral and inspected him (from inside the corral). We were about twelve feet apart.

"Hello, old boy."

He stood in profile to me and did not turn his head, but I saw the small eyes in the golden Guernsey lids roll around to look at me backward.

Bulls always do that.

The most dangerous animal in the United States, so say the records, is not wildcat, panther, mountain lion or grizzly bear, it is the thoroughbred dairy bull.

The first bull I had for my dairy I raised myself, and named him the *Deercreek Challenger*; for short, *Cricket*.

The raising of a bucket calf is strenuous and undignified and must be done in blue jeans.

The point is to make him drink out of a bucket at an age when it is natural for him to raise his head and suck. You've got to get his nose *down* into a bucket of milk; at the same time have something in the milk that feels like a teat for him to get hold of; and at the same time hold him where you want

38

him; and at the same time prevent his vigorous butting from knocking over the bucket.

You straddle the calf, back him and yourself into a corner, hold the bucket in your left hand and with your right force his head down into it. He smells the milk, gets excited and starts butting in every direction. Now you hold him very tight with your legs, set the bucket on the ground, put your left hand down into the milk and let him suck your fingers. Doing this he draws in plenty of milk at the same time.

It usually takes three or four days of starvation and a session morning and evening before the calf is so hungry that he gets the idea—and the milk.

After that it goes easily.

That is the way I raised Cricket; and for a twelvemonth afterward he would run to me wherever he saw me, holding out his nose; and if I extended my hand, he would seize my fingers in his mouth and suck; and so I could lead him anywhere I wanted.

He never outgrew this, or the desire to do it. But he grew big; and little by little running *to* me began to seem running *at* me; and I wished he wouldn't.

When I came back one spring after having been away all winter, I went out one evening to bring the cows in for milking, and I came home with my heart in my throat. There was a monstrous, black bull loose in the herd who insisted on paying me the most unwelcome attentions.

I had been obliged to get a stick and make threatening gestures at him.

"Get away, Cricket!" This, as he was nosing up behind me, with funny little grunts, his nose outstretched, reaching for my hand!

I brandished the stick. He gave a squeal, turned, kicked up his heels and careered away with a stiff tail in the air, but soon was following me close again.

"He was playing with you," said Michael. "That's a fact. He hasn't seen you all winter, and he was excited and affectionate."

At two Cricket may have been excited and affectionate. At four he was a menace everyone felt.

Fortunately he did not jump fences but he ranged along beside them (if you were walking on the other side) bellowing and pausing now and then to paw the ground.

Michael says this is to veil himself in dust and make the flies get off of him. With Michael, the animal is always right.

Cricket could see a person moving two miles away and would begin to bellow and make his way to them with an air of terrible deliberateness.

This, say the books, is showing a good herd instinct. A proper bull must be on the alert to protect the herd, resent intrusion of strangers, be ready to charge.

Cricket certainly resented intrusion and gave every evidence of being ready to charge.

One summer when Eugenie and little Jean were at the ranch, they went fishing down in the Calf Pasture. Nobody happened to remember, when they started out, that Cricket was in that pasture.

They arrived back at the house hysterical with fright. Cricket had seen them as they walked along the stream; came hurrying up to them and bellowed and pawed the ground; and when they fled, followed close behind them. They ran. Eugenie's hook caught in Jean's dress, and Jean's in Eugenie's. Jean began to scream.

Michael and I agreed that Cricket would have to go. No use waiting until something terrible had happened.

So, in town one day, Michael spoke to the Hebrew Rabbi to whom we sell our beef.

When the Rabbi came out to make the appraisal I drove him in the car to a vantage point on the hillside above the pasture; and we sat in the car looking down at Cricket a quarter of a mile away.

The Rabbi wanted me to take him on foot into the pasture. "But he's dangerous," I said.

"I'm not afraid of bulls."

"You wait a moment. Wait until he catches sight of this car up here. He'll know there's a stranger in it."

The next moment Cricket saw us. He became motionless, his head alertly raised. He stared, sniffed, listened; then he started

40

in our direction with that terrible deliberateness, never taking his eyes off us.

Presently he paused, lowered his head, pawed the earth and bellowed.

I don't know how lions sound bellowing on their native heath, but I have heard them in the zoos; and the sound is nothing to the deep belching roar, breaking to a furious squealing falsetto that is the bellowing of an angry bull.

"He can't get to us. There's a fence between," I said.

"But I can't appraise him without getting closer to him—much closer." So I drove down and around to the fence on the far side of the pasture where the ground is flat.

We got out and stood against the fence. Cricket, twenty feet away on the other side, was quiet now that he had us under his eye.

The Rabbi was guessing at his weight. He crawled under the barbed wire fence and walked closer; Cricket lowered his head a little. They looked at each other. The Rabbi circled him, looking him over. Cricket circled too, keeping his head low.

I kept my eyes on both.

"Eighteen hundred pounds, maybe," said the man at last, and turned his back and walked toward me.

"Run!" I screamed as the bull charged.

One backward glance, and the Rabbi exploded into huge leaps; he dropped to the ground and rolled under the fence.

As he stood up and brushed his clothes off he said, "You tell the mister to kill that bull. Don't bring him to me alive. I don't usually allow an animal to be brought to me dead, but that bull is likely to kill someone if he ain't killed first."

So now I have the Roamer who moans instead of bellowing, and runs away, but has never charged anyone. Still—

He was waiting there at the fence for the cows to come up from pasture for milking.

I saw them coming, scattered, some lagging, still nosing at the grass, some walking purposefully with nodding heads. They had fed all day. Their stomachs were full. Many of them stood relaxed, chewing their cuds.

41

As I walked across the corral to open the gate and let them in, the Roamer jumped the fence into the corral.

The short chain did not impede him at all. I saw how he did it—just tossed the chain up by a swing of his head and in those few seconds before the chain fell again, his great weight lifted easily over the fence sideways, like an expert college hurdler, and dropped lightly on the near side.

I stood at the gate while the cows filed in. The Roamer stood still, watching me. I made a bee-line for the barn door, but quietly. (No panic.) His head turned slowly; his dark eyes, troubled, puzzled, crafty, never left me. Then he moved to the small wooden box where his grain ration would be poured and sniffed it.

In the barn I found Felix and Missy, already in position, waiting for the cows, and in a moment heard the clattering of milk pails and the voices of Riley and George as they came down from the bunkhouse to milk.

I'm sitting on the terrace with my portable on my knees, just looking at the Green and enjoying it and being glad that we didn't build the house somewhere removed from the farm activities but right here in the middle of everything.

Chapter 6

The well has come in with a fine flow. This is a triumph; but the inlet is so low the water will have to be pumped up to the level where all the pipes are.

This means a windmill. It will cost two or three hundred dollars.

There is another worry. Just where shall it be placed? Everyone has a different opinion, and all the talk is about underground waters and overground air currents.

The bed of Lone Tree Creek is the very lowest level of the ranch. From that the meadows and range sweep northward to the railroad tracks.

It rises southward, too, in a series of swoops, to a sharp timbered ridge that has a cut in it just big enough to hold our ranch. Wonderful shelter! Then up again across pastures and county road to a higher ridge, long and undulating. This is the saddleback. Then another scoop and more and more, each one with a crest of a different line and color all the way to the Buckhorn Mountains of Colorado. Behind all, towering, sunlit, the Neversummer Range, snow-covered most of the year.

That cut in the first ridge is a cosy spot for our ranch. It is shaped like an hourglass and our gorge is the narrow waist of it. Through the gorge runs a foot path and a trickle of water. The fairly steep timbered hills that enclose it on either side widen out for the stables above and the ranch building and Green below.

Because it is a passage of the winds, we hang our meat there when we have butchered and have a sheep or side of beef to keep. We put it in a cage of fine wire mesh and hang the cage from the branch of a pine tree. The cage swings in the wind and the meat is preserved from flies and birds and dries and

43

cures richly. This is where Michael wants to put the windmill.

But old George insists the windmill must be high up on one of the timbered hills, not down in the gorge. And Michael says that cinches it—it must be in the gorge because George is always wrong.

George resents Michael's authority and acknowledges an order with a sort of mumbling snarl. But when he speaks to me his voice is so changed it is almost hushed. To western men, chivalry is very real. They have gentleness and deference and tenderness toward "the missus." Nothing could make them give it up.

George's teeth are very large, very store-bought, very assertive. He has no hair at all. Teeth and bare skull conspire to give him the look of a death's head.

He would tell you he's a cowboy. In his day, he has been. Even today he likes to catch up old Baldy, put a big comfortable western saddle on him, step into the long stirrup from the top of a rock, and go ambling about.

On most ranches (all except the big beef-raising outfits) "cowboy" and "hand" are synonymous. George is now a "hand."

We inherited him when we bought the ranch, like the IZ and the Jewish A. In the winters, if we don't need him here, he gets a job in town as janitor of a small hotel. In the zero temperatures and the heavy snows he is in the cosy dry basement; he sleeps on as good a bed as he has ever known and near the furnace. He eats from the hotel kitchen. His personal needs— tobacco and occasional replacement of blue jeans, shoes and lumberjacks—are supplied by his salary. The salary is fifteen dollars a month.

Now Michael has taken the three drillers to town in the car and the place seems very quiet.

The windmill, Michael has decided, will be in the gorge.

George goes around prophesying doom, but the windmill crew have arrived and have started to put it up.

I cannot rest.

I change my clothes, wash my hands—change my clothes, wash my hands—

44

This is a sign of mental confusion and always afflicts me when I move from one habitat to another. Apparently I am a limpet. Give me a chance to cling, and how I will cling.

I marvel at myself. I simply cannot stand the days; suddenly cannot stand this life or any life.

The endless flux; endless search, change, restlessness; nothing ever right, nothing truly assuaging. I thought I was coming home, but it doesn't feel like home. I think it's the music.

To write stories or music one withdraws from life and becomes an observer, an onlooker. When one has, in this way, been adrift in dreams too long one cannot get back. I would like to be anchored. Right in this house, this chair, this dress; and eat and feel warm or cold, and never move out again into the unreal, but I know I will.

A tide of cosmic misery wells up inside me and my dis-ease becomes acute despair.

I tell myself that I am simply making adjustments. For four months I have been a certain woman, living at a certain pace, among certain vibrations, in a certain locality. Now all is changed, and not the least of the changes is that I am lifted from sea level to this high altitude, called by the trainmen of the transcontinental railroads, *the big hill*. This is their quaint name for the Rocky Mountain Divide.

So I start to put the laundry away and lose it; find it fifteen minutes later on the dining room table; find myself standing before my bureau drawer, hunting and hunting, and suddenly realize I don't know what I'm hunting for. I go up to the corral to see what horses are in, and up there remember what I was hunting. I return—have forgotten it again. I open the drawers and look; give it up; change my clothes; wash my hands—

. . . two of the yearling colts are missing. Michael and Riley have been riding for hours, hunting them.

. . . every day I struggle with clothes. Blue denim Levi's are classic on a western ranch; but when new they are stiff and heavy, and even when softened by wear and washing they are tight—I have heard it joked that you need a button hook to get into them. So I wear linen jodhpurs of different shades—blue or

45

white or tan. These have to be bought in New York, as nothing of that kind is worn in the west except by "dudes." Then the leather belt and gloves, jodhpur boots and a linen hat (I never go out without a hat to keep my hair from blowing away) and it is a lot to have to wear just to go up to the stables. Long before the day is over I'm tired out by my clothes.

After all, you associate very intimately with your clothes—they have to be compatible. Also, your husband has to like them. If Michael doesn't like my clothes he just gives them away. One fall in Los Angeles a friend came to see me and I sat looking at her dress, puzzled by something familiar about it and finally I cried, "Why that dress! I have one just like it! I bet you bought it at Robinson's!" And she gave a little shriek and said, "Why, Mary, it's *your* dress! Michael gave it to me. Didn't you know?"

In New York I had to shop hurriedly for New York clothes. And I did make some plans for the ranch, some things half made to be supplemented with this or that. But then came *Joy in the Morning* and I have forgotten all I planned.

I look at a bundle of material rolled up with a string around it, and can't think what was to have been done with *that*. I get on a cotton skirt, socks and sandals and heave a sigh of relief for the lightness and freedom; then ransack all my drawers and find nothing suitable to top it with. No sweater is the right color. The halter I bought in New York to go with it turns out not to fit. Besides, it looks like a piece of underclothing.

So I'm back in jodhpurs and spurs again, and the contents of my chest of drawers are spread over my room.

I have been to town to put in an order at the employment office for a cook.

I saw a man about selling some of my cows, as I have more than I need.

I bought supplies.

I went to the nursery and bought all the plants for the window boxes and flower pots.

Two scarlet geraniums for the two little brackets under the pine room windows; a dozen dark salmon geraniums for the long ultramarine-blue window boxes; two vinca vines for the wall pots on the front of the house where the pergola over the terrace gives us an outdoor living room.

Then a mixture of things for the old black Dutch oven that Michael found on a dump heap and which now hangs from the pergola. One ivy, one vinca, a lantana, pink and white phlox, ageratum, purple and rosy morn petunias, and a single zinnia of an unusual cerise shade.

. . . now I have planted the flowers and, as I write, am sitting out on the terrace under the pergola. It has not yet got its summer awning on, and when I look up I see the pretty square lattice against the cloudy sky.

The Dutch oven, hanging at the edge, looks charming with all the new plants crowded into it and dripping over the sides.

The grass on this terrace was so long Michael turned some horses on it last night.

I heard them climbing up and down the stone steps, clumping about, squealing, knocking over chairs.

Today, the terrace is shaved clean. Michael has been over it with the trimming shears. Tonight we will put the sprinklers on it.

The flower border is full of light-blue meadow iris. The four big clumps of lilac are just getting ready to bloom.

Up here, with the high altitude, the seasons are two months or so behind New York. This year the spring has been unusually late; the frost was hardly out of the ground before the end of May, and Michael only yesterday weeded and hoed the borders and dug up the ground around the lilac bushes.

The big cloud is right overhead and thunder is rolling.

Milking time again, and the cows are standing in the pasture near the corral, lowing. The Roamer is with them, of course, and now and then gives that deep moan.

Three tiny calves are tied on the Green. Since something keeps their mothers away from them they are dejected and stand with hanging heads.

The dogs are lying near me. Bunny, the brown cocker, and Rachel, my white setter. She is eight months old. I sent her to the ranch from Los Angeles when she was a baby of three

47

months—a highly bred, valuable Llewelyn setter. I wanted a dog big enough and strong enough to follow my horse on long rides, as Bunny's little short legs get tired. I thought a setter would be just right.

But Michael had to leave the ranch soon after her arrival, and she has grown up with no training and no manners. Hardly knows her name! Knows only one thing, that life was made to do as you please in, and this means, for her, to run and run and run. And the more you are called and commanded to return, the faster you should run away.

As a result, she is as thin as a little snake. And nervous and timid and wild.

Michael is apologetic. The damage was done before he got back to the ranch. He has tried locking her into the tool house for days at a time, and she did eat better and picked up a little, but to keep a young dog shut up is not fair.

I look at Rachel, quite despairing of her; and as if she knew it, she rises, drops her head, and slinks out of sight.

But Bunny, so overjoyed to have me back, bursts into ecstatic tail-waggings every time I move or look at him.

Tomorrow I shall go to town again to get the cook, whose name is Etta Biggs, and on the same trip take down our yearling steer to have butchered, hung and stored for beef for us, during the summer.

It has rained.

I moved in with the typewriter.

Michael and Riley have returned. They did not find the two lost colts but spent an hour mending fence.

Michael looks burned, hard as nails, happy, and about twenty years younger than he really is. He has the physique of a college athlete.

The rain stopped and the sun came out and there was a rainbow.

"How," demanded Michael, "did all that short grass get into the bathtub?"

"Well, the terrace is covered with short grass; and after I had my sun bath on it this morning, I went up to the bathroom and rubbed myself off with the bath towel in the tub. A lot of the grass you had cut was sticking to me."

"You mustn't do that. The grass will wash down the pipe and clog it."

"But it was just a little bit of short grass; and the pipe's *so* big—" I made a big round with my hands.

"*So* big," he corrected, making a small round.

"I was going to scoop it up anyway."

"You don't have to. I scooped it up."

"Thanks. Am I a disorderly person?"

"Well, I wouldn't call you exactly orderly."

"My room's tidy right now."

"Well, you're not disorderly either—but it doesn't matter. A little disorder is permitted, you know, to a genius." There was a twinkle in his eye and good-humored mockery in his voice.

"Well, anyway," I declared, "you haven't got any ticks on you." We were standing in his room while I examined his bare back for ticks.

The other day, working on the dam in the meadow, he got two ticks.

I kissed him good night.

"How about you?" he asked.

"I haven't got any either."

"How do you know?"

"I'd hear them ticking." I grinned. "Will it keep you awake if I go down and play the piano?"

"Not a bit."

"I'll shut your door."

"You don't have to. I like it."

This kind word for my music warmed my heart, and I played an hour or two. Typed some more.

I'm going to bed now. I feel more calm than I did.

I don't like ticks. I do feel itchy. . . .

Chapter 7

No chance yet to tell Michael about my music.

Communication—I think of the African drums that shake a countryside just to communicate a tidbit of gossip. Or the Indian sign language—a series of suave gestures by which anything can be told. Sometimes the mere meeting of eyes delivers a shock of communication that can hardly be borne.

It links us, one to the other. So we must tell. Until I do, if it's only to pages of paper, it doesn't seem quite to have happened to me. So now I shall put it all down in this journal.

All my life I have been making things. Houses and gardens to live in. Things to wear and things to eat. And love and marriages and children and many Hollywood screenplays. But not, so far, a serious career as a composer.

Some time ago, I received a letter from Vernon Spencer, saying in effect, "If you haven't lost the urge to compose, or the ability, you ought to get at it again as there is now a good market for teaching pieces but very few good pieces. It is a crime—what they put out for children to learn. You have a charming vein of melody, and not enough education to make you turn up your nose at the idea, so get busy!"

There are two photographs of Vernon Spencer in my desk. One, as what the Germans call a *jungling*—and how dear a word, especially if translated *youngling*. It is the picture of a sixteen-year-old boy, or eighteen, possibly twenty. He has an arch, bright expression; candid expectant eyes behind studious spectacles, amazing big ears sticking out like small sails, and a sweetness over the whole face that is benign and almost beautiful.

50

The other picture (as he is now) is not beautiful and there is no resemblance to the *youngling*. This is what unremitting intellectual labor, plus genius, does to a face. If one did not know him a genius his signature in the right-hand corner of the picture would be proof of it. No one but a genius could write like that. But in Los Angeles and Hollywood, proof is not needed. He is the *maestro*. Besides, he admits it. Recounting some achievement of his own, he adds brightly, "Sheer genius, isn't it?"

Above the signature he has written a characteristic gibe, *To the only Mary I have ever loved.*

I gave his suggestion considerable thought, then decided I still had the urge and the ability, and if there was even a faint prospect of a market, I would certainly get busy. So I wrote eighteen teaching pieces, and now Schirmer has accepted four.

For years Spencer has been begging me to stop composing long enough for him to teach me how to compose. . . . *You should have studied as a schoolgirl, a child; did no one recognize your talent? Was there no one interested?*

And I hear my father's voice from long ago: "If you will only be serious about your music, Mary, I will not insist on your graduating from school; and when you are old enough I will send you to Europe to study."

But I was not serious about a career. I just loved music as I love breathing air and living life.

Continuing, Spencer said, "You could be at least as distinguished a composer as Chaminade."

I simply could not believe this for when I was a girl I and all my friends were playing Chaminade. *The Flatterer, The Scarf Dance.* Why!—she was famous on two continents.

I had first gone to Spencer because I already had a big pile of compositions and hoped to get them published.

He examined some themes I had written and burst out, "Every one a gem! Valuable work which, if developed, would be instantly accepted by any publisher. I can't stop playing them. Take this thing. Make a climax here, like this—simply superb! With a male chorus singing that it will lift you off your feet!"

But he qualified his praise. There were faults in all of them, he said; phrasing omitted; rests placed incorrectly and not of

51

proper duration. As they were they could not be published. Therefore, I must—I simply must—study. I had no choice. And he could promise that in three years I could learn all I needed to know.

It made me feel faint. I could not see myself as a career woman. I already had two children. But the divorce—that had changed things somewhat. It had left an emptiness. Perhaps some sort of serious work . . .

So I placed myself under Mr. Spencer and he began me on four-part harmony.

They always begin with that. The four parts are the four human voices, soprano, alto, tenor and bass. Hymns and chorals. Sung by oratorios or chorale societies or church choirs, these are magnificent. There probably were no happier moments in my childhood than when I stood in my father's church, singing the well-known melodies, watching my brother Reese up there in the choir—the soulful look in his eyes under the soft straight blond bang, mouth wide open above the black windsor tie, hymn-book in both hands—and all the rest of the choir, men and boys, so ordered, so dramatic in their black cassocks and white cottas, all their mouths wide open and the great and glorious roar going up.

But choirs and organs are not accessible for practice at home, nor for lessons in the teacher's studio. And the music as written in hymnbooks for just four notes is unattractive on the piano.

If you could use all ten of your fingers instead of four, and all over the keyboard instead of only two octaves, it could be made to sound like something. But no—just four fingers. And to accomplish this meager and miserable sound you have to memorize innumerable rules and exceptions to rules.

Arduous, unpleasant and unrewarding. All the same I worked very hard.

Spencer was excited by my work and said I was covering what would ordinarily be five lessons in one.

After six weeks the baby got diphtheria and I was quarantined for two months. Lessons had to stop.

During quarantine I had fun, composing. I completed six teaching pieces for piano as Spencer advised, and sent them off

52

to John Church Company. To my surprise they were accepted. When quarantine was over I wrote three more, a little more advanced. These were also accepted, and the largest music store in Los Angeles completely filled its window with the compositions of this new composer.

Spencer called me up and told me to go downtown and look at it.

I stood before that big store window marveling, not believing it was really me.

I decided to continue my study with Spencer. But just then I received an offer from Metro to go on their staff as special reader. The salary made the greatest difference in my small household. I began to look ahead and see good private schools for the children, summer vacations, . . .

And from that I went to scenario writing, ten years of it, with surprising success. Then my marriage to Michael, and never again an opportunity to study composition with Vernon Spencer or any other. But I continued composing. I couldn't help it.

We have kept in touch. He has never ceased to exhort me. But in late years there has been less peremptoriness. Less hope, I suppose. And I notice he has changed the tense. He no longer says, If you would only study—he says, If you had only studied.

Is it then really too late? This challenges me.

A girl marries, has children, makes a home, brings up the children. Pretty soon half her life is gone. The children like birds crowd to the edge of the nest and fly away. My daughter, in Los Angeles now under the care of her father, is studying piano with Vernon Spencer, studying voice under Mara Kempbal; she has a voice like an angel and red hair and long legs and sings in the choir and her two first names, like mine, are Mary O'Hara but we call her Pat.

And my son. Before he went to West Point he was all long loose legs and arms. They seemed without bones. To see him put his six feet two into a chair one wanted to lean down and lift certain parts he had left behind and help him get all together in the chair.

Then, once when I visited him at the Academy, we were walk-

53

ing around and suddenly he said in his dreamy way, I think we're going to get caught. He explained the ceremony of the sunset gun and the lowering of the flag.

As he spoke there was the boom of the gun. His hand snapped to the salute and his body faced around and froze to attention— my ungainly colt and his undisciplined arms and legs! And so he stood, drawn up tight, molded to significance, every inch of his body obedient, while the National Anthem was sung and the flag lowered and I struggled with tears. Anything beautiful makes me cry.

So now, it's no longer I who buy his clothes for him (that magnificent uniform!). And those three years of study that would be needed to make me a second Chaminade—I have them now.

But more would be needed than time. Money would be needed —a good deal. Spencer is an expensive teacher.

He has a large house in the Los Feliz district. It is built on a steep hillside overlooking barancas, hills, and those abrupt craggy peaks that shoot up on the edge of Los Angeles, making everything look like an illustration on a poster.

His studio is a long room with one side half filled with plate glass through which he can see that extraordinary view. He sits at the grand piano, a little left of center middle and gazes out that window while his hands are on the keys. To the left of him is a second grand piano, the Erhard, for the pupil. (For me?)

But we are economizing. And even if I were for a sufficient part of the year in Los Angeles, it would be pure self-indulgence to place myself at the Erhard for a course of lessons.

There is something else. One hears that to train a musician who is already composing is not always wise. For, they say, if first you compose, then go to school, you will learn rules, a dictionary of musical terms, forms and methods, but you won't compose any more. (Always this strange opposition between knowing and doing.)

In New York one winter I heard of a man called Bleeker, organist and teacher of teachers, and wanted to hear some of his lectures on improvisation. I called him up, a little at a loss

54

how to introduce myself, and said, "Well—I'm a composer—I've had a number of things published, but I'm very ignorant, and I—"

I was interrupted by his chuckle. "An ignorant composer! That's the only kind there are!"

On the other hand, the editors of all the publishing houses are graduates of the music schools; they catch the least divergence from the rules, and it is by them that my compositions are judged —either accepted or refused.

So I am buffeted from one position to the other.

One thing I know. I am in confusion and uncertainty. The music keeps pouring out, but anyone can convince me it is worthless.

It is time to do something about this.

So, in New York, I did two things.

I went to Schirmer's and inquired about text books. Whose books, whose system of study was best? Dr. Percy Goetschius, I was told, the strictest teacher of all, the one from whom all other methods derive. I have a picture of him, the distinguished, earnest, kindly, bearded, German face; and underneath the picture, the list of his university degrees and achievements in the world of international music. He, like Spencer, is a graduate of the Leipzig Conservatory.

One hears that brains deteriorate as one gets older. Well, I could put that to the test this summer. Perhaps one is slower, memorizes less easily, but youth has disadvantages too. It is preoccupied with the biological urge. It takes everything seriously, especially itself. It is apt to be touchy. It gets its heart broken. It has much to lose; it must succeed.

But let the years accumulate, and disappointments and failures too, and soon one is traveling light indeed. For is not everything lost already?

Anyway—determination's the thing—I ordered the books. *Tone Relations, Lessons in Form, Elementary Counterpoint, Applied Counterpoint.* They were to be sent to me at the ranch.

The other thing I did was to write Spencer and suggest that since he has a sixteen-year-old son, and I have this summer camp

55

for boys, would he not like to send Jimmie here for the camp term and so arrange a credit for me against lessons next winter in Los Angeles?

. . . can't wait for his answer to come. . . .

"What's your letter?" asked Michael, bursting out of the door.

I was sitting in the hammock, the mail in my lap, a broad grin on my face, already seeing myself seated at the Erhard in Spencer's studio.

Michael held a sandwich in both hands. Chopped onion and a fried egg between pieces of rye bread. So then I told him about everything, the pieces Schirmer had bought, and that Jimmie was coming to the camp. I showed him Spencer's letter. "Please let me have a list of what Jimmie will need . . . linen, blankets, toilet articles, clothes . . . bedroll? Rifle? And if you have any new compositions ready for criticism send them so that extension lessons can begin immediately. . . ."

"So you see," I finished, "that will mean a credit, and music lessons from Spencer for me next winter when I am in Los Angeles."

"How big a boy is he?" asked Michael finishing his sandwich and going down the stone steps.

"Small for sixteen."

Michael got the shovel and went about cleaning the manure off the Green. "By the way, I've had Madame Pompadour brought in and put in the Stable Pasture for you."

"Oh, good!"

"Be careful. She's been on the range all winter."

"I know." Pom is a dark blue roan. Almost grape-colored, with a full black tail and mane and the wild look in her big dark eyes that is characteristic of so many horses that have spent their lives on these upland ranges.

She is nervous. She bolts. She runs away. Sometimes she rears and goes over backward. We forgive rearing, which is just exuberance, but falling over backward is going to extremes, and we don't like it.

I am crazy about her. She has wonderful gaits. We are good

56

friends. I am, to my chagrin, very soothing to all horses. When Michael rides them they are gathered, they prance, side-step and appear to be on the point of exploding.

Michael put the shovel away. "I think," he said, "if Jimmie Spencer is a little fellow, that dark, three-year-old bay would be about right for him."

"The mare?"

"Yes. I forget what you named her."

"Princess. Prinny for short. But she's not broken yet."

"No. I've got to get at those broncs right away."

I sat there a long time dreaming about music.

The sun was setting. Long level rays struck the opposite cliff.

I heard the clatter of some shale and small rocks cascade down into the rivulet at its base—some horses are picking their way across the face of it and now I see the blaze of gold on their bright hides.

Michael is always wondering if he could not somehow lift that water to the top and persuade it to leap down in a long arching ribbon of whitewater.

When the moon rises, we see it first over the cliff there—just the thin gold edge. Then as you watch, it pushes up and in less than a minute it is sitting there, a big round golden Japanese lantern with the black branches of the jack pines laced across it.

How fast the earth spins—

Chapter 8

Driving out yesterday with Etta Biggs, my new cook, she suddenly said, "Thing that worries me is, are you and I going to clash over the food?"

Astonished, I asked her why we should.

"Because you're an easterner. Do you like the way we cook in the west?"

"Well"—I hesitated, thinking of some of the heavy floury gravies, like paste, the thin, dry, fried steaks, the heavy flapjacks—"perhaps there are just a few things I would like done differently; steaks, gravies, and so on. But supposing I just tell you if there's anything I would like different. Otherwise, do it your own way. You don't mind being told, do you?"

"Not if you tell me nice like," she answered with dignity.

Then she told me about herself. Most of her bodily ailments, she said, came from not having been properly taken care of when her children were born. The story expanded and grew, and it appeared that every single misfortune that had come upon her was due to neglect, or abuse. She fairly blazed with indignation over all that had been put upon her; and put upon others too. People on relief rolls should get more money. Much more.

"People should be took care of," she said. "And not so skimpy, neither. It's more than just rent and food and clothes they need, by the time they have their laundry sent out and something for pocket money—"

I listened.

"And the thing that makes me the maddest," she said, "is when I see people having one child right after the other. I could just get right up and fight—what right have they to make these

58

children be born? I know I never forgave my parents for having me."

"Are you really sorry you were born, Etta?"

"I sure am. If I'd had anything to say about it, I wouldn't have chose the parents I had; they never gave me no advantages. And if I'd known as much as I do now, I'd never have had no children myself."

"Wouldn't you really?"

"I sure wouldn't. Whenever I see a hearse going by," continued my cheerful domestic, "I think, there's luck for you. Why couldn't it have been me?"

Whether or not it was this conversation that caused my morale to slip, I do not know. At any rate, I found myself again in the same dreary confusion I had been in a day or so before.

After having settled Etta in her quarters and given her directions for supper, I wandered out to find Michael.

I found him submerged in the problem of finding a particular shape and size of a bit of lead pipe to make the fountain fount.

He sat in the tool house over a pile of junk, fingering this one, then that one, muttering to himself.

I sat down nearby, discouraged. One might as well have hoped for small talk from an Indian Yogi.

I began to mutter to myself, too. "As long as Pom is in the corral, I would go for a ride if it weren't so foggy and cold."

He pricked up his ears at mention of a horse. "Don't let a little thing like fog stop you!"

I sat thinking, and he again fell into his abyss.

I wandered away.

I went slowly upstairs, intending to wash my hands. I pulled myself up short. "None of that!" I said.

With determination I got into riding clothes. The cold was really bitter. I put on a woolen polo shirt, over that a sweater, over that a leather jacket, and pulled my woolen ski cap on my head.

Pom was very fresh after her long free winter on the range and it was all I could do to hold her.

First I took her down into the Home Meadow, for I wanted to practice some jumps on her. I made her jump the creek where

59

it's narrow there, back and forth a couple of dozen times, and I found out what it is that unsettles me with this horse. It's the way she abruptly changes her gait for the take-off rather than the jump itself.

But Pom wanted to go, not to be reined in and forced here and there, so I left the meadow for the upper ranges where the fog would be thinner and I would have a chance to look for the lost colts. I had asked Riley which they were. Playboy and Floss. Those two beautiful little sorrels, inseparable friends. You never saw one without the other.

I rode upward through the Home Pasture—the acreage immediately surrounding the house and the Green.

Wind was roaring in the pines on top of the cliff so that, as I rode through them, it sounded as if I were by the sea with an equinoctial surf in my ears.

I felt the endlessness of the sea.

The smell of the jack pines, wet in the fog and mist, was delicious and clean beyond words. I breathed it deep.

A bluebird, color of larkspur, became interested in us and followed along, flitting from one bush to the next, keeping just abreast of us. Such a small thing, he. Such big things, Pom and I. But he had the advantage; free, light, powerful.

He cocked his head and peered at me. I peered back. I am always expecting to exchange greetings with the birds and animals when I meet their eyes. Sometimes, very rarely, it seems as if I do. And if it happens, something more happens—I feel a little pang and a bond is forged between us. I have often looked into the Roamer's eyes but have never really met them. Because I am afraid. If I could do that we might be friends.

I went on up through the Stable Pasture, crossed the county road and began to mount the saddleback.

Pom's body gathered and her pace quickened. She is tireless, carries me like a feather and would take hills at a gallop if I would let her.

On the upland, the mists and clouds rolled about us. The wind still roared. It had a pounding rhythm in it, as if I held a shell to my ear and was really hearing that strange echo of surf and sea—and suddenly I felt despair. Oh, why? It should delight me, but no—it is too big. It is epic, and when suddenly there was a break in the coiling fog and my glance pierced through, following undulations that went on to a distance no eye could reach—here again was endlessness—all—all so beautiful it whips the heart out of you and makes you one with it—but it is a graft; done with a knife—blood and anguish.

Rachel and Bunny had started out with me but were soon led away by their hunting instincts. Bunny showed up every so often, as if knowing that he was in duty bound, but after one or two flashes of Rachel through the fog, during the first mile of riding, running like a mad thing, I lost her, and Bunny and I went on alone.

I pulled up near the crest of the saddleback and sat there a long time scanning the world, but saw no colts—no life at all.

Pom looked too. All the horses get terribly excited when they are on these high places. Her body quivered. Her proud neck was straight up, her ears sharply pricked. I let the reins lie loose on her neck and she kept turning her head first in one direction, then the other, with small, abrupt jerks. But fog closed over us again.

It was impossible to see.

I returned to curl up in the corner of the sofa by a roaring fire with a book on rhythm by Lussy in my hands, and to wait to see what Etta would produce in the way of eastern cooking by supper time.

. . . very late . . . a little white ghost outside the door. Rachel. Muddy, bedraggled, thin and wild beyond description, her flanks heaving in and out, her tongue hanging like a long wet streamer from the side of her mouth.

I have fired Etta and telegraphed to Hilda in San Francisco on the bare chance that she may still be able to come to me for the summer.

Apologizing, Rachel creeps up to me to be fondled.

All dogs love this, but in Rachel it is too desperate a need. After a moment or two I take my hand from her head and tell

61

her to lie down. But, cringing, she creeps to Michael and begs of him. Then she's off to Riley where he stands watering the Green.

I have seen her at lunch time, seated between the knees of one of the windmill crew, basking and blissful under the heavy, fondling hands. And if anyone raises his voice to her—let alone shouts—she goes into a state of shock.

All children shout at dogs, and nearly every dog begins life in a home with at least one child in it. And in the country everyone yells at them.

One calls. They do not appear. One calls louder and louder, one shouts. If it is cold, standing there, and one has left a good program on the radio or an interesting book or conversation to come out there with the food and call the dogs, some impatience enters the voice. If you are masculine, you get profane. At last one bellows.

The dogs do not mind. When, having at last heard those calls, they come as fast as they can, tails are wagging, eyes are adoring, they are ready to leap and love and to be fed and caressed and taken inside and comfortably possessed.

The shouts mean nothing to them. They are sure of the love that is underneath the noise.

But Rachel minds.

How can all this be stopped for her? All the men call her and shout at her.

How she skedaddles. How angry they get.

I see her hiding somewhere in the shrubbery, looking out, seeing all, determined and ready to run away. Her timid manner, I am sure, comes not so much from fear as from guilt. She has no intention of obeying and is crushed by her own wickedness.

She is not even properly house broken.

In the country where doors are often open and everyone goes in and out, where dogs are outdoors more than in, it is natural for them to attend to their own needs without asking permission. Strictly their own affair. And all's well provided the doors do not by some mischance remain closed longer than usual.

Rachel will have to be house broken and she will have to learn to come when she is called.

I am planning a special call of my own to summon her, a sound that shall be nothing like all these other shouts and calls that she has been running away from for so long. I would like to use a whistle, but cannot, as the horses are trained to come at a whistle. So I shall call her on two notes, two high chest tones, pitched on the fifth then the third of the scale of D major.

This small third is a plaintive interval. Children, calling to each other from one hill top to another, are apt to use it.

In Switzerland and Germany the yodels one hears bouncing from one mountain to another contain it. And I can always hit it exactly because orchestras tune on that A.

Now today the fog has gone and it is warm and clear. All the colors are intense. I've been lying in the hammock at the end of the terrace, basking. No loneliness today. Respite. I like to catch a glimpse of Riley and George going here and there—barn, corral, spring house, bunkhouse—the sudden bursts of sound that drift down from the windmill crew—the slamming of a door—

Across the Calf Pasture, up on Number Sixteen, I saw a sudden flash of color—the yearlings streaming down over the range to the creek for water. They are the fastest things on the ranch. They don't run, they just *pour* over the ground—across the little swales and draws—up or down hill means nothing to them; sorrels, bright bays, chestnuts—they blaze with color when the sun strikes them.

Now the day is waning and the light changing for sunset. Soft and lovely. No clouds. Just a clear emerald green—and the evening star big and golden.

The windmill will soon be finished.

Chapter 9

When I am improvising at the piano and certain sounds emerge which enthrall me—sometimes just a short progression of chords, or a change of key, or a bit of melody—I play it over and over, taking the most intense pleasure in it.

A sort of hypnosis results; at last I am oblivious of everything around me and I see visions, nature pictures: sea, mountain peaks, flower faces, sunsets. As a child, I called this going into another world, and knew that certain sounds let me into it. This would exhaust me emotionally. My father would look at me long and thoughtfully, and say, Mary, you look as if you had been drawn through a knothole. I would feel guilty and ashamed and hang my head.

I always know when this is going to happen. I become intensely susceptible and aware and know that I am going to enter that different world (which now I call *Shinar*). The nature-visions play upon me with great power, sometimes frighteningly.

The light, for instance, the strange way it alters in mood from dawn to dark.

First that light of early morning which I have written about in *Joy*. So innocent and gay and heartfelt, with the birds singing all together in a rapturous concert, "Here it is again! The day! The sun! And air and wings!" The whole world a cup yearning upward, lifting and opening itself for more light, and more and more—

And more light pours down until the vast outpouring of noon; and then it begins to be cruel. No cranny is spared. In early afternoon it is crushing. No faintest line of shade. Then, slowly, the sun rays tilt a little and become oblique and each sharp edge is softened by a thin strip of shadow. Now the whole world is etched with ever-widening lines of blue and purple; and watching the shadows grow you begin to smile and wonder and feel a mystery. And through all the upper air is a breath of relief that softly deepens into sadness as the day wanes.

Twilight is enchantment and magic and exciting and full of things. And birds sing dramatically in the twilight, one at a time, as if making important announcements.

Quite often, out of one of these semi-hypnotized experiences at the piano, comes a new composition, as when I wrote *Enchantment of Dusk*. I have often thought the piano itself has something to do with it. Not only the limpid beauty of tone and matched-pearl action, but something more.

For this particular instrument is special. It has a history.

It is a grand—the largest size the Mason and Hamlin company makes—and was selected out of stock by the famous composer and pianist Leopold Godowski for a young piano pupil of his. (This was in Los Angeles, a good many years ago.)

The boy was considered a genius. The Polish father who supported a whole brood of children by his position as typesetter on the Los Angeles *Times* made superhuman sacrifices and the piano was bought and installed in the living room of the little Hollywood bungalow where they lived. There was no other furniture in the room. None of the other children was allowed to touch the piano or even enter the room. This piano and the boy were the whole promise of their lives. The future.

For a year the boy studied with Godowski and the piano was never silent. Then it was closed and locked.

Interested philanthropists, persuaded by Godowski, were taking charge of the young genius. They would send him to Paris to be educated. When he returned he would be a world-famous virtuoso and would no longer need this piano. The greatest of the piano manufacturers would be vying with each other for the honor of supplying him with an instrument.

In those years I too was living in Los Angeles, and I was looking for a piano as fine as the one on which I had played as a child.

In the Brooklyn house where I grew up, music was taken very

65

seriously. This was because my maternal grandmother lived there with us, and she was as full of music as a rose is of perfume.

She owned a harp and played it beautifully. A harp is a story-book instrument. In fact it comes out of the Bible and is preached about in church. Of course it is golden and encrusted with cherubs and angel heads. No one could possibly have been more suited to be the companion of cherubs and heavenly instruments than my stately grandmother. Occasionally I was gathered into this celestial association by being placed on the floor as she played, delightfully mixed up with her long black silk train, and permitted to shift the pedals when the key was changed.

There was another imposing instrument in that Brooklyn drawing room. This was a Steinway piano, concert size, a gift from my grandmother to Elma, who was studying piano "seriously."

As soon as I was tall enough to stand alone and get my hands on those keys, I did so. To hear a fifth played low down on such a piano with the lid up is an experience for anyone who has ears to hear. For a musical child, for me, in those first years of my life, it was a quickening; it committed me to music.

When my grandmother played she would allow me to sit close beside her on the piano bench. As long as she would play I would stay there. She would glance down at me with her look of combined sweetness and quizzical amusement, and I would watch her hands and learn the tunes. And as soon as she had left the piano, start picking them out myself.

I learned by listening. Soon I was playing many things by ear.

Anyone who, from infancy on, has played on such a piano as that is spoiled for anything inferior.

So when I married and moved to Los Angeles and rented a Knabe grand, I was soon dissatisfied, and sent it back and rented a Baldwin. Then sent that back and bought an old Chickering.

I was still dissatisfied. I played on all the pianos in the Steinway salesrooms, but none compared to Elma's. The music companies and salesmen became accustomed to my search for just the right piano.

66

Onc afternoon, playing there alone, I noticed a small door in a corner. Opening it, I found myself in a sort of attic. There was nothing in it but one piano. Here was the twin of Elma's. Long, black, closed, majestic, waiting. It truly was waiting.

This was the concert piano held in readiness by the Steinway people for visiting virtuosos.

I slipped onto the bench, lifted the lid, and played that deep fifth, the low D and A. And there was the magical, reverberating sound that had awakened my soul in childhood.

They let me play there as much as I wanted.

One day a salesman called me to tell me he thought there was a piano in a little bungalow in the Hollywood Hills which would interest me. He told me how to get there, for there was no telephone.

So the practice piano of the young Polish virtuoso (who, alas! never materialized) is now standing in my living room here at the ranch. It was shipped from Los Angeles in a crate the size of a small hut, put off at the Buford station, then carefully hoisted into our big hay wagon. Two work teams, Jock and Ginger, Fanny and Cap, drew it at a slow walk over the plains to the house where piano movers from Denver were waiting to set it up.

Enchantment of Dusk was written late one fall soon after we had come to the ranch.

Michael was ill when I composed that piece.

I felt guilty, working so steadily at the piano, probably driving him half crazy when I should have been up there nursing him.

So I went up and aired out the room for a few minutes, pulling the covers up to his chin until I shut the window again. I freshened his pillows, brought him fruit juice, pulled up a chair and took my sewing.

He turned his face to the wall. "Go down and play," he said.

"Do you like this piece?" I asked at the door.

"Yes."

"What do you like about it?"

No answer. He did not turn.

I waited a while, then started to leave and heard his voice.

"It is such a—lovely—free—wandering thing—"

I cherished the words.

When it was done I saw that it had glamor and a mood. It truly was pervaded by that strange light of dusk. There was enchantment in it, and one of the birds calling in it was a hermit thrush. They are never near, never in your garden or on the edge of a woods, but always buried in the heart of it; and someone hearing the piece cried, That bird! *so remote—*

Michael's throat got worse. It was quinsy and his fever kept going up, so the day came when I helped him bundle up and I drove him to the doctor's office in Cheyenne.

Because there was no room to park I drove the car around and around the block while I waited.

Michael went in and sat down in front of the doctor who is a great friend of ours, a Hungarian. He speaks perfect English but in a strange nasal whine.

The doctor directed his small glaring headlight into Michael's wide-open mouth and exclaimed, "What—a—beauty!"

(When Michael told me this afterward I knew just how he sounded.)

Then he picked up his lancet and the nurse moved in with the basin.

In fifteen minutes Michael was on the street, holding a wad to his mouth and looking up and down the block for me.

In bed again at the ranch, pillows behind him, a pain-killer inside him, an extra strong highball in his hand, the open fire flickering, and the delicious comfort of painlessness oozing from every pore—it did me good to look at him.

The piece—*Enchantment of Dusk*—has had a small career.

I took it to New York one year and offered it to the Sam Fox Publishing Company with an alternate title: *Twilight and Birdcalls.*

Mr. Fox has music in his soul, and when his editor is playing a piece for him to hear, he walks up and down the studio, concentrating, listening intently, and illustrating the ideas that are

68

suggested in the title by making expressive gestures with his hands and body.

An enchanted dusk with birds calling in it would be quite difficult for even a trained actor to act, but Mr. Fox was nothing daunted.

Tall, very handsome and always dressed in London-tailored tweeds, he stood quietly waiting while the piano performed the birdcalls. It was the dusk that intrigued him, and the enchantment.

"Now this is the enchantment beginning," he exclaimed and began waveringly to progress around the room, lifting his arms and allowing them to float about like seaweed under water.

Then the piece traveled still farther.

A friend of mine in Holland showed some of my piano compositions to a Dutch piano virtuoso, Pierre Palla. He chose *Twilight and Birdcalls* and played it at a concert in The Hague.

Chapter 10

All the animals love music, I find. When I sit playing in the living room, the top half of the Dutch door is open. Beyond that is the narrow terrace held up by a two-foot dry stone wall (beautifully laid by Michael), then the flower border, then the Green.

There the animals foregather. Sometimes they come up onto the terrace, to the very door. Birds come, perch on the pergola, hop and twitter, and often burst into such loud singing it seems they are trying to drown my piano.

Only since I have returned has music entered Rachel's life. I think it astounds her.

When, for a pause and a breath of air, I rise and go to lean on the lower half of the Dutch door and look out, there they are.

Glancing down, I see both dogs on the door mat.

"Why, here is Rachel!"

Bunny wags his tail violently. *I brought her.*

Felix and Missy are sitting in the sun at the far end of the terrace washing themselves.

There have been occasions when, sitting at the piano, I have turned my head and seen the pricked ears of young Rheingold at the door.

No sign, as yet, of the lost colts. Today it is brilliantly clear. I shall try again.

I made a wily plan. I would pay no attention to Rachel, but would call Bunny to me. This was treachery, for Rachel, having followed Bunny from infancy, has the impulse to come whenever he is called.

Michael would help me. Then we would grab her and lock them both into the tool house, and so I would save her from running still more flesh off her bones.

But I was already in riding clothes. Would she notice?

She watched Michael as Bunny ran to him, and when Michael called, "Here, Rachel! Here, Rachel!" she turned and fled.

Michael shouted commandingly. I shouted. Riley saw her streaking past the bunkhouse and *he* shouted. The men at the windmill shouted.

Several darted out and tried to catch her as she whipped through the gorge. She ran low on the ground like a weasel, her long tail so far underneath her body it could have touched her chin.

Michael lost his temper.

A few more terrific shouts and we all acknowledged defeat.

Rachel was sitting in the aspen grove above the stables, a vantage point from which she could see everything, particularly the corral in which I was saddling Madame Pompadour, and from which she could take off speedily into the wide wide world if the slightest move were made to capture her.

Riding up the mountain I wondered how I could make her love and obey me. I saw her streaking past.

She raised her face to me, not triumphantly, but just so happy that the joy spilled over. She is mad for freedom, but she's anybody's dog. She has no confidence. The frightened, cringing, crafty, slinky way she looks around! Like a wild animal without home or friend or owner.

I let Pom go up the saddleback at a canter. Rachel was already out of sight.

High on a ridge behind Section Twenty I pulled up and sat scanning the world. Thirty miles east, in Cheyenne, there were slabs of pure gold in the sky—that's the gold-leaf dome of the Capitol. Stretching both east and west was the railroad. I marked it by the trains on it—tiny toy trains. Going west, climbing the "big hill," two locomotives pulled them—I could see the clouds of smoke; but going the other way, east, that was downhill; and they balled the jack and had no extra locomotive. It is a busy road. A train passes, so they say, every three minutes. I could see the white jacket of a Pullman porter as he stood on the dining car platform.

Ringing the scene, far away, west and south, were the mountains—the Snowy Range, the Neversummer Range—so the Indians named them. Fourth of July they always have a ski meet in the mountains down there in Colorado.

No storms today in any direction—just fleets of white clouds sailing—but straining my eyes to those far peaks, I saw there was wind there; for as I watched I saw a feather of snow whip up, like smoke from a chimney; and I knew it was a mountainside that had been torn loose and hurled aloft. I saw it hover and spread and whirl—yes, a wild wind—and then slowly disintegrate and melt away. All was calm again.

I rode on, holding Pom to a walk. Suddenly she stopped, her head came up with a sharp jerk, and she whinnied. An answering whinny came from behind a low hill to my left. I squeezed my leg against her, we moved forward around the hill, and there was the whole band of yearlings, all heads up, watching us, ready to fly off. One little blue roan came out to meet us; and suddenly he and Pom were in an excited dither of reunion. This was her yearling colt. The other colts milled about us. Rachel had found them long before I had, and was seated on the opposite side of the little draw, calmly watching.

I had time, now, while Pom and the colt were nickering and playing around each other, to look over the others. Rachel vanished.

The colts are always rough in the spring with long fur that's beginning to come off in patches. Sometimes they have changed so in color and size during the winter that I can hardly recognize them.

I expected two to be missing from the original sixteen, but, counting, made it fifteen. This puzzled me. I counted again. Fifteen. How could Playboy and Floss both be missing unless a strange colt had got in with our bunch?

Looking at the sorrels, one of them seemed to me remarkably like Playboy. But Floss, who had unusual markings, was undoubtedly missing.

Riding home, I smelled carrion on the breeze.

The smell was strong.

I drew rein and looked about, then saw Rachel on the brink of a little gully, looking down.

I galloped up. There lay Floss. Hard to think that was all

72

that was left of the lovely little filly—the body already half rotted away, the hide burst, shrunken and dried, the teeth bared, the lovely cream-colored tail that had given her her name (for it had looked like a skein of embroidery floss) just a tangled, matted switch.

All sorts of things had been at the carcass. Mercifully, it was still half covered with unmelted snow.

I reconstructed the accident. All the colts racing across the prairie together as they constantly do. The ground covered with snow. The gully partially or fully filled. Unable to see just where there was firm ground and where not, Floss makes the leap, either miscalculates or her foot slips or the bank gives way with her as she lands. And she's down.

Back at the corral I told Riley.

"But there's two missing."

"Only one, Riley. Playboy's with the bunch."

"But we didn't see him."

"You were looking for the two together. When you didn't see Floss you figured he was gone too. But he's there."

I unsaddled Pompadour.

"How many colts was there?"

"Fifteen."

Riley scratched his head, mystified. He is a comic. He has short bowed legs and always a surprised questioning grin on his Irish face.

I walked into the living room to find Michael standing before the fireplace, a wild look on his face.

"I'm in the doghouse. You came just in time."

"What's the matter?"

"The windmill is up but it doesn't turn."

"It doesn't turn!"

I was aghast. Then remembered with relief, "But there's no wind today."

"A little. Enough. It ought to move, but it doesn't stir. Here is all this time lost, so much to do, no water in yet, and I don't know what to do first, where to begin. Should I try to siphon the water? Or buy a pressure pump?"

73

He had the Montgomery Ward book in his hand open to the page where the pumps were catalogued.

He was distraught. My heart began to beat. I felt it was a catastrophe.

"Floss is dead," I said. "I found her skeleton up in Section Nineteen. Playboy's with the bunch."

I wish the windmill would go.

We stood and looked at the lazy windmill.

Now and then, with a strong gust of wind, the arms would turn for a few moments, and pump a little water.

"Yay—ay—ay—" Michael would shout.

And I too. "Yay—ay—ay—" And the dogs came running at these strange sounds and leaped and barked and wagged their tails.

Then it would turn slower and slower—become motionless.

"Anyway," I said, "it's not a major disaster."

"It *is* a major disaster!"

"No. If we had drilled for water here, there and everywhere, and found none as many people do, *that* would have been a disaster. But we found this good flow without much drilling. Now if we can't pump it with the mill and lift it that way, we'll lift it some other way. This simply means delay."

"The boys'll be here in two weeks and I've got three horses to break and train before they come." His voice was desperate.

"It won't matter so much if the water is not running when they get here. The horses have to be broken—that's important."

We have to get a windmill expert out; see if eight-foot blades instead of six-foot will do the trick. If not, see if the water can be siphoned from the well into our spring, a pressure pump put into the basement of the house, the mill taken down—

When anything stumps Michael he gets sick. So this time he has neuralgic pains on one side of his face, a slight cold; hoarseness.

He has tried to siphon it.

It won't siphon.

74

He blames himself passionately for everything that goes wrong.

"This time I thought I had taken every precaution; gone over every possibility before I ordered the mill; and *still* I was wrong!"

"But," I cried, "how could you tell in advance about the wind? You spotted the water all right; that's the main thing. And there always seemed a good draught of air through the gorge."

"I could have tried out the air currents more thoroughly. Should have. Could have run up flags there, day after day, to just that height, before ordering the mill."

So his cold gets worse.

Old George goes around looking very smug.

The windmill man has come with another "expert." They have inspected it thoroughly, inquired into the reasons of its coma, taken pulse and temperature, decided that, after all, there would have to be a pump to lift the water from the well to the big tank on the hillside above, from which it will be piped down into the house.

They retired with Michael and the Montgomery Ward catalogue into his study to choose the pump.

Michael wrote out the order and they took it to town to mail.

Before leaving, however, they replaced the six-foot blades with eight-foot, just to see what would happen.

Nothing happened.

Michael, having ordered the pump, feels much better. His neuralgic pains are gone and his voice is as usual.

He tells me happily that the pump will be in and the water running in the house by Sunday.

This is of course impossible, as today is Wednesday and the pump won't arrive for several days.

But at any rate, things are moving.

Where is the good-looking, well-dressed man who met me at the bus station in Cheyenne when I arrived from New York? His riding boots were polished and his whipcord breeches immaculate. That thick blond hair flat and burnished with much brushing.

Army life not only gives a man a fine physique and carriage, it is apt to make him a bit of a dandy, too. I thoroughly approve. Men need to enhance their appearance with clothes and grooming as much as women do.

But besides grooming of course he is very good looking. People turn to look at his hard bronzed face with the big white-toothed smile, those keen—very keen—never-smiling ice-blue eyes. The nose, blunt and abrupt, is the giveaway of his temper.

But now!

His work clothes consist of a battered, perspiration-stained hat; baggy old trousers covered with patches and discolorations; a drab gray flannel shirt open at the throat; heavy, shapeless, square, farmer boots with elastic sides; coarse white socks crumpled above them.

I never see him when he isn't carrying a hammer, files, pieces of wood or iron. His handsome, square hands with their strange wide fingers are always grimy, always cut or bruised as he goes about setting things right for the summer; rearranging the tool house, chicken house, stables, machinery. Besides the big things like the windmill and the horses there are endless details to be attended to. And when the work, for the moment, is over, he reacts into semicoma, sitting there by the radio smoking his pipe, motionless, staring, no light in his face, dark hollows under his eyes.

Hilda has come.

And now everything is changed.

I have put my room in perfect order. The little sewing table by the window with yellow flowers on it. My desk, so neat, with all the papers tucked into racks. I have filled the rest of the house with flowers. This is because now we're a team, Hilda and I. And you must pay attention to your team work. But when you're alone, you can get very slack.

I have been to town and bought three dresses for a dollar each. I have one on now—red, with a small white polka dot, a little sash in the back and a zipper all the way down the front. It is light, cool, easy to get into, and has an air of insouciance. So I feel insouciant.

76

Chapter 11

There are lots of fish in Lone Tree Creek and the water has not yet been taken out of it and diverted into the irrigation ditches that run along the shoulders of the meadows.

This will be done when the dams have been repaired. Then the ditches will be cut at intervals and the water will pour down over the meadows and flood them and so force the hay.

Until then the meadows are dry; the brood mares and their foals and of course the stallion are still in winter quarters—the aspen grove at the far end of Castle Rock Meadow.

The meadows, each one a long eliptical saucer, run the length of the ranch and are connected with dams.

So if I don't go fishing now before the meadows are flooded I'll probably miss it altogether.

The sky is overcast today; good weather for fishing.

The first thing to do was locate Missy. She is as determined to accompany me on my expeditions as the dogs are.

I found her sound asleep in the corner of the sofa in the living room. She was on her side, curled up like a caterpillar, her innocent face slightly upturned, eyes tight shut and four little paws dangling and limp against the creamy fur of her belly.

No human infant wakes when his mother moves him. Nor do my animals startle at my touch. When I passed my hand lightly down Missy's soft fur, from tip to tail, there was not the quiver of an eyelid. So I went out and called George and told him to dig me some worms.

Michael would be surprised, I thought, as I started off, when we had trout for supper. I would tell Hilda not to cook them in corn meal, but just in salt pork fat and in the open air so they would have the taste of wood smoke. The dogs appeared from nowhere, leaped all over me, then took off on a fresh rabbit trail.

I know where the trout are, close under the bank at every turn.

As I fished I was thinking back to the beginning of the ranch.

It must have been this creek. Without the creek there wouldn't have been the dams. Without the dams there couldn't have been the hay. Without hay, no Mary-Dairy, nor boys' camp—in fact, no ranch.

And I wouldn't be standing here now, fishing in it.

I felt a strike and jerked my line out with a ten-inch rainbow trout on the end of it.

Four things happened at once.

Missy shot out of the bushes behind me and leaped at the wriggling sliver of silver. The trout fell off the hook. The dogs, unaccountably, were there, saw the trout go into the water and plunged in after it. I dropped my can of worms.

As I stooped to gather them up I felt a Presence and turned to look. The Roamer stood behind me, watching, the short chain hanging from his nose.

I stood petrified. The dogs came out of the water, got as close to me as they could, and shook themselves vigorously.

From infancy on, one is taught not to show fear. One is even told not to *be* afraid (and how silly this is!). All the same I instantly knew that the Roamer had no evil intentions. He was curious. He saw that something was going on and he wanted to know what it was. Besides, he didn't want to be left out. Animals are congenitally lonesome and seek companions. (Unless they are sick. Unless they are about to die. Unless a female is about to give birth.)

In one other respect they resemble their human big brothers— they seek security. Let some human being take over, speak with authority, show willingness to seize and possess them, and they will fling the burden of themselves and their whole lives upon you with love and gratitude.

As my fear subsided I turned to Missy with exasperation. She could and probably would spoil everything. If she accompanies me on a fishing trip she usually sits on the bank motionless,

78

right under my line, her eyes directed down into the water. I think she can see the fish swim up, nibble, taste and take the bait. The moment my line jerks him out into the air she competes with me for possession.

I called her, "Here, kitty," my hand held out.

She can never resist my hand and ran to me with her sharp little cry of love. I lifted her and put her against my left shoulder, where she assumed her usual snuggling position with one arm flung around my neck.

As I walked up the creek the Roamer followed and soon was joined by Rheingold, junior stud.

The dogs ran ahead, torn between the desire to keep track of me, not miss anything, and yet be off on every hot scent.

I took my stand at the next bend. The dogs sat down, watching me, their tongues hanging out, whimpering with eagerness for something to happen. But nothing happened, except, far away, some movement in the grass which I could not see, and they were off again.

I now caught three beautiful trout in quick succession. Each caused a commotion because I had to protect the fish from Missy and get it off the hook and into my pocket. The last time I dropped everything, including Missy, fell on my knees, almost lying on the fish, Missy jumped on my back, Rheingold stamped and clattered, the Roamer gave a deep rumble, both dogs came dashing back, hot and panting, and lay down in the creek to cool off.

From now on they dropped other interests and paid attention to fishing, running ahead of me upstream, spotting likely pools and bends. They would turn and look at me with bright inquiry, their tongues hanging out, and when I said grumpily, "No, not here," they would proceed upstream with unflagging optimism. How I managed to catch two more fish! I thought of supper. My mouth watered. A good mess of trout.

I came at last to the fence between Crooked Meadow and Castle Rock Meadow. At the far end is the great towering pile, once, of course, a small mountain. Through the ages it has been consumed by erosion until it is stripped of everything except its rocky skeleton; and there it stands, a turreted castle with battlements and towers and many roomy caves underneath. Not too inviting, these caves; animals, small and large, choose them to die in or devour a kill; and they are full of skeletons, and odd pieces of bone and hair—here and there a skull; always the ugly buzzing of blow flies.

But the meadow is a beauty, not only rich with the leavings of last year's hay, as they all are, but provided with fine shelter by the grove of young aspen which straddles the Creek at the far end, near the Rock.

Standing where I was, my hand on the gate, I could see no sign of mare or colt, but I knew they were there. They must then be hidden in the aspen grove.

It is well, on a ranch, always to remember just where you are, where the fences and gates are, and just what stock is in the enclosure with you.

If I opened this gate and went into the meadow, my escort would expect to go with me.

I turned and looked at them. The dogs knew they had to be patient while I thought. They waited, sitting, their bright faces lifted to me. Missy was in my neck. Roamer and Rheingold also understood I was thinking and were patient, hoping it would come to something.

I knew that only by force or quick maneuver could I keep Roamer and Rheingold from following me if I opened the gate in the barbed wire fence.

Blazes would come galloping up from the far end of the meadow to inquire who was invading his domain and probably eighteen mares and seventeen foals would accompany him. There would be wild nickering and whinnying, especially over the reunion of Rheingold and his mother Juanita.

For Juanita is in the brood mare bunch.

She is also Michael's particular favorite mount, exactly balanced to his height, weight, style. She is really head girl.

It was I who brought Juanita to the ranch.

It was several years ago and we had too many dairy cows and heifers and not enough saddle horses; and I told Michael that a dairyman had stopped me in town one day and said that he had a saddle mare he would exchange for a dairy cow, if I'd like to make the trade.

Michael pronounced it an excellent idea and suggested that I inspect the mare and make the deal.

I did not feel enough confidence in myself as a judge of horses to do anything so important, but Michael was too busy to bother; so I arrived one day with car and trailer at the little dairy farm north of town looking with great doubt and some distress at a tall, raw-boned mare, which the owner assured me was broken to the saddle, but which he appeared afraid to mount.

She was a rack of bones. Her hide would have been black had it not been for what seemed the dust and dirt of years ground into her. She had an ugly cyst on her nose, size of a big plum. But she was unusually tall, and it seemed to me, looking at her this way and that, that she had a fine head.

Being by nature credulous, I believed the owner when he said she had been considerably ridden, and I thought she would be of more use to us than one of my spare heifers.

Perhaps what decided me was the fact that she was in a parched hillside pasture without grass, water or shade.

I brought her home behind the car in the trailer, and as I drove (not being able to see her) I forgot the bones, the dust, the hanging head, the wart, and fell in love with her. I thought I was bringing home a glossy black mare, smooth and fine-limbed, with lovely spirited head, a fiery, intelligent eye, and good saddle gaits.

I gave her a name befitting a Spanish princess. *Juanita*.

My heart beat with pride and excitement when I stopped the car in front of the terrace of the ranch house.

They were all there. Michael, some of the boys, Eugenie, and some friends.

They said, "What's that in the trailer?"

They shrieked.

Even Michael, who can smell good horseflesh a mile away, was stunned.

I turned to look at her. She was standing, as tired horses often do, with weight on one hind leg so that all her bones (and you saw them all) seemed askew and lopsided.

81

Her color was rusty black and dun. Her weary head hung dispiritedly over the side of the trailer. Her eyes were half closed. Her wart very conspicuous.

Where was my Spanish princess? I had to laugh myself. We laughed until we ached. It was one of those times when you just can't stop. And of course I knew the laugh was not on Juanita, but on me, for they kept shrieking, "Mary! How could you?"

But in the end, she was Juanita, the Spanish princess.

Broken, trained, schooled, well fed, groomed, cherished— "You'll know her from the other mares," said Michael not long ago as he directed a man to go out and bring her in from pasture, "because she's the one that looks like a race horse."

She adores giving birth and is never dry. Every spring she drops the prize foal of the bunch, never like herself but reproduced in the image of the Sire—a golden chestnut. And they are as alike as peas in a pod.

She raises them beautifully while she is being ridden by all our heavyweights, jumped over hurdles and taken on pack trips. On the Suicide Ride she is way out in front carrying Michael. This is the follow-the-leader run, down steep hills, up and down banks, over streams and hedges, always at a fast gallop, which is the last wild ride of the camp term.

Rheingold was one of her children and she would be thrilled to meet him. I could imagine them rearing, nipping at each other, interweaving their heads and necks. But what about Blazes? How would he receive his well-grown three-year-old son? Usually, when the young colt is two, his Sire doesn't want him around any more and drives him—with mean bites—out of the band.

Well, I thought sulkily, intent on getting to just that certain bend in the creek where there is always a good-sized trout under the bank, I don't need to open the gate, I'll just roll under the fence.

But I knew the result would be practically the same. Blazes and his mares would come rushing down the meadow. Roamer and Rheingold on *this* side of the fence; Blazes and his gang on the *other;* myself in between, and undoubtedly those bad dogs would begin to bark frantically and even chase the foals.

At the exact moment I came to this conclusion and decided I might as well give up my fishing trip, my escorting animals knew it. Roamer dropped his nose and began to graze. Rheingold did the same. The dogs removed their attention from me, trotted about, smelling out rabbit trails.

I realized it had grown much darker and looked up at the sky. That heavy cloud was overhead, and suddenly lightning split it. I was going to get a wetting, I saw, unless I hurried home.

I quickly reeled in my line, but it was too late. Masses of dark clouds were boiling up. There was a crash of thunder. Missy leaped from my shoulder and vanished. It began to pour. I tucked down my head to protect my eyes, pressed my can of worms to my bosom and plugged homeward. Streams of water were running down Roamer's white coat. Rheingold had turned a dark, soaked brown. Stoically, they both lowered their heads and hunched their shoulders. There were sudden, surprising blasts of wind. Bitter cold struck through me, the skies let loose one crash of thunder after the other. Lightning played all around me. I saw the field covered with little bouncing white marbles, which quickly became ping-pong balls, and looking up to see what on earth was happening, I caught a chunk of ice on the cheek bone.

I made for shelter—that outcrop of rocks there—and as I squeezed under the overhang a little cottontail fled out from it. I tasted salt blood from the cut on my cheek.

Presently I walked homeward in bright sunshine. The fields steamed and glittered with diamonds. All colors were intensified; green of grass and trees, red of roofs, blue of sky; and as I looked, a rainbow came into being—the perfect arch, spanning the saddleback and the ranch; and then as I watched (no one can look away from a rainbow for a single second), another rainbow above it, again the complete arch. And then, unbelievably, the third.

I stood at the cattle guard—staring.

"Hilda! Hilda! I'm drenched! Throw some sacks down on the kitchen floor!"

She was horrified at my bloody face and chattering teeth.

"Goodness sakes, Mrs. Bergwin!"

Homemade rolls were baking in the oven and the room was warm. Hilda got my big bath towel and I stood in front of the hot stove and pulled off my dripping things.

One of the trout was a beauty—twelve inches long.

Hilda cleaned them and we had them for supper.

Chapter 12

I suppose it is Michael's experience in the Remount Service that has given him his skill in moving large numbers of horses. He needs no one to help him; in fact, doesn't want anyone around.

The ranchers hereabouts comment upon it.

"He's right handy with a horse," they say.

They cannot do it themselves. They collect neighbors to help and they all yell and gallop and get the horses running like mad. It takes half a dozen cowboys to keep them headed where they are meant to go.

Not only Michael's ways with horses, but our ways with all the animals, in fact our ways in general—ranching, planting, cooking, managing, everything is commented upon via the country grapevine.

This country, which appears so empty, is simply sizzling with gossip and gossipers.

We have no close neighbors. Ranch houses are miles apart and have no telephones, but they are linked by communication lines as effective as the African drums.

Any telegram we send or receive is read aloud to anyone who comes; so, if we buy or sell a share of stock, it is known; if we have more or fewer boys for our summer camp than we had counted on, whether or not we will clear expenses is thoroughly gone into. Just how many hired hands we employ, what time they start work in the morning, how we feed them. And, if you should happen to drop in at the ranch just at dinner time, could you count on being asked to dinner? A good dinner? (This became a racket.)

Greenhorns are always fair game and we didn't mind. Sometimes we got a laugh ourselves when the tales came back to us.

"How d'ye think they planted their potato field? *With French-fried potatoes!*"

"What do you think she said when I went over there one day and told her one of her cows down in the meadow was wantin' a bull? She said, *'How do you know?'* "

It got about soon that I knew nothing, not even the facts of life, would believe everything I was told; and that I was easily frightened, particularly of bulls.

I became accustomed, after smiling a greeting at some familiar face in the Cheyenne grocery, or garage, or at the Granite Canyon Post Office, to see several heads pressed together, faces contorted, and to hear the particular kind of sniggering laughter that always means someone is being ribbed.

Strange things happened which purported to be accidents.

"A bull, you say, Mrs. Bergwin? A strange bull on your ranch? Why how could such a thing happen? Must have been some steer just happened to wander in."

"No, a bull."

"I bet it was a steer."

"No, a big red bull."

"A steer 'ud be just as big and red, but only—"

"I tell you it was a big Hereford bull—I heard him bellowing down in the meadow."

Glancing about, I caught the look on the listening faces, red with pent laughter, and realized it had all been staged. But I was launched on the tale and couldn't stop. Polite questions prodded me if I paused. And I told how I had been sleeping outdoors, my cot under a tent fly that hung over a pole suspended between two pine trees; and that I was wakened early one morning by the terrible bellowing of this bull. He was quite far away —down in the meadow. And I lay there trying to figure out what bull that could be. Then he stopped roaring and I wondered where he was going. There's a little path that comes up from the meadow, behind the house, to the stable corrals. My cot was right beside that path, and if he did follow it, he would end up here at my bedside and, maybe, be enraged by the white

tent fly and charge it. There had been silence for some minutes
—I wondered where he would be right now—and suddenly leaped
out of bed, swept aside the tent fly and all but hurled myself
upon his horns!

My listeners exclaimed, "Tck! Tck! Tck!" and put on expres-
sions of horror.

To this day I don't understand about that bull, for we have
met again and again.

One night about midnight I was lying awake, unable to sleep,
and heard a group of riders coming in the ranch road. They
made no effort to muffle their steps or their voices; they shouted
and joked and galloped past the house, up the gorge and on
up to the corrals.

I thought perhaps some men wanted a short cut between the
highway and the county road and had come through our ranch.
No one is supposed to do this and it would have angered Michael.
But he did not wake and I soon fell asleep.

In the morning we found that same big Hereford bull shut into
our corral.

Old George, very excited, recognized the bull. A killer who
had been put off his owner's ranch years ago. No one would have
anything to do with him or take the responsibility for him. Everyone was afraid of him.

We put him out on the county road. I saw him there for
weeks afterward, grazing, quite alone, wandering up and down.
If I was on horseback I would stop and look at him and he
would stand quietly and look back at me. With his immense
body of beef, his little short legs, and stumpy horns sticking
straight out sideways, he bore little resemblance to my Roamer.

At last he disappeared.

There is one advantage greenhorns have. They get scientific
advice from the County Agent and read the government bulletins that are freely handed out. Local ranchers seldom do.

We had a whole shelf of those bulletins. There was not one
piece of information a greenhorn might need that was not given
us in a short well-written brochure. Here was the agricultural
brains and know-how of the country.

So when I was faced with the extraordinary sight of three

87

immense hog carcasses—pink and hairless—laid on the grass before me, and heard the hired man say, "All ready for you to can, Missus," and had recovered from my initial astonishment (which provided amusement, via the grapevine, for the countryside), I merely went to the bookcase, extracted the brochure entitled *How to Put Up Your Hog,* commandeered a couple of hired hands and the use of the bunkhouse kitchen for a couple of days, and *put them up!*

The article promised superlative results provided directions were followed and this proved true. Never was such richly flavored sausage meat, never such tasty bacon, never such tempting head cheese, or appetizing jellied feet. And the hams! Here the brochure outdid itself. It stated that if you want to get your banker on your side for the rest of your life, just give him one of the hams when they have been rubbed with black pepper and sage and neatly sewn into tight jackets of white linen and hung from your kitchen rafters for six months!

And so, likewise, with the potato planting. Right out of the book, that planting! And the resulting prize crop.

I have always thought Michael escaped razzing because of his horsemanship. This, they simply could not laugh off. And in this country it means something.

Burt Langley, our neighbor twenty miles south, came to visit us one day. Visitors came just to look around and see what we were up to, frequently to borrow equipment, or discuss a fence line, or just to cut through from one road to the other.

Langley was a big red-headed fellow with a poker face. He was always needing a shave, always chewing. It might have been gum or tobacco but the jaws swung as my cows' do.

When he was ready to leave he rode his horse down on the Green and put on a bucking show. The horse performed every trick the horses do at the rodeos. Langley sat him without difficulty and kept casting challenging glances at Michael and me.

Michael scorns the immense western saddle which, he claims, is like a rocking chair into which the rider is practically fastened to keep him from falling off. He scorns the way the westerner mounts—his back to the nose of the horse. He scorns the way the horse is allowed to start off before the rider is in the saddle. (The first thing Michael teaches a horse is to obey the command, *Stand!*) He scorns the constant whooping it up, lashing, spurring the horse to buck and rear and show off.

He scorned everything that Langley was doing and did not disguise it; but of course I was impressed, and this disgusted Michael still more. I smiled in amazement and clapped my hands, and Langley was pleased as punch and rode off with head up, chewing his cud vigorously.

Another neighbor, Reuben Haygood, is quite different and has become a friend. He uses horses in the human and humane way we do ourselves and Michael often hires him to come over and help out with our haying.

I remember him last year when he was cleaning up Crooked Meadow with a rake team, his Nig and our Baby harnessed together—expertly combing it with the rake, piling the greeny-yellow hay into shaggy piles.

He stopped the team as I greeted him.

"Good morning, Mrs. Bergwin."

"Good morning, Rube. How are you today?"

"Well, I don't feel so good. How do I look?"

"Why you look fine to me, Rube."

"Yeah. That's the way. See how I handle this team, Missus?"

"Yes. I was watching you. You handle them as if you know just what you are doing."

"And by talkin' to 'em. I don't hit 'em. That Baby of yours now, you notice by pullin' at her you can't get her over, but just by talkin' you can do it."

He passed on. And I heard him talk to them. "What you doin' there now, Nig? Don't get to fightin'. Now, Baby, look out, Baby, swing over now, Baby—" And obediently the horses would climb into a small stack and over, while Rube expertly lifted the rake and dropped another mound of hay on the pile.

Baby was one of my favorite horses. Heavy enough for work, not too heavy to ride. Her dull brown coat and coarse black mane gave her an undistinguished appearance but I liked to ride her.

Michael disapproved. Horse must balance the rider, rider must balance the horse. This was why the Prince of Wales took so many falls—he rode horses too large for him.

But whether we balanced or not, Baby gave me a thrilling ride, for she was eager to go; she had smooth gaits; and she had an affection for me. Under such circumstances I would enjoy riding an elephant.

Chapter 13

Now Michael has distributed all our horses—about a hundred—into the correct pastures for summer use.

He brought the brood mare bunch—mares, foals, stallion—up from Castle Rock Meadow, moved them through the other meadows, then through the Home Pasture, up through the gorge and Stable Pasture, across the county road, up the saddleback and out onto Section Twenty. There they will spend the summer in charge of the stallion, out of the way of the boys and all the riding and shouting near the house.

Blazes will see to it that the mares are always where grass is thick and rich. He will hold them in sheltered draws during storms; take them to water holes; repel intruders.

Two cowboys, working all the time, could not take as good care of these mares and colts as one good range stallion.

Riley and George had orders to be invisible throughout the day. Not one head must be seen. Not one shout be heard. The dogs were locked up.

The trek involved the opening and closing of about six gates. I offered to do this but Michael preferred to do it himself. He would ride Gold Coin, our big sorrel gelding. Gold Coin's gaits are nothing to give a rider pleasure, but he is wise. He could almost do this job himself.

The next bunch he brought in were the eighteen two-year-olds from Section Seven. Ten of these were fillies, eight were colts.

In the corral, he separated them, drove the fillies out to Section Nineteen and left the eight young stallions who are to be gelded, in the Home Pasture, convenient for the veterinarian when he arrives.

Then from the main bunch of saddle horses and geldings and work horses he cut out the three three-year-olds who are to be trained immediately for use this summer. Diabolo, Wing Ding and Prinny.

They were halter-broken when they were two, but they've never been ridden. To have them ready for the boys to ride ten days from now means gruelling work.

Here in the west horseback riding is no sport. Riders—cowboys and bronco busters—break horses in order to use them in their work. They do it as quickly as they can; violently, sometimes cruelly, but efficiently.

Often the horses are found, rounded up and corraled in one day, broken the next, used under the saddle or in harness the next.

The horse is fought to a finish and licked. There is that one thing he has to learn—that he must submit to a master. Then he is ready for work.

For days before, the horse is half starved so that he will begin the fight already weakened. Then he is lassoed, his feet are tied, when he struggles up he is thrown again. Then he is sacked out. This means that he is flicked and whacked continuously with a blanket or sack; banged on one side of the head then the other, until he stands without a quiver no matter what happens to him.

Horses are extremely intelligent. Their scientific rating places them right at the top. They soon know the signals. In one of these fights, right at the beginning, they find out they can't win and so they give in. After that comes good treatment, oats, kindly words and they discover that life can go on as usual. But they never forget that first defeat and know better than to invite another.

Cowboys feel that no horse is safe to be ridden unless he has been licked once.

There is, however, the occasional horse who will not give in—he'd die first. And so he dies.

Michael will not tolerate this method. "Something goes out of him," he shouts, "and he'll never get it back!"

So he allows more time, subdues the horse more slowly, and it usually works. But cowboys don't trust it. One of them told

92

me I was riding a horse not yet ready to be mounted by anyone.

We are now working with these three broncs every day.

Diabolo is wicked and has learned to toss Riley just about every time he gets on him. He does not toss Michael. And I am not allowed to mount him.

Wing Ding is the biggest. When full grown he may be sixteen hands. Michael thinks he may do for the army. That would mean a good price. Michael is being very careful with him. The trouble often is the rough treatment a horse gives himself, banging about, throwing himself down. For if he gets a bad cut or scar, the army will not take him, no matter how well trained he is.

Prinny is not very well grown. Both Michael and Riley are far too heavy for her back, so she is my job.

The Goetschius books have arrived from New York.

Michael brought the package back from the post office and handed it to me. "What is it?"

"The Goetschius books! Music! Remember—I told you about it?"

I grabbed the package, rushed into the house, tore off the paper and sat down in a corner of the sofa.

Counterpoint is the most difficult department of the study of harmony because it is so precise and mathematical. I knew that, so decided I ought to begin with it. I opened *Elementary Counterpoint*.

Without pausing to study or do exercises I rushed through the book to get a general idea of the whole and to understand Goetschius' plan for the student. I discovered that each chapter was a lesson. At the end were exercises to be done and then corrected.

When I finished the book and put it down I already knew a good deal about counterpoint.

I have always loved a horizon. No matter what it is, the flat monotonous line of the sea, or the skyscraper line of New York, it fascinates me.

If the line were not solid but made up of a succession of little dots, and if there were two of these dotted lines, two different horizons running along together, one over the other, so that opposite (or counter) to each little dot (or point) would be another point—this perfectly illustrates two-part contrapuntal or horizontal music.

Romance enters in with the beautiful word *fugue,* for the points do seem to fly. They do not begin exactly together. One line starts running across the page of music (or across the world, or the keyboard) and a little later the other line takes off after it.

Each of these lines, explains Goetschius, must be a beautiful melody in itself, and to achieve this you must be obedient to rules. In addition, when they are joined in a partnership of flying, they must be beautiful as a duet as well as two beautiful separate solos.

Ah! They have to get married, these two horizon lines! Not only one beautiful creature plus another beautiful creature, but a beautiful relationship as well!

But what is beauty? Who can say that there is such a thing? I can say it. For me, there is. Swift, graceful movement is beautiful. Flight, *fuga,* is beautiful.

One summer one of the boys said to me, "But Mrs. Bergwin, how can you be so sure? How do you *know* there is a God? Supposing there really isn't? Or supposing you couldn't believe there is?"

"It wouldn't make any difference to me."

"Why not?"

"I would worship just the same—worship goodness, worship beauty. I *know* that's true because I see it all around me. Look around. Don't *you* know it?

A warm color flooding his cheeks answered me. "But is that really *IT?*"

"It's enough, isn't it?"

"Enough for what?"

"To let you out of prison."

"Prison?"

"The prison of the flesh—of the merely physical, of the material."

He sat wondering. "But you said worship—all this isn't God, is it?"

94

"Funny you should ask that. St. Augustine asked it about fifteen hundred years ago. He tells about it in his book."

"And what was the answer?"

"He said that just by loving the physical world so much he was asking it if it was God. And its beauty answered, 'No! But He made us!' "

He looked baffled.

Since Goetschius undertakes to impart a technique he begins, as all schoolmasters do, with an examination of the classics.

Look, for example, at one of Bach's Two-Part Inventions, which are short fugues. The horizontal lines of notes start at the beginning and fly without pause to the end.

Analyze each line and you will see that it comprises two kinds of music which could be called positive and negative. Positive: fragments of very pronounced character called *motifs* which are repeated throughout the piece in different keys. Negative: rambling interludes that have not much character or originality but merely serve to connect the *motifs*.

So before you attempt to do two related lines, write just one line of correctly mingled positive and negative music. And before that, write one *motif* (anywhere from three notes to a couple of measures). And before that, make one note move beautifully and obediently to the next!

It is astonishing how many things you are forbidden to do if you are to get from one note to the next in accordance with the rules of strict counterpoint.

It seems like a stunt such as children set themselves to do. Tie your hands, blindfold your eyes, put your legs into a sack, and then see if you can make it from here to there.

Bach considered his *Inventions* stunts. He says he wrote them for exercises.

Now I have done the exercises at the ends of Chapters 1, 2, 3.

The eight young stallions who are to be gelded are out on the Green, drinking at the fountain and playing with each other. I've just been standing at the door watching them.

95

You can almost see the hot sap pouring through them. Their coats, gleaming and iridescent as if they had been oiled, are golden, and black and blood bay. Manes and tails do not just hang—they seem to have a separate life, every hair springing out, strong and erect. Mostly the colts are on their hind legs, their forefeet high in the air, flailing at each other in play. Little squeals and grunts come from them.

They won't be like this when they have been gelded.

There is one among them, a black, whom I did not name till he was nearly full grown.

Horse breeders are always looking for that one outstanding animal who might found a dynasty. Such a one as the little Morgan horse who has given hundreds of his progeny his own name and fame. (Occasionally there is a genius in an ordinary human family.)

This colt has been outsize from birth; his coat shines like jet; he has unusual lift and spring in his action. But it is his hair that is phenomenal. His immense tail sweeps the ground; his mane is full and billowing and blows around as wild and high-held a face as I have ever seen. He is like a wind rushing over the plains.

It is my habit to name them from some early, spontaneous observation. As when I said to one youngster, "No shenanigans, please!" (Name, Shenanigan—Annie for short.) Or, "Oh, you're very hifalutin' this morning, aren't you?" (Name, Hifalutin'—Falla for short.)

But I could not name that colt. I struggled for something that would suggest greatness, or lordliness, like Eagle, or Bugle, or Chieftain. He came down those hills blaring like a great horn.

Finally I named him for that—I named him Trombone.

Now Trombone is out there with the other two-year-olds, waiting to be gelded.

"What would you think, Michael, if we didn't have Trombone gelded? Suppose Rheingold doesn't pan out as stud? One can never know in advance—"

He said he'd think about it. It causes a lot of trouble to have young ungelded colts growing up on a ranch with a lot of fillies

96

and mares. Sooner or later there's bound to be a fight between the stallions.

Michael saw such a fight in Belgium, during the war. One stallion killed the other. They have exact, precise fighting strokes, which could be named like a boxer's.

Rear—reach over—hammer stroke on kidneys.

Sink, snake head forward, crunch foreleg.

Up—bring hoof down—cleave the skull.

I have seen all these strokes delivered; I have seen a whole complete fight, but performed by the little foals in play. Just shadow-boxing.

I've been on Prinny. Nothing has happened yet, but it's rather scary sitting on a horse that you know may simply explode any minute. She keeps her head turned, watching me, and her back is humped a little under the saddle. That's close to bucking.

I spend all day in riding clothes, too tired at night to change. But I continue with the counterpoint.

Michael can't make it out.

He stopped beside the piano. "What *is* that?"

"Counterpoint. You remember. I told you. The Goetschius books."

Seriously, not trying to be funny, he asked me, "Is it music?"

I burst out laughing. "Honestly I don't know! What do *you* think?"

"It sounds like something figured out with a slide rule."

"And it is! Bach called these *Inventions*. But there are whole concerts of it. Big orchestras and virtuosos play it!"

"But don't you *compose* any of it? You know—*create* it?"

"Yes. About six notes at the beginning. The *motif*. All the rest is what they call *manipulation*. Slide rule."

Michael, now that he has ordered the pump, is no longer disturbed by the windmill.

Every time we go up through the gorge to saddle a horse we pass it. Like a languid lady posturing with a fan she stands gracefully; now and then as if to tantalize us, waving her fan a

97

little in one direction, then the other. Then she stands motionless, smiling.

She pumps no water.

"Will we have to pay for it?" I hazarded, thinking of several hundred dollars.

"Certainly not!" Michael glared. "It's no use to us, is it? And I've ordered the pump. He can take the windmill down again and use it on some other job. It's new."

"But—the labor. Putting it up. Taking it down. Who'll pay for that?"

"Not I!"

But my heart sank. In the end, I knew, we'd have to pay for the labor. And the pressure pump still to buy—it hasn't come yet.

I feel I am making a little headway with Rachel.

I've discovered she loves raw eggs. These she takes from a little blue bowl that I hold in my hands.

Bunny, like most cocker spaniels, is greedy.

If we do not watch, he gulps his own dinner, moves towards Rachel's and gives a low growl. Rachel immediately steps back, Why, certainly, Bunny, if you want it. I was through anyway.

And he eats it while she stands watching him, her long feathery tail waving gently. So we worry for fear Bunny gets most of her food.

And then, too, she is often far from home at feeding time.

Or perhaps she is close at hand, but will not appear because she has been called in too peremptory a manner.

So a bowl of food is left out for her at all hours.

This does not work very well because of Bunny, or because of the cats who also love corn meal and cracklings, or because of the ducks who love it too.

But we have discovered that Rachel feeds herself. She insinuates herself like a little snake between the bars of the calf pens and eats their raw ground oats. She drinks the sour milk that is put out for the chickens. So we have directed Riley to leave a bucket of sour or buttermilk accessible to the dogs at all times.

Rachel eats what and when she pleases. It is the wild running that keeps her so emaciated.

The raw eggs she licks up out of a little blue pottery bowl on the front terrace just after breakfast every morning.

I hold the bowl in my hands. She is extremely dainty and gentle about it; casts many glances at me as if to say, "Are you sure this is for me? If there is any reason I should not take it I won't give another lick—"

I smile down at her. Her eye catches the smile and her brush waves a little as she cleans out the bowl.

The dogs usually spend the evening in the living room or on the terrace with us. At bedtime we go out with them, let them have a little run, wander around a bit ourselves, then call them and put them into the tool house for the night.

That, at least, is the program, and Bunny follows it. But it is seldom that Rachel is not off like a shot the moment she realizes that bedtime is approaching. Bunny, then, is shut into the tool house alone.

When Rachel returns, perhaps at midnight, when the whole ranch is deep in sleep, that is when she really has fun.

Her bark, or rather, barks—for they always come in a barrage (especially in the middle of the night)—are sharp and nervous.

She sounds like a woman who simply can't stand it another minute.

No human being could sleep through her barking.

She places herself at a high vantage point where she can see every part of the ranch spread out below her in the bright moonlight; and her rule is, if anything moves, bark at it. If a leaf is swung by the wind, bark at it. If a cloud goes over the moon and all the *chiaroscuro* is changed, bark at it. If a horse, grazing on the Green, takes a step, bark at it.

At the first bark I am sitting up in bed, holding my head in despair. How long before Michael wakes? Is there any use in going out and trying to stop her? No, there isn't. She won't come if I call. I can't catch her. No use.

After about half an hour of her barking, Michael is thoroughly awake, angry, determined.

Michael does not accept defeat as easily as I, so he goes out. There are gentle calls, "Here, Rachel, here, Rachel, come, puppy, that's a good little girl! Here's a biscuit for you, Rachel!"

She thinks this over in silence for a moment, then looses an outburst of barks.

The same soft, beguiling voice calls, "Here, Bunny, here, Bunny!"

She stops barking, sits there on the hill, watching Michael.

He calls again, still softly. The horses hear his voice and move toward him. Rachel forgets all about Michael and gives the horses a piece of her mind.

Michael shouts. Rachel disappears.

He yells at her—that commanding yell; but she does not return until, disgruntled, he has gone back to bed.

Then she comes back, sits on the hill, and barks some more.

Just caught a glimpse of a familiar apparition on the sky line. Diabolo cantering jauntily along with an empty saddle. Where is Riley? He trudges in, usually, about an hour after Diabolo has got back.

Chapter 14

I have come to the chapter in *Elementary Counterpoint* where the student must begin to "manipulate" motifs.

The motif is given in the book. The student must work out a correct counterpoint to it; then a counterpoint for the counterpoint. This constitutes the thematic (or positive) material of the piece and is repeated once or twice in different keys. Though the motif is short, often only two or three measures, yet there need be no more thematic material in the whole piece, only "negative" music to link the motifs together.

I have discovered something interesting about the motif. If it is ugly, the counterpoint to it is uglier, and the counterpoint to the counterpoint still uglier. The whole piece, then, is a masterpiece of ugliness and very painful to work on.

But if the motif is beautiful, as in most of Bach's contrapuntal works, then the counterpoint to the motif is beautiful, and the counterpoint to the counterpoint, and so the whole piece.

How strange and wonderful! These little scraps of music—one measure or sometimes even part of a measure—how can it be that in them is contained the whole beauty that finally is deployed in a three- or four-page Invention? But so it is, as (I explained to myself) the whole oak is in the acorn, and the whole beauty of the whole oak!

The examples of motifs given in the Goetschius book are very ugly indeed. And I manipulated them bravely and ended up with one horrible piece of counterpoint after the other. And I suffered.

So when I came to the page that directed the student to invent

101

his own motif and then manipulate it, I was happy. Now I would show them.

With confidence and excitement I set myself to invent a beautiful motif.

Ah! How strange! It's not so easy after all! How altogether incomprehensible! I have not been able to do it! With all the abundance of my musical imagination and my free-flowing inspiration I have not been able to create one single tiny motif worthy of manipulation!

This is an immense surprise to me, and I remember that Vernon Spencer once said to Michael, "Your wife knows a great deal, but not as much as she thinks she knows."

I work harder. I struggle mightily. I write motif after motif. *Let me just create one—musical—acorn!*

But I cannot. I too get sick. My head aches. My voice is hoarse. I am half blind.

It's a warm cloudless summer day—almost the first we've had.

At Michael's orders Riley and George took the big rug, the curtains and upholstered pieces out of the living room and cleaned them. The whole house is spanking clean.

Late in the afternoon Michael came in. I was standing before the fireplace, very morose because of counterpoint motifs. He was jubilant.

"Well, I've had a good day. I got the tank scrubbed out, all the holes in it soldered up, made the new cement platform for it farther up on the hillside so we'll have more water pressure, set the tank on it, pipes all connected. Now *that's* done! George has made two big batches of butter. I've got the colts in, looked them over and fed them oats. And the pump ought to arrive in a day or two."

He kissed me.

He looked terrible. Unshaven. Ragged. Dirty.

I had to laugh.

"Aren't I a horrible-looking thing to be coming around to kiss a lady?"

"This," I said, "is to celebrate the plumbing? Or the plumber?"

Riley has come in with the mail. There was a post card for

102

Michael to say the pump from Montgomery Ward has come. Now Michael will have to take the trailer over to the station, pay for the pump (C.O.D., of course), have it loaded on the trailer and bring it home, then install it.

But suddenly she's whirling like a Dervish! There's a good wind blowing right there! The long blades are almost invisible in the air.

The piston rod goes up and down, pumping water up into the tank!

The lady is laughing at us, up there in the gorge. She's having fun, whirling her fan. We're having fun too, watching her.

"What about the pump from Montgomery Ward, Michael?"

"It can go back," says Michael blithely.

"Will we have to pay the freight charges?"

"Not I!" (But we will.)

"I'm going to town."

"By the time you get back there'll be water in the house and a hot bath for you."

Michael is usually overjoyed to see me when I have been away, but this time, when I returned, I found him distraught.

"I'm in the doghouse again."

"About the water system?" I asked in alarm.

He nodded.

"What's the matter now?"

"It runs down into the basement but not up into the kitchen or the upstairs. Can't understand it. Runs into the bunkhouse too, and that's *higher* than our upper story."

He explained a little more, then in exasperation flung the subject away. He built a fire and lit it. "Let's not talk about it or think about it. I don't give a damn. I'm going to take a long day of rest soon."

I stood watching the flames, thinking. In my mental vision I saw the network of pipes underground and tried to figure out the different levels, the pull of gravity. "How strange," I said thoughtfully.

"I said we wouldn't talk about it," he snapped; and I turned

103

away, put on the radio, sat down on the couch, feeling rebuffed.

There was a long silence. The fire sparked a little. I couldn't think of a thing to say.

His eyes drifted to me across the room and he asked softly, "Tired, honey?"

"Going to town always makes me tired."

"I'm tired too. Dog tired. I'm going to have a drink." He went to the kitchen and came back with two glasses, handed me one and sat down.

We sipped our highballs while the fire slowly burned down.

Then he said, "Before I go to bed, I'm going up to see if the tank is overflowing. The mill has been pumping water all day. I don't want it to undermine the dirt foundation."

Soon he came back. "Well, I've found the trouble. The tank is empty. The water has all run out. And down here in front of the house, where the pipe turns to go into the basement, the ground is soaking. That's where there's a big leak. Either in the joint, or the pipe has burst."

"Oh, that's fine," I cried. "Isn't it? Now you know where the trouble is and you're out of the doghouse!"

"No, it's not fine," he said violently. "It's a pain in the neck."

I was silent, trying to figure it out. "Do you think the pipe froze?"

He nodded.

"How deep was it?"

"Three feet."

The way he looked at me, I knew he felt guilty. He's been told that, to be safe, they must be five feet down. But he's put them one foot, two, three, as it were, fighting every inch of the way. They've all frozen and burst.

He and Riley have dug up the pipe, found the leak and put in a new length of pipe. Water came into the faucets all over the house, upstairs and down. Eureka!

"Then you're out of the doghouse!" I said joyously.

"No, I'm still in the doghouse."

"What now?"

"My hot water boiler in the cellar has burst."

104

There is a man called Williams who goes around buying horses from ranchers. Michael hates to sell to him because he offers so little; but often we have to.

He came yesterday morning when Michael had driven down to Castle Rock Meadow to inspect the dam.

I told Williams I'd go down and get Michael, but he said he'd come back tomorrow.

I walked down to the meadow myself to tell Michael the good news, but Riley was working there alone. Michael had taken the car and gone up the range somewhere.

I walked up the slopes of the saddleback, wondering if he was watching me from somewhere. He has hawk's eyes. If he was, why didn't he come to meet me? Probably a little more inspection of the fences, the water hole, the grass, or what-not. I reached a high point and looked around. Then I saw the car circling far off, winding in and out the gullies and ravines. It takes expert driving to drive the range. It looks like an almost level expanse, but it is really a succession of undulations melting into each other, some shallow, some deep, some concealing little springs, runs, rills, groves of trees, fields of green grass, even a house or small building.

As I looked, the car disappeared.

I stood waiting, determined to stay right there until he found me.

I tilted my head back and was lost in the vast blue sky. There was more sky than earth.

How still the world. I looked slowly all around. When one stands quietly out there on the range, one is watched by many eyes. Listening, you can hear the voices—the little pipe, the chirp, the far whistle, the cry, the sudden rustle nearby.

My eye caught a little movement—I looked closer—two antelope not fifty yards away. I would not have seen them but for the flash of white under their tails—a heart-shaped plastron.

They stopped and turned to look at me, then moved away again. They have a strange sliding gait, as if they were rolling on wheels. They are most exquisite little creatures and look like porcelain figurines, quite unreal.

Suddenly the car slid out of the ground right there to my left,

105

and came toward me as if to run me down, with Michael's big grin over the wheel.

I jumped in and as we drove home told him about Williams coming and that he was on a horse-buying tour.

"Isn't that keen?" I yodeled.

Michael glared. "Just when I've moved them all out to the farthest section."

All the same, when we got home, he put on breeches and boots, rode out over the saddleback, cut out twenty horses, brought them in and left them in the corral.

Williams never came back.
Michael moved the horses out again.

The veterinarian came and gelded the young stallions. There was one casualty.

Sometimes, for no special reason, one takes a fancy to a particular colt. Perhaps, with Star, it was because I had so often felt him give me a little nudge in the back if I was in the corral with all the colts milling about me.

When I am making friends with a horse I turn my back so that, freed of my eye, he can come up behind and get to know me by smelling me. And first he touches his muzzle lightly to my shoulder blades, sniffs, blows on my nape, then gives a few snorts and prances away, only to come back and give me the big shove in the small of my back which means he likes me and wants to be friends.

But it is more than that. He wants the excitement of my eye on him. When a horse first feels the human eye, it is almost unendurable to him. He goes half crazy. But what he at first fears he comes to tolerate and finally long for.

I would turn and look at him, wondering which one was making advances to me; then see the bright white star on his forehead, and recognize his comic, inquiring face.

Something about him always made me laugh.

Here on the ranch we see death often and close. When an old horse or cow takes the last step and sinks down, one does not grieve. It is good and right to sleep at the end of a long day. But

106

when it is a little filly like Floss, or a boy like Star, it flings a heavy pall.

I stood outside the corral looking at the rest of them. Hanging heads and bloodied legs. Where was Trombone? There were only six.

Michael, I saw, had gone down to the house to get the car. To drag a dead animal through the pastures and across the range and up the hill to the shaft of the old gold mine in Section Sixteen is a job that he hates, but no one else can do it.

The car backed up to the corral gates.

I ran to the window.

"Trombone?" I asked.

"I put him out on the range," Michael answered. His scowl did not lessen. He probably felt he was shirking a duty.

So he's out there still. Still sailing over the hills with his head way up, a wild question in his eyes, and all that hair ballooning around him.

I have acquired a second maid. An attractive Japanese girl whose name is Fumiko.

Chapter 15

Michael and I have spent a day in the car driving across the state to retrieve three saddles he lent a man last fall. A hundred and fifty miles to get there, a hundred and fifty to return. He hated to take the time but we need the saddles for the boys.

Mostly, we short-cut across the plains on old dirt roads.

The whole day was like a dream in which we traveled strenuously and got nowhere. Grass and sky. Clouds and shadows. They held our eyes. They made the dream. They made us silent and spellbound.

Strange, that all over the world the American west is typified by guns and bandits, holdups, rough riding, when the truth of it is this wide rolling emptiness, this incredible beauty.

The horizon line was never without a little cluster of dark lines, a windmill and huddle of buildings all off the square. When one faded into the distance there would be another coming into view. Sometimes there were several.

Those old windmills are made of wood. They sit on squat wooden towers and look like sturdy athletes, twirling Indian clubs. But modern ones are like ours—made of fine strands of white metal, as delicate as spider webs against the sky.

All day the car hardly varied its fifty-five-miles-an-hour pace; the landscape hardly changed.

Here was the same view that had welcomed me on the fourth day of the long bus trip from New York. I had watched one state after the other pass the window. When we began to be lifted up into the high altitude, into that down-curving dark blue sky, I was hypnotized again as I always am after I have been away. And remembering the way it feels to have a horse under me on those plains, cantering on that cushiony grass, I began to be excited, I felt the rhythm, clop, clop, and presently I was composing a song.

I named it *Green Grass of Wyoming* and decided that it could be the theme song of my Musical. Mr. Fox would publish it, I felt sure.

The Musical exists at present in a box filled with different folders that contain songs, dances, theme books filled with melodies and musical ideas to be developed later.

The box is labeled in good-sized black letters, FOR THE MUSICAL.

The music in it has been accumulating since I was eighteen when Schirmer returned a song I had submitted to them, saying, ". . . this is musical and has charm . . . the composer should study composition."

Yes—for half a lifetime I have had this dream. Is it a dream? Or an intention? Is there a difference?

When my sister Elma, aged thirteen, declared she was going to be a Medical Missionary and spend her life doing good in foreign lands, probably working among the women confined in the *zenanas* of India, she was not taken seriously; and yet, one by one, she took those steps that finally made her head of a hospital in Shanghai, that put her in a pulpit to preach sermons in Chinese and a classroom in which she taught modern obstetrics to young Chinamen.

And when, aged fifteen, I said, "Someday I'll write a Musical," neither was I taken seriously, even by myself, and yet have never ceased taking steps to fulfill that dream.

The compositions have steadily accumulated.

When I was in New York I showed a few of the dances to publishers and was told that if I could get a well-known choreographer, a man, say, like the famous Russian, Chalif, to make choreographies for them, they could be published.

It is not easy to get a prominent artist's attention, to make him really listen, to overcome that habitual listlessness and lack of expectancy which inevitably comes to be the chronic attitude of everyone who achieves eminence.

I saw Chalif and told him the proposition. He put me off from day to day. He had a class. Or the pianist was not there. "Where is Nelson? Do you know where Nelson is?" He got everyone in his large suite of rooms in Radio City hunting for Nelson.

"Can you not play them yourself?"

I shook my head sadly, knowing how easily all my skill deserts me at a crucial point. At last one day, when again Nelson had vanished I undertook to play them on that frightful piano—many keys missing—all the others a dark brunette—pedals squeaking—and outdid myself.

"You play very well," said Chalif. "I do not know why you are so modest."

Then he made a gesture, and said, "Your music has this."

He clenched his fist before his face, stiffened his whole body, thrust up his fist an inch or two and gave a little stamp.

Oh! that stamp!

My eyes suddenly burned.

I could not conceal my emotion, my excitement, or restrain my smiles and tears. And he beamed at me understandingly and it was as if he took me in his arms and patted me and said, There—there—

He then carefully went over each dance with me, explaining with an artist's patience and precision just what each one was.

"This *Ski Waltz* is an exhibition waltz. Just two people on the stage dancing together, dressed in formal evening dress. This *Dancing Dolls* (which I like very much) is a whole *ballet*—about six minutes and a half—at least six people on the stage—"

As he explained, I saw each dance—all performed so beautifully on the stage of my Musical. I wondered why I had not seen all this myself, from the start.

No deal resulted, of course. The choreographies would have cost too much money; but I went out walking on air. Oh, that clenched fist! Oh, that stamp!

The dances and Chalif's directions as to what to do with them are all there in the box, and now the theme song too.

On this long, all-day grass-drenched ride with Michael, I began to think about the story.

Story ideas—the best of them—come to me when I'm not trying; when my immediate attention is directed elsewhere, as, now, I was watching the horizon and the moving, changing shapes of the cloud shadows.

Ideas come, then, from that lower level of the mind where the subconscious moves freely, whimsically and erratically; and the conscious mind watches and takes note of them with surprise: "Why! See here! Look at what's drifting up!"

Henry James said it was like watching a pot boil. You lean over the stove watching the stew: "Ah! there's an onion! A carrot! A chunk of meat!"

A story for my Musical boiled up. Half a dozen stories boiled up.

It would be laid in Wyoming, of course, a sort of folk tale. And long ago, when we were raising sheep and there was a herder in charge of them, I had been surprised at his face, a distinguished, aquiline face. And I had made inquiries, and had been told tales that you could believe or not, as you chose, but immediately I put the tales into the mouth of a character in the play, and it went like this:

"Wyoming sheepherders? They bin written up in the newspapers! Big bugs—that's what they were once! Seen better days! Most of 'em come f'um the east. Git into trouble, hightail it to the west and hide away on the sheep ranges. Cain't say as I blame 'em. Eff'n you got to run f'um the law, run as fur as ye kin!"

And so I would have three of these, and they would be funny men. And there would be one more—the hero, who had come west not because of a disgrace but because he was hunting a lost grandson.

Suddenly I had my story in a capsule. *Story of a lost boy*. And he would be the *young* hero, who couldn't marry the girl he loved because he was a "catch colt"—Ah! Here's the title—*The Catch Colt*—and it's absolutely true of this boy, because no more than the catch colts on the range who are caught and tamed because they are handsome and have points although no pedigrees, does he have any background or knowledge of his people. And then I would have to get grandfather and grandson together! And I'd have to have a chorus, and remembered that

111

when I had bought the Roamer the owner of that famous Colorado herd had told me he never allowed a milking machine or a male milker in the barn—just women or girls. So then I saw half a dozen pretty milkmaids. And the ranch would be a dairy ranch—

Sometimes the ideas boil up so fast it exhausts me. I hurry to a typewriter and jot down an outline, a sketch, a bit of dialogue, the description of a face or type.

All this would go into The Box as soon as I got home.

Michael did not succeed in getting the saddles. The man had sold them. He and Michael got in a fight. Michael's fist is still sore. All the way home his face had *that look* and I grieved.

So today he took the long day in town he has been promising himself. And I spent the time at my desk making an ink copy of *Joy in the Morning* to send to Mr. Spencer. I resent having to do this, but he demands it. It is the Leipzig idea, the German idea. Make everything as difficult as possible. It tires my fingers and stiffens my neck and gives me a cramp in my foot. Besides, it makes it too final. So far, I think I have never played this piece twice the same. Still experimenting. Does it sound better in this register? Or this? Better with the melody in single notes? Or octaves?

It is only a couple of months old. Many of Chopin's works evolved for ten years. Brahms's for ten. Beethoven's never less than one.

As for the counterpoint, I cut the Gordian knot. Since I am unable to compose a motif worthy of being developed I did as so many composers do—stole one. It is all right to do this, I have discovered, provided only that you announce it in advance.

The title of my piece of counterpoint is *Two-Part Invention in G Minor*. And above the first staff I have put a bit of a miniature staff and the words, *From a Bach Bourrée*—and then I wrote on the little staff the four stolen notes that constitute my motif. D, G, D, E flat.

From there I have no difficulty in continuing. I know that I have a worthy musical acorn, and that in due time (and considerable work) I will have the oak.

112

I took a walk after supper. A beautiful balmy evening. Then put the dogs to bed in the tool house, then went indoors. The living room was dark. I sat down in the pompous chair and turned the radio on and sat listening awhile—but just nonsense. Turned it off. Sat there a long time in the empty room, the dark, the silence. I could see the French windows opening out onto the terrace; the square panes of glass, so soft and pretty, were faintly light—was that starlight already? I went out again and wandered around.

There is a night light that I do not understand. Not moonlight or starlight, but the whole sky luminous—a pale burning blue over an earth dark as an ink blot. I stood in that black gulf looking up. What was that fire?

The mysterious light faded when the stars came out, one by one, and the earth emerged from its blackness and I saw the familiar shapes of hills and woods and plains. They crowded the sky, those stars, shouldering each other, pouring down light—

After a while I went in again, lit the lamps.

Now it's nearly midnight. I feel wide awake. I don't want to go to bed and try to sleep and nap a little and wake up with a jerk to look at my watch and wonder what the time is.

"And now—" said Michael, after telling me about how first of all he just went to a café and sat without moving for a couple of hours with a cup of coffee before him (he often does this when he gets away from the ranch) and then went hunting around and found some pretty good army saddles at a second-hand shop, and then did the rest of the errands (there's always a long list) and then went out to the Post and Lieutenant Hotchkiss was there and they went to the Club and met some other officers and had drinks and went down to the Plains Hotel for dinner—

"And now what did you do? Did you ride? What did you have for dinner?"

"I had Hilda make a creamed macaroni."

"Creamed macaroni . . ." Michael repeated dully.

"And a chocolate cake for you."

He didn't answer. His eyes went to the fire. He looked sunk.

113

"No, I didn't ride," I said, "I went for a long walk and took a book along. The dogs were out hunting across the creek so I was alone. And I stretched out there on the saddleback and just watched the sky for the longest while. There was a hawk up there. He was patrolling a big section. He saw me. He would slide down and circle away and up again and give that faraway lonely cry—"

I glanced at Michael. His shoulders sagged a little more. I went on: "Then I fell asleep and when I woke up I propped myself on one elbow and began to read. Then I heard 'Yip, yip, yip,' and I looked down the hill and there was Rachel coming a mile a minute, Bunny behind her. So then I came home with the dogs. . . . What about bed? It's long after midnight."

He roused himself and said, "Yes!" with sudden violence.

I took my book and we went about blowing out the lamps.

Chapter 16

Reese has written that he is sending Jerome out a little before the camp term opens.

Jerome is really our number one boy, not only because he comes nearly every summer but because when my own children are not here he is the son of the house, being my brother's second wife's son. He calls us Aunt Marie and Uncle Michael.

When Reese and Eloise got married Jerome was eleven, and it had long been the desire of his mother's heart that he should learn to ride horseback.

Jerome has always been phenomenal, the kind of child who is recognized as a genius in kindergarten. Give him paints and brushes and he immediately paints pictures people want to hang on their walls. A year's piano lessons and he plays like a professional. Having learned chess, he beat all comers. But he had never welcomed opportunities to become better acquainted with horses.

"What about Mary's ranch?" said Reese (very anxious to take Eloise to England for a long honeymoon). "There in Wyoming everybody rides. It's the way they get around. And she and Michael always have boys visiting in the summer."

It seemed made to order.

He's a handsome boy with dark skin, dark eyes, dark mops of hair—a streak of Jewish in his ancestry and another of Mongol. I remember Reese leaning over his wife's chair one evening in the drawing room of his New York apartment. She was in a lovely evening dress of rose-colored chiffon. From above, he arched his hand and placed two fingers on her high cheek bones. "See that?" he said proudly, "Mongol."

A faint smile appeared in her narrow and mysterious eyes. We had just come out from dinner. During the meal, Eloise's

115

Siamese cat had reposed, motionless, in the center of the table.

When we rose from our chairs Eloise picked up the cat and draped it over her shoulders, like a fur piece.

Mongol made me think of Genghis Khan, and I saw a vision of the mad chieftain and his hordes galloping all over Asia and Russia. But here sat Eloise in conventional evening dress, serene, faintly smiling and complete mistress of New York social amenities.

Still—there was the cat on her shoulders. Her Siamese cat.

When Jerome arrived and I looked at him, shadows of inscrutable Siamese cats flitted across my mind; and galloping hordes; cruel arms upraised, cruel knives flashing down. But what I actually saw was an overgrown child wrapped in a sort of sulky protest, already defending himself against conventional pressures. Through this, I felt something gentle and appealing reaching out.

He aspired. This was the innermost truth of him.

I asked him how he managed always to have such high marks at school and he told me, "I couldn't bear not to. The minute the master gives out an assignment, then I can't do anything or even think about anything until I've done it."

We soon became aware of his unusual abilities. He soaked up knowledge about everything, and his mind roved, seeking more. He painted pictures. He played the piano. And at the evening games of chess and checkers he was champion. He was passionate, noisy and violent. He had a distinctive laugh, a soft chuckle sustained quite a while all on one pitch. I loved to hear it and kept listening for it.

Michael gave him old Baldy to ride. Baldy would know all about Jerome when he had carried him for five minutes. Baldy would do, at all times, whatever he himself thought was right and proper.

At the ranch, that first summer, Jerome wore habitually a small red felt cap, like a skull cap. I used to wonder why it never blew off, but it clung to the hair, and the hair clung to it.

My counterpoint has gone well. The little musical acorn contributed by Bach did all for me that I thought it would.

116

I applied the slide rule. I manipulated, shifted the key of the motif, mingled together proper amounts of positive and negative music, invented the counterpoint of the motif according to strict rules out of the book, and then the counterpoint of the counterpoint, and finally drew the two heavy vertical lines that announce, "It is finished!" All without any emotion at all.

Can anything truly alive be born without pain?

When I am doing one of my tone poems or even one of the little teaching pieces it is wrung out of anguish; ecstasy too. And sometimes I clap my hands over my face and burst into tears.

In the writings of the Saints I have seen that they call emotion a "movement of the soul."

There is none of this in counterpoint. No movement, no soul. I don't see how there could be. But it is precise, it is correct, it marches terrifically. Done by a master, it is magnificent.

Mathematics versus soul. It would be interesting to pursue this idea further. Does it mean physical versus metaphysical? And do they, somewhere in infinity, merge and become one? I think so.

I wonder what Vernon Spencer, who, after all is professor of Counterpoint and Fugue at the University of California, would think of my *Two-Part Invention in G Minor*?

It occurs to me that, without waiting to finish the ink copy of *Joy in the Morning*, I will send him this little bit of a machine-made thing and give him a surprise.

The Roamer's gone again. The fence between our land and Haygood's is broken through.

Riley, Michael and I got on our three broncs and went hunting for him. This kind of riding is good for the horses—stopping for fences (three were broken), in and out of streams, slithering down banks and cliffs, clambering up—after all, this is what they have been used to since they were born. They relaxed and seemed to know what we wanted. Even Diabolo behaved, and Riley's comical face wore proud grins.

Wing Ding is superb. Well, of course—look who's riding him.

"What boy will have Wing Ding?" I asked Michael.

"Some kid my height—my weight."

I thought them over. Evidently Michael did too, for presently our eyes met and an impish grin spread over his face.

"Jerome—" I said, and felt some consternation.

The Roamer was traveling fast. He had gone up over the saddleback toward Langley's ranch, which seems to have a special lure for him. Is it some particular cow? Or just any cow in heat?

We saw him at last far off. There's nothing else on the range as white as he is.

It took a good deal of shouting, of maneuvering with the horses, and use of Michael's whip to turn him. Once that was done, he seemed to know the jig was up and trotted briskly homeward. Finally broke into a lope and we made the rest of the trip at an easy canter.

When we rode through the Calf Pasture, the cows had come in for milking and were waiting there. When the Roamer reached the corral he began to moan, then to bellow, then put his head down and pawed the ground.

Michael made Riley get off and open the gate onto the Green. They made the Roamer go up near the tool house.

They put the long chain on him again, and now he's in the same old place in the meadow by the stream, not moving or eating.

A wonderful day today. And all's well with the water system. The wind blows. The windmill spins. The tank fills. Water runs through all the pipes and out of all the faucets in the house and bunkhouse. The fountain founts. The new hot-water boiler is installed. Tubs fill with hot water. The pump has gone back to Montgomery Ward. *Invention in G Minor* has gone to Vernon Spencer. Wing Ding, Diabolo and Prinny are ready to ride. And in no time at all, this morning, I composed another invention— motif and all!

It happened like this.

I was waiting for Michael to come down to breakfast.

I sat down at the piano and played *Invention in G Minor* through like a piece, up to time, trying to make it sound as stunning as I could (and it's quite stunning). Then I began to fool around, looking for another motif. Instantly I had one. I am astounded by this. How can I have learned how to compose good motifs just by working out one Invention? But there it is—a good, two-measure motif, plus its counterpoint, plus the counterpoint of its counterpoint. This one will be *Invention in D Minor*. I began to manipulate it immediately. Negative material came of itself. I could almost have improvised the whole thing through, in correct form, to the end. I shall not have to steal motifs any more.

There is not much satisfaction in these things. They leave me empty and lonesome.

I keep playing *Joy in the Morning* over and over as if this were my last chance.

Everyone likes it. Heads are poked into the room, people stop to listen and say, "What was that little rippling thing you were playing? Seems to me I have heard it before."

Vernon Spencer once told me that when one writes something that hits the popular taste, it always seems familiar.

The ink copy is not nearly finished yet. A piece with a gay ripple that goes on for pages and pages means hundreds of notes.

After breakfast I worked some more.

I went to the door for a moment's rest and a breath of air, and looking down, to my surprise, saw Rachel on the door mat. And she had come of her own volition, for Bunny was not there.

Had she been chasing rabbits? Had she been hunting among the rocks on the top of the cliff, whimpering with her irrepressible eagerness, nosing, scratching—and then the wind brought her the sound of the piano? And was she, too, seduced by the sweet sound of *Joy in the Morning*?

As I looked down at her and met the happy look in her up-turned face, I was encouraged.

I said, "Would you like to come in, my sweet?"

Yes, please.

I let her in and went back to the piano.

She moved restlessly about the room for a few moments, collecting olefactory bulletins of Bunny, herself, the cats, Michael and me.

Finally she flopped on the rug under the piano, stretched out and was in complete repose. A beautiful white china dog.

Chapter 17

Jerome has arrived.

Michael presented him with Wing Ding.

"Let's see you try him out."

Jerome vaulted onto the horse without using the stirrup. He arranged the reins, his knees dug in. He grinned at Michael as his heels touched the flanks and the horse started forward. Leaning in the saddle, to swing his mount in a circle, he looked back at us over his shoulder and Michael walked carelessly away.

"He's all yours."

I wondered about fear. How completely can it be eradicated?

That first summer, before Jerome came to the ranch, Eloise wrote me to tell me about certain of his difficulties. He didn't get along too well with other boys. He wouldn't go out for athletics. He went his own way and there was something sulky about him.

We discovered this ourselves. He would start out on an expedition with the other boys, but soon turn back and come home—always with an excuse. He had got a barbed wire scratch getting through the fence and knew he ought to put mercurochrome on it right away. A thorn in his finger, a cut, tear, bruise, and he was filled with consternation. He habitually wore patches of adhesive and bandage—dots of medicinal color.

At first I did not take it in. In our childhood we had thought nothing of falls, even broken bones.

Then I noticed that the teasing of the boys was really jeering—and I heard Riley say, "Why that kid's afraid of his own shadow."

One day, out painting, carrying paintbox and glass cup of

water, he slipped and fell. The cup was broken and Jerome's hand quite badly cut. It bled freely and he came rushing home, unashamedly howling.

While I washed, stanched, assuaged and bound up I was silent, waiting for the uproar to cease. But it did not cease and he continued to seem on the point of fainting.

"But Jerome, what is the matter? It's not really hurting now, is it?"

"Well—no," he groaned.

"And I assure you there's nothing in the least dangerous about it."

Sobs that seemed to tear his breast.

"Is it the blood?"

"Well—I—don't—know—"

The immediate emergency passed, but I worried. I could not bear to think of a child in a chronic state of fear. Under Michael's commanding eye Jerome had to groom and saddle Baldy, mount him and ride him out of the corral, bring him back after the ride, unsaddle him and lead him to pasture. He had to listen to wild talk of the other boys about the rides they would be having before the summer ended. He would have to listen to evening gab fests when the boys would persuade Michael to reminisce about the war.

Some fear is necessary. We could not live without it. No one wants a child around who hasn't sense enough to be afraid; but courage is necessary too. After all, we live in a world that can wipe us out as easily as we draw a breath. This fact we have to face, get used to, then dismiss.

I began to talk about it with Jerome. We took our afternoon rides together. I let him set the pace. (We ambled.)

We talked about fear and what was the use of having too much of it and letting it make you suffer, because no matter how carefully you guarded yourself, something would happen you couldn't foresee and you were finished anyway. And we each contributed a number of such macabre instances. To come out with these did not frighten him but seemed to relieve him.

And we had instances of courage too, and we talked of the beauty of it. Nobility. Heroism. And he kindled to this, the color

121

came up into his face. I told him how the Indians valued courage; and how the young braves must prove their bravery by climbing to the eagle's eyrie on top of the cliff and bringing down an eagle's feather as trophy.

"And I've got an eagle's feather, Jerome. Not that I climbed a cliff to get it, but it's a true eagle's feather. And I'll give it to you. It'll help you to remember about this."

He sat up there on Baldy, and turned his face to me and smiled. I smiled back at him. I felt clouds of pain rolling away.

He said, "If Mother could see me now—riding along like this—wouldn't she be pleased?"

And we broke into a gentle trot.

I fastened the eagle's feather in his red felt cap in such a way that it could be turned straight up—very jaunty and victorious—or tilted despondently down. It could even be worn at half mast.

"Now you grade yourself," I said. "I'll always be looking for the eagle's feather. When you ride in with the other boys I'll see if it's up or down—and I'll know how you're getting on—" and I thought to myself, self-examination, and self-knowledge and confession—the wig-wagging of this eagle's feather will tell it all.

I saw many a trailing feather that summer, with sheepish, hangdog looks from Jerome; and I saw the feather up, too, with a look of victory. This is so beautiful on a young face it makes the heart burn to see it.

Eloise was, indeed, very pleased when she heard of Jerome's riding. And more than pleased when next winter the headmaster at his school told her that the summer on the Wyoming ranch had "put Jerome over."

I wanted to know in what way it had put him over. All I could elicit was that he had "taken hold." He had been elected president of his class. He had gone out for football and had been made the captain of the team.

Jerome, fifteen now and as big as Michael, is still more child than youth, unless conversation becomes intellectual or touches on art. Then his look changes. A depth opens in his eyes. His thoughts are worth knowing.

Michael has put a ping-pong table on the Green way over beyond the fountain. Michael is quite a champ at it and proud of himself. He's out there now, playing with Jerome. Jerome, as it happens, has never played ping-pong before, but Genghis Khan is winning.

Now they have all arrived—seven new boys, and seven old. Young voices shouting and chattering everywhere, doors banging, groups wandering around, trying to get acquainted with each other, with Michael and me, with the lay of the land. The old boys guide them around, explain, warn, tease.

They take easily to me. I am just another Mamma. But they don't know what to make of Michael.

Hearing the old boys call him "the General" they catch on to that. Then, hearing that there is an "officer of the day" appointed every morning, to inspect "quarters" and be Michael's "aide," they realize the camp is run on military lines. Then they discover that a large part of their lives is arranged for them; that in the mornings they do some sort of worthwhile ranch work—repairing roads, mending or setting fences, cutting posts; that after our midday dinner there is an hour of compulsory quiet, reading, writing, resting in their cabins; after that an hour of compulsory horseback training, nothing less than true West Point "monkey drill"; and only after that are they allowed to take their horses and go off and do as they please. This adds up to a great deal of conforming and obeying. Now and then we have a boy who seems never to have obeyed anyone before.

I always wait to see how long it will be before they begin, in a natural and unconscious manner, to gravitate toward Michael. What is it? There's such an *up* about him. It is hero worship, I think, and I've always considered it one of the most important experiences of adolescence. If a young person misses it, what a loss! Like, later on, missing being in love.

If Michael is in town for a few hours, the boys just sit around in a slump, waiting for him to get back.

One after the other comes to me. "Mrs. Bergwin, when will the General be back?"

123

Or, "There's no chance of his not coming back for supper, is there?"

Michael makes all the noise.

That this is a virtue and something to brag about I had not realized until one summer when I had come from New York to Wyoming by bus. Three young girls kept the passengers awake with a running fire of talk and laughter all of one interminable night; and when the bus stopped at dawn, and they jumped out and were met by friends, they boasted loudly, "We made all the noise, all the way from Omaha!"

There really has to be someone to make the noise!

We have a daredevil, Harry Brimmer, a smallish boy of fifteen with a crew cut, a sudden rough loud voice, very thick eyeglasses and a constant, delightful, Puckish smile. He fell off Diabolo before they had got out of the corral. Mounted him again, was spilled again. By that time Harry was really intrigued. I think he's going to provide a lot of the fun this summer.

The youngest and smallest, Scotty, goes on practically our largest horse, disregarding all rules of balance. This is Baldy, who put one ear back as the little fellow was lifted to his back, and thereafter knew he was on his honor.

So far, Jerome has had no trouble with Wing Ding, but I wonder how he really feels? There is no eagle's feather to tell me.

My own preoccupation, these first days of camp, is the food. I am the caterer, shopper, hostess, housemother, trained nurse and confidante.

Every other morning I sit with Hilda for an hour at the red checked table in the kitchen and make out the menus for two days.

"What will we have for supper, Mrs. Bergwin?"

"What will we have for dessert?"

These two questions have often stumped me, not dinners. Beef, lamb, veal, chicken, pork, ham, game and the vegetables of the season and then around the circle again. But desserts and supper dishes! The only ones I can think of are the ones we had yesterday, the day before, and the day before that.

124

I look pleadingly at Hilda and am secretly outraged by her expression of untroubled expectancy.

But now I have solved this problem. Last winter I gave myself with all seriousness to research in the matter of desserts and supper dishes.

Confining myself to recipes that could be made without using all the utensils in the kitchen (and this rules out magazine recipes) I collected twenty-eight.

As our camp term is eight weeks, there need be only one repeat.

So now when Hilda asks me those disturbing questions, I turn the pages of my kitchen book and feast my eyes on the typewritten lists. Dutch Apple Pie, Caramel Rice Pudding, Applesauce Cake—and if Hilda has forgotten how to make them, on the following pages are the simple directions.

I type the menus and pin them on the kitchen wall. From the menus I make my shopping lists. I go into Cheyenne three times a week with the trailer hitched behind to bring back bushel baskets of spinach or corn or beets.

Michael and I now live in different worlds and it is lonely.

He seems quite in his element. I think he is back in the war again and these are his "boys" to think for and care for. But me—I feel let loose in a crowd of leprechauns who dance and prance around me, laugh incessantly, shout meaninglessly, talk in a language unknown to me (it cannot be English).

At meals, if Michael and I speak to each other, it is a public announcement down the length of a twelve-foot table, he at one end, I at the other. The boys sit on each side.

There is a smiling face down there at Michael's right who really has the look of a cherub. His forehead is framed by flat clustering curls of light brown hair. His eyes are dark blue. He makes me think of a woman who lives in Vernon Spencer's house who has the beautiful name of Ruth. She has a beautiful face too, particularly the smile. Her teeth are large, flat, perfectly even and dazzlingly white. Of course she is the wife of Spencer and this is their boy, Jimmie.

Jimmie is all lightness and easiness, all calm content. His smile is his mother's smile. He is no musician. He is fascinated by trains, tracks, engineers, railroad systems. He would rather, he tells me, be a brakeman than Paderewski. I wonder what Sheer Genius will do with this?

He sits a horse, says Michael, like a sack of meal. This is the highest praise, for if the rider is relaxed, so is the horse.

Prinny took to him immediately.

Jerome said, "Aunt Marie, can I have the piano every day in the quiet hour after dinner to practice the way I did last year?"

"As far as I'm concerned, Jerome, you may. But ask the General."

"May I, Uncle Michael?"

Michael gave permission.

There is one boy who worries me. "Bobbie, why are you so thin? Did you have many bad colds last winter?"

"I'm always thin, Mrs. Bergwin. I eat like a horse, too."

"Have you an overactive thyroid?"

"I've had a metabolism test and I'm all right. And I haven't got a tape worm either. Dad and Mother have given up worrying about my being thin."

"I think you ought to put on weight. Everyone gains here at the ranch."

Perhaps the rich milk will do it. There are always buckets of creamy milk standing in the cold running water in the spring house, ready for the boys when they come in, hot and thirsty, from riding, late in the afternoons. They dismount, tie their horses and gather in the dark coolness inside. From the terrace I can hear their voices—arguing, laughing, gossiping—

I once said to Elma, who, after all, is a doctor, "I think the boys drink about a gallon of milk a day."

"A quart, you mean." (She is used to prescribing a quart a day.)

"No, a gallon. They drink three or four glasses at every meal. And three or four dippers from the bucket in the spring house."

Missy presented herself to me as I sat at the window reading, and announced that she was going to have kittens.

This was no surprise to me.

She made petition to have her confinement in the house, pref-

126

erably on my lap. I put her out and closed doors. She made the rounds of everyone on the terrace, purring, winding herself around legs, telling about the wonderful thing that was about to happen, then vanished into the darkness.

Now she has reappeared, slim as a movie star. She is detached, demure. The boys tease her to show them where the kittens are, but she sits quiet, washing herself, *What do you mean kittens? I know of no kittens . . .*

Chapter 18

I have these two typewriters. The portable, which I take every-where with me; out onto the terrace; or it sits on my lap during a long evening in the living room or out driving. Michael has spoken of building a little table for it in the car, beside the glove compartment, so that when we take our long motor trips across the continent, I can just reach forward and pull it out.

The big L C Smith is on a permanent table in my bedroom.

Sometimes they are both up there, at right angles to each other, a sheet of paper in each—writing a story on one, this diary on the other.

I have noticed that whenever I tell people little anecdotes about the ranch life here, particularly the horses, they listen with interest. So I think I'll try that next. Just a short story—about five thousand words—about one of my horses, perhaps a little filly.

The boys are intrigued by the typewriters and my screen career. Particularly Ham (Hamilton) Parks who, one evening when the talk was all about future careers, announced that he was going to "be" an author.

Ham is swarthy, heavy-set, something of a football star al-ready and a true extrovert if ever there was one. His choice of a career surprised me.

Now if it had been Billy Allenger—

Billy is seventeen, goes to college next year, and is our tallest boy: six feet two. He is pale and rather distinguished looking, wears dark-rimmed glasses, seldom speaks, never smiles, looks like a New York businessman of about thirty—one of "these sad young men."

I asked Ham Parks about his writing.

"Of course," he said modestly, "I don't know how yet, but I'm going to major in it."

I then asked him whether he had written short stories. Articles. No—what then? His shoulders lifted superciliously.

"Just whatever I had to do at school."

"Are you a good letter writer?"

He delighted the boys by making the face of one about to throw up.

"But then what do you mean—about becoming an author?"

He was patient with me. "What I said—I'm going to major in it."

"Why choose that if you already know you don't like it?"

"There was an author who came and lived near us in the country one summer. He had a Pullman trailer hitched to his car. He had to live where he was alone. I like the woods. I like to fish. What a snap!"

I asked Harry what *he* was going to be.

"A psychiatrist." Harry's near-sighted eyes, through those heavy-lensed glasses, peered inquiringly around, but no one laughed at this. "My Aunt Jennie went to a psychiatrist every day for a year. And my Dad said she paid him a fortune. All he did was sit and listen to her talk."

They have all been to psychiatrists or know about them, and enjoy explaining about their complexes.

Presently I was asked if I never wrote screen stories anymore.

"You have to be in Hollywood if you write for the screen. Here, I'm writing for magazines. Trying to, that is—"

"How do you mean? Trying to?"

"Trying to get them published, I mean."

There was a puzzled, disapproving silence. This was not the way a successful career should go. So I added, reassuringly, "And I think I'm getting close."

"How do you mean—close?"

"Well, now I'm getting rejections, and that's really very close to succeeding, you know, just one step away—"

Murmurs of disgust. Success should come, of course, like afternoon tea being wheeled in on a tea wagon.

"One step!"

"Yes. I've taken all the others. Thought up the story. Played with the idea. Decided against it, decided for it—a dozen times. Finally wrote it. That means paper, typing, carbons, revisions, time and work. Then getting an envelope, finding addresses, weighing and stamping, mailing; then getting the script back. That's a lot."

"And the one step more?"

"You get a check instead of the script. And a different kind of letter."

They mulled this over.

"*You* could tell Ham how to write, couldn't you, Aunt Marie?" (Jerome has done considerable writing himself.)

I laughed. "Well, I could tell him a good many ways *how not to—*"

They all wanted to hear how not to.

"Well—*do not* be: literary or academic or precise or stilted or precious or woozy (not too woozy) or wordy or repetitious or long-winded or childish or kittenish or cute or clever—"

"Gosh! What does that leave you?"

"But tell us what *to do* then."

This was harder. Actually two or three tips have pulled me through many a jam. When I first began, in the Hollywood studios, to translate a novel into a screen-continuity (which is a succession of meticulously described photographs), I asked a veteran, "But how do you ever know how to begin?" And he answered, *"Just tell your story."*

This never fails. In imagination I place my small boy across the room from me, direct my eyes on that eager listening face, and begin.

Rule Two I got out of an English book that had a writer for heroine; and once, all tangled up, she said to herself in exasperation, "Now can I put a few simple thoughts into plain English or can I not?" And she immediately found she could.

When I passed on these two invaluable rules to the boys they found them very disappointing, as all true observations seem to be.

Bobbie asked, "But what if you get stuck? I'm always getting stuck somewhere in my compositions."

"Well, then, if I'm at the typewriter, I change to lying on the bed. Or the hammock. Or going for a drive—getting wheels under me—"

A gabble broke out which I finally interrupted by: "It's perfectly true. If I've invented something when I'm lying on the bed, and then try to expand it when I'm sitting at the typewriter, I have to go back to the bed to get the rest of it."

More of the gabble, through which Jerome's charming, sustained chuckle persisted. He finally said, "Aunt Marie, isn't that being woozy?"

"It certainly is."

"Just what is *woozy*, Mrs. Bergwin?" This from our usually silent Jimmie.

"Well—let's investigate this word by finding all its opposites."

This precipitated them into a wrangle in which I could eat a few mouthfuls in peace, while I listened to words emerge. Factual. Cut-and-dried. Precise. Mechanical.

With some steering from me, they finally came up with physical and metaphysical which I approved, and then asked if anyone could define the point at which physical passed over into metaphysical.

Just before we left the table I gave them my opinion on this —that there is no such exact point—and Jerome contributed the final words, "That's why you can be a little woozy?"

At first the boys are scornful of taking a rest in the middle of the day, but gradually they come to like the quiet hour. Many of them fall asleep. The biggest boys sleep the longest.

Each cabin accommodates two boys. The floors and the lower half of the walls are of wood. Above that is wire screen. A roof pole and rafters support a canvas tent fly with side flaps that roll down in case of rain.

The little encampment is in a grove of young pines, on the gentle slope of land behind the house. It is kept in good order under the eye of the Officer of the Day.

At the end of the summer, when the boys have left, I sometimes go up there and stretch out on one of the cots. I hear the murmur of the pine needles and smell the sharp tangy resin. That sound, that smell, takes you away from any city. It puts you out of doors, and far away and alone. I found this out early in life, when as children we would be taken to the woods for part of our vacation. The boys will never forget it.

The first week or two of camp, there is considerable strain for both Michael and me. I can see it on his face—a hard look. It is not only that it takes time for him to get them really in hand, there is constant worry about the horses and possibilities of accidents.

Riding comes after the quiet hour.

One boy is appointed to bring the horses in from the Stable Pasture. It is a mile square and full of rough hill-and-dale terrain, and the horses are scattered. But they know they will get oats as soon as they reach the corral and are eager to come. The horse ridden on this daily round-up is always Gold Coin, a wise old fellow who knows every trick and could almost do the job alone.

The boys love this assignment, and it is excellent training for balance and hands.

I enjoy being in the corral to watch the fourteen lively broncs sweep in at a gallop.

Then every horse is haltered, his nose bag of oats put on; he is tied to a post of the corral fence and groomed by his rider.

We have one fifteen-year-old boy, Redding Brewster, who has already done a good deal of riding. He is blond, handsome, well set-up. Michael has given him Rheingold; they are very well balanced and look magnificent together.

The other day Rheingold was misbehaving, pulling at the rope as Red tried to tie him in his place. He balked, braced his legs, wig-wagged his head and acted, in general, as if he had never even been halter-broken.

The punishment for such behavior is to be tied for a while to the snubbing post in the middle of the corral—a sort of dunce's stool.

Rheingold was thus humiliated and stood quietly now, with his nose slightly elevated and tied not more than a few inches from that unpleasant Post. Then, when at Michael's orders, Red untied him, the stallion seemed to attack his young master.

They've been arguing about it ever since—did Rheingold really intend to strike Red down, or did he just rear over him? At any rate, the horse jerked loose and reared; Red turned to get out of the way, but slipped and went down on all fours as the big hoof came down.

I was there. There was a sound—sort of groan or exclamation from everyone. Michael scooped Red up, held him hanging face downward over his left arm while, with his right, he tore off the slashed blue jean trousers. I could see the awful dread on Michael's face for that second in which he expected to see the sort of wound that would be made by a down-pawing stroke of a stallion's hoof.

But Red was unhurt—there was not even a scratch on the smooth white buttocks.

Rheingold had plunged off sideways and was standing in his usual place against the corral fence, subdued now, and waiting to be curry-combed. His head was turned around and his ears pricked to see what was happening back there at the snubbing post.

Michael set Red down and he stood grinning, embarrassed for his bare behind. Someone yelled, "Where's your pants?" and when Michael jocularly draped the torn blue jeans over the snubbing post there were whistles and cheers.

No more trouble between Red and Rheingold.

While the boys groom their horses, Michael goes from one to the other, giving directions. The curry-comb and brush must be run down the hind legs. This is hard for the broncs to endure. It tickles them. Michael teaches the boys how to stand while they do it; they must be on the alert, ready to dodge; above all, they must hang on to the horse's haunches so that if there is a sudden kick they are not in just the right place to receive it.

Nose bags and halters are then removed; bridles put on, and blanket and surcingle. All the exercises are done without saddles.

Mounting from the ground with no saddle is difficult. Many a boy is left in the corral, struggling to get on his horse, when the rest of the troop is riding down to the practice field.

133

This is a level area of the meadow between cow barn and creek.

The drill actually quiets the horses. Standing in a row or circle, knowing that the reins are loose, feeling the boys slide all over them, slithering off, climbing on again, the broncs get completely relaxed and enjoy themselves.

I can see the field from the terrace, and at this hour I usually am there to watch the maneuvers.

The boys do "scissors" on their mounts—Michael doing it first. This turns them so they are sitting facing the horse's tail. Then they do it again, to bring them facing front.

Then Michael does a handstand, placing both hands on the horse's withers, leaning forward till all his weight is on his hands —then the slow lifting of his body from the back of the horse and gradually up in the air, till his legs are straight, pointing upward. The boys struggle with this. Occasionally there is an expert gymnast who can do it.

There is frequent falling off, which Michael intends. He disapproves of tense clinging to the back of the horse, anticipating the disaster of "being thrown." For if your balance is lost you're already thrown, in a manner of speaking, and you'd be better off than on. The rider should slide or jump to the ground, leap on again. So they practice jumping on and off at a walk, trot, canter.

This adroitness is learned gradually, through the summer. It is referred to in our advertising folder under the heading of The Study of Equitation.

When the hour of drill is over, the boys are free to do as they please. This usually means more riding, probably to some distant spot. They have visited every ranch around.

The first few weeks most of them return to the stables and saddle up. But gradually, as they feel more secure, they just turn from the practice field, kick their horses and tear off bareback, whooping, galloping like a band of Indians.

I finished the ink copy of *Joy in the Morning*, mailed it at Granite Canyon, and brought back the incoming mail. I always sit down in my hammock to distribute the mail, and the boys

134

cluster around. I noticed a large envelope with the address written in the handsome caligraphy of a genius.

I wondered what he could be sending me and opened it to find my *Invention in G Minor*. He must have sent it back almost by return mail. There was not a correction on it, only one big word scrawled across the bottom of the page, STUNNING. And there was a short letter: "If your *Invention in G Minor* had been handed in at the University it would have won the prize in Counterpoint. Who has taught you Counterpoint?"

I am thinking seriously about this. If the second one, *Invention in D Minor,* is on a par with the first, and I feel sure it is, then it seems that this is fairly easy for me to do. If I composed a dozen of them they might be offered a publisher as a series of modern contrapuntal pieces for a student to work with before tackling Bach. But this would be quite a job—and I do not particularly enjoy it. I will wait to discuss this with Mr. Spencer when I get to Los Angeles.

So now I shall take up the study of Thematic Development.

I have books by Goetschius and de Lavignac on this.

De Lavignac says, *Early in the piece the composer makes a note of those scraps, fragments, tag-ends of melody which, later, he will use to develop his themes and fill out the body of his work.*

This is something I have always done unconsciously. But to know what I am doing and why, to become acquainted with the classic forms and patterns will, I believe, greatly shorten my labors.

So I am searching, now, for some piece in my reservoir of manuscripts which is ready and waiting to have its thematic material "developed."

I am thinking of *Bagatelle*.

I composed this some years ago in Los Angeles. When I played it to Mr. Spencer he completely mystified me by shouting, "You savage!"

He hurried to the door of the anteroom, flung it open, and called to the waiting students to come in. I had to play the piece again for them.

Afterwards I asked him, "But why savage?"

"Because you broke every rule in harmony with that descending run in parallel sixths and justified it by making a tremendously effective passage."

As I was playing this over, Jerome burst into the room. "What's that? I like it. Play it again."

If, long ago, it made Mr. Spencer cross the room—if, now, it has made Jerome come running—it must have something.

"But I don't like that title—*Bagatelle*," said Jerome. "It sounds as if it was trifling, but it isn't."

No. It has a hard, driving vigor.

"I'm thinking of making a big piece out of it—perhaps a recital piece."

"I'd like to learn it."

But I cannot decide. It seems just right as it is—three pages long; and to tear it to pieces—"develop" it—would destroy its bold free flight.

Oats, say all the government pamphlets, are best for feeding young stock; calves, dogs, horses. (The Scots raise their tall hardy men on oatmeal.)

"Bobbie," I said, "I notice you take oatmeal for breakfast. Do you like it?"

"Yes, I love it."

I serve the breakfast cereals in colored bowls of Mexican ware.

"Could you—er—eat more—if you had a bigger bowl?"

With some embarrassment Bobbie answered that yes, he thought he could.

Now I have substituted for his red bowl one of the yellow mixing bowls from the kitchen. He fills this with oatmeal, adds a cupful of thick yellow cream and a cupful of brown sugar. This he takes as a preliminary to his breakfast of bacon and eggs, toast, milk, fruit.

Chapter 19

Michael and I drove over to Granite Canyon for the mail and I waited in the car while he went into the Post Office.

When he came out he thrust a parcel at me. For a moment I could not think what it was, then saw the name Schirmer, and remembered.

"Oh! It's my pieces!" I cried. "My complimentary copies!"

"What pieces?"

"My four teaching pieces that Schirmer bought!"

Michael was interested. I tore off the wrappings and we examined them. Schirmer had put them out very nicely; very artistic, really, a cunning little picture of a "Papoose" in swaddling clothes. A wee vignette of a tree "Blown by the Wind."

Michael seemed really impressed.

Later he asked me indignantly, "Why haven't you got your pieces out on the piano?"

"What pieces?"

Still more indignantly, "Those pieces Schirmer just published."

"Oh! Do you think I ought to?"

"Certainly!"

So I put them out.

"Now play them."

"*These?*" I was surprised. "Why they're just tiny things. Nothing at all really. And you've heard them over and over. They're nothing worth listening to."

"*Play them!*"

I opened the pages of *When the Wind Blows* and set it on the rack.

I had forgotten it long ago and had to read it. I am a poor

137

reader at best—frightful at worst—and this was the worst, with Michael expecting something marvelous just because Schirmer has published them—expecting to be bragging about them to the boys in another minute.

I stumbled through it, wondering why on earth Schirmer had bought it. It was correct, rather clever, really had something, but still—

When I finished it I turned to Michael and said, "I can't see why they bought it."

Then I realized his face was convulsed. At my remark he burst into stentorian shouts of laughter, nearly sobbing. "I can't either."

He laughed until he almost cried. I couldn't help laughing with him, but I felt a small misery and a large confusion.

Several of the boys came into the room. Quiet hour was over and they were getting ready to ride.

I played the piece again, blaming the poor effect on my bad reading. Jerome stood beside the piano listening attentively.

"It sounds like a fugue right there at the beginning," he said.

I felt supported. I noticed that in spite of the small size of it, so bare, unornamented, stripped down to its bones—just music in miniature really—it did have feeling. And a sort of significance.

I played it several times. The other boys left with Michael. Jerome stayed.

I began to feel irritated that all its values were only hinted at. I suddenly pushed the music away and played it by ear with as effective an arrangement as came easily to my hands. I was surprised at how free and rampaging it was; quite a dramatic little whirlwind of a piece, suitable to the title, *When the Wind Blows.*

"Worthwhile that way, isn't it?" said Jerome.

This is what irks me about these teaching pieces. Good material, good musical ideas, just thrown away. And why do I do it?

For these four pieces Schirmer offered me fifty dollars cash. I replied that I would prefer royalties. They replied, "No royalties." Fifty dollars take it or leave it. I took it.

And when, long ago, John Church Publishing Company published my collection of six teaching pieces called *Summer Days at Deercreek* (and the biggest music store in Los Angeles filled its window with them) I was paid twenty-five dollars for the six. No royalties. And for the three a little more advanced which were published subsequently, fifty dollars.

I am delighted to find that we have another musician on the ranch.

This is little Scotty. He has got this nickname because his family is Scottish—last name McCollister. Scotty can sit down at the piano, reach for the pedal and play *The Happy Farmer* with accuracy and spirit.

This sensitive child is carrying a heavy burden. He is the youngest and smallest boy in the crowd. He is on a horse that is always given to baby beginners. He cannot get on him alone.

Every other boy can annihilate him with a word. No, they don't need a word. Just by being what they are, bigger and older than he, they demolish him.

Harry has only to look at him brightly, the corners of his Puckish mouth turned up, and say in a kindly manner but in that loud voice which makes everyone turn and listen, "Well, Scotty?" and every boy at the table bursts out laughing.

A scarlet flush creeps up Scotty's neck and cheeks and his eyes fill with tears.

He is not afraid—these are tears of helpless rage.

What can I do about this? Nothing, that I can think of. Scotty sits at my left at the table. I feel we could converse very comfortably if he were not every moment under siege and in an attitude of defense.

But now, with the music, we have really got together. There is one of the teaching pieces which I think he could learn.

When I was working on them last winter I placed them in groups of six. Six bird-song themes. Six little nature studies. And the group I called a *Musical Travelogue* was a set of national dances. I completed a German, a Swiss, a Spanish, a Scotch, an Irish, and I wanted a Swedish.

This series was written not from authentic folk melodies, but in the style of the folk music of each country.

Mädchen Tanz (Schirmer used English words instead of German) is a little spinning German waltz with a few measures of the *Blue Danube* in it. *Kilties* was a Scottish march. ("See the kilts swing!" cried Reese when I played it to him.)

I knew no Swedish music nor had I ever heard their folk songs. How should I get the inspiration for a Swedish piece?

Spencer once said, "Anything resembling folk melodies is difficult to compose. They are not *made*. They just grow. If you write anything like that you've done something."

I have thought a good deal about the manner in which a folk song could come into being. The seed of it, the soil, the growth.

Surely the seed is emotion—hot from the human heart.

If I myself, in a mood of loneliness and longing, stood at a window and reached out my arms and cried, "Oh, come back to me! Come back! Come back!" it is almost a song already. If such a cry should become rhythmic, then immediately it *is* a song.

It would become rhythmic if it were accompanied by some routine action. If she were not standing at the window but were seated, holding a child in her arms and rocking him and humming. Then to make it rhythmic—then to find the words—

> Ship she sailed, across the sea,
> Goodby my lover, goodby!
> It's taking my lover away from me
> Goodby my lover, goodby.
>
> By Oh! My bay—bee!
> By Oh! My bay—bee!
> By Oh! My bay—bee!
> Goodby my lover, Goodby!

(I used to sing that to a little figure in long white nightdrawers—his bullet head pressed on my bosom, my arms wrapped around him, the rocking chair swinging back and forth, the day waning and the blue dark beginning to fill the windows.)

Songs that go with rocking the cradle and burying the dead,

140

with grieving and loving, with greeting and leave-taking and planting and harvesting and merrymaking and fairing—these are folk songs.

The book *The Negro and His Songs* by Howard Odum and Guy Johnson tells of a university don who wished to study the songs of a gang of Negroes working on the road near his house. So he took notebook and pencil and sat himself on a rock wall near them; and after long listening made out the words of their song:

> White man settin' on the wall,
> White man settin' on the wall.
> White man settin' on the wall
> Just wastin' his time—
> Wastin' his time!

How should I get the inspiration for a simple Swedish folk tune?

We had at that time a Swedish foreman whose name was Nels, and I put it to him one evening up in the bunkhouse that I was sure he knew all sorts of Swedish songs and dances and tunes.

But Nels shook his head shyly.

"Oh, yes you do, Nels! You know—at the fairs, at outdoor dances, how did they dance? What kind of steps? What kind of songs? Did the boys pick the girls up and throw them around? Did they run? Or stamp? Or what?"

Suddenly Nels put down his pipe and jumped up. Not only did he get to shouting and dancing and stamping on the bunkhouse floor but he told me what actions went with the song.

Bonde Danse means *farmer dance*. And it would be in the spring, after plowing and planting, that they would all gather in the birch groves, and the young girls and young men would sing and dance.

He described the clothes they wore; the full brightly colored skirts of the girls, and how, when they whirled, their drawers would show.

Nels's face became pink and sentimental when he described the two-inch wide band of handmade lace on the edge of the drawer legs, for, all his childhood, he had seen his mother

141

crocheting this lace, and as they grew up, his sisters too. It was to be sewn on innumerable pairs of knee-length white linen drawers.

I once heard my grandmother exclaim in a tone of horror, *"Just think!"* and roll up her eyes and toss up her hands, when someone told her of a friend who had seven daughters.

"Think of what?"

"The drawers!"

I wrote the little Swedish piece, following the exact rhythm of Nels's stamping feet, called it *Bonde Danse,* placed it in the *Musical Travelogue* group, and felt it was the best of the lot.

Evidently Schirmer did not, for it was not one they selected.

I could see everything in it Nels had talked about. The birch grove with the fluttering green leaves of spring, stampings and leapings of the tall, stalwart, tight-trousered young men, whirling skirts of the girls, and the happy, laughing, screaming young faces—the marvelous thrust and spring of the hot blood of youth carrying them all off the ground and into the air—and this was mixed, in the peculiar way in which a human mind can mix up its visions and dreams, with the sight of our own Nels, stamping and leaping there in the bunkhouse kitchen, lit by a few old oil lamps, and the striped dish towels hanging by the sink behind him.

"Come, Scotty, see if you'd like to learn this little piece I composed. It's called *Bonde Danse.*"

Scotty slid onto the piano bench. I set up the music.

Harry stood by, squinting and listening, mouth drawn up in his Puckish grin—all ready to spoof.

I remarked, laughing, "Harry, you couldn't learn this if your life depended on it. But now you watch Scotty."

Scotty learned it without difficulty and it gave me a peculiar pleasure to hear a little boy play it and interpret it in his own individual way.

Harry listened for a while, as we worked at it, then grinning, squinting, drifted out to the terrace.

Scotty played it one evening after supper with everyone listening and sitting quietly, at Michael's command.

While he played it, I leaned on the side of the piano, hearing all that could have been in that music, but was not.

I was thinking of Liszt's wonderful concert pieces, the Hungarian Rhapsodies. These had been developed from simple little Hungarian folk tunes. In the extraordinary way in which one can remember music—whole long pieces, every note present in one's mind simultaneously—I remembered those concert pieces as I have heard them played many times in Carnegie Hall (and with them always a surge of excitement in the audience) and could excise out of the concert arrangement the simple little tune that had given them birth—now the *theme*—

There was an example of Thematic Development!

How had he done it? How had he been able to take small jingles that could be played by children's little hands and evoke out of them these massive, thundering, reverberating, soaring mobilizations of harmonies and melodies?

I listened to Scotty play the *Bonde Danse,* and began to note what de Lavignac had named the "scraps, fragments, tag-ends of melody which, later, the composer will . . . develop . . . to fill out the body of his work," and I did truly begin to notice them, and they began to leap and plunge in my mind like unruly horses. I could hear the chords crashing, the girls whirling, the boys leaping. All this, I knew, was a concert arrangement, parts of it, and that my work would be to hear it, unite it into a whole, bring my critical powers to bear on it, shape it to a classic pattern; and finally write it down.

It was overwhelming. And I felt as if I had received a shock, when little Scotty finished and rose from the piano bench and stood there a moment, facing the room and the burst of applause.

His cheeks were pink with pleasure.

This afternoon, in the corral, I noticed one boy helping another to mount. Red was helping Scotty.

There is a look of responsibility about Red unusual in a boy of fifteen. I have asked him if he has a lot of younger brothers and sisters; but no, he is an only child.

Red opened the strap of Baldy's stirrup and let it down, then helped Scotty to get his foot into it. Then as Scotty was clawing at various parts of the saddle, yelling, "I can do it! I can do it!" Red, with a clutch on the seat of his pants, gave him just the boost he needed.

Now that all these boys have joined our family group, Rachel is completely out of hand.

I had particularly made up my mind that since she is quite large she must be trained to keep off sofas and beds; she, of course, would like not only to jump on beds, but sleep on them. Fourteen boys—fourteen beds—all the boys aiding and abetting her—

All she has to do is disappear at locking-up time, stay away until all lights are out and all danger of capture past, then go to one of the cabins and whine.

Next time I go to town I shall buy a brush with stiff bristles suitable for brushing the long curly hair of an English setter, and a leather harness and leash.

And I shall roll up a newspaper with which to smack her.

Everyone fondles and pets her, everyone feeds her, no one has ever raised a hand to her.

So now I shall make her love me.

Chapter 20

To a city dog the sight of a harness and leash can only be a delight. But a country dog is out already and owns the world. How could I make Rachel fond of her leash and harness?

The hour of training takes place on the terrace.

At that time of morning when the boys have gone off to work and the house is empty except for Hilda busy in the kitchen and Fumiko doing the upstairs work, the sun is lazy and warm, there is not simply *too* much distraction all around, and, really, there is no better place to be than right here, with the box of biscuit, the blue bowl, the eggs and *me*. Not that this last as yet means much, for she loves everybody, but it is evident that there has begun to be something a little special about me. There are also some strange and peculiar-looking things on the terrace, which she has never seen before. She sniffs at brush, leash, harness suspiciously at first, but soon gets used to them.

The brushing comes first. I allow her only a few licks of egg, then explain that now she must wait a little for the rest. I lift her to the bench, hold her with one hand, and begin the brushing with the other, talking to her, explaining.

Now and then her hind quarters collapse and I must lift her again by jaw and tail into show-dog position and shame her a little with my voice. There was some whimpering protest at first, and a few times she turned and snapped at the brush. But a dog loves all attention and handling provided it is done with gentleness and love. My voice comforts her—also occasional licks from the blue bowl.

Next, the harness.

She got used to seeing it there mixed up with the biscuits and

145

the blue bowl. One day, after brushing, when we were both lying on the grass I made passes at her with the harness, and she responded with licks and waggings. I slipped it over her head, snugged it around her and fastened the catch.

She showed curiosity, sniffed at it, turned a couple of circles, then forgot it and sat down on me again.

I pulled her around by it to get her used to the feeling of the straps on her body. She did not mind. Obviously I was just playing with her.

Then I attached the leash and stood up. We went for a short walk.

I dreaded the first violent check.

The moment came. She scented something, stood quivering a moment, then launched herself and was almost thrown on her side by the leash. Recovering and realizing that she was not free, she stood trembling, and strained, her eyes boring into the distance. Then she flung herself on me with a barrage of pleading cries. Please! Oh please let me go!

No, Rachel. You're going to stay here with me now.

A moment or two more of that taut trembling, then she gave up and forgot it. We returned to the terrace.

I sat down again, she sat close beside me, and when at last I slipped the leash off and set her free she was not aware of it.

The four short stories that I have had out knocking at the doors of the magazine publishing houses have now all been returned.

The last one came today and with it a rejection note from the *Atlantic Monthly* which said, "The manuscript which we are returning to you has been among those in which we have taken a special interest; and if through press of work it is not possible for us to write you a personal letter, we hope you will realize that we have enjoyed your work and are greatly obliged for your courtesy in sending it."

As I know from experience that the *Atlantic Monthly* has other less encouraging form letters, this offers a whiff of encouragement.

What I have neglected to do is to "slant" my offerings to the proper magazines. "Literary" stories should not be sent to the "slicks" and vice versa. But most of my stories, I think, are somewhere in between.

I doubt if the literary story is for me. I like to tell a real tale, create a little suspense, make the listener open his eyes. So I have to put my point of view into it.

The literary story of today, it seems to me, deletes the point of view (à la Chekhov). I have heard the typical Chekhov story described as being a presentation of life without any intrusion of the author at all. Just show your people, make the reader watch what they do, hear what they say, and let the reader draw his own conclusions. Lest you have, at the beginning, set down anything that might *introduce,* or at the end, anything that might *interpret,* chop off the beginning and end of your story.

Now this does not fit *my* idea of a *story* at all. This, I claim, is a vignette.

Vignettes are fascinating.

I was all agog one day in New York listening to snatches of conversation I heard on the streets.

"A hundred thousand, I tell you!" this man behind me exclaimed. "Yes, siree! One hundred thousand buttons! And I—"

Or, two girls walking together, one saying, "Can you *imagine*? And I had gone to him for *consolation*!"

Or, one young fellow telling another, "My job? Just pickin' 'em up and puttin' 'em down, pickin' 'em up and puttin' 'em down—"

And Eugenie, telling me about a dinner party she had gone to. And when I asked her if they had played bridge afterward, said, "No! *What* do you think we did all evening?"

I could not guess. It turned out they had amused themselves by looking at what I shall call vignettes of real life. It was a hot night. They turned the lights out, sat in the dark, watching what went on in an apartment across the street where the shades had not been pulled down. Definitely Chekhov.

There is a vignette that appears to me on certain occasions here on the ranch. It is when I am sleeping in the pine room downstairs.

The windows there have very deep embrasures; the casing

is of light pine. Outside the window, just below the sill, is a little wrought-iron bracket with a ring which holds a pot of geraniums.

When I wake early in the morning and see by the soft glimmer that the sun is just rising, I sit up against pillows and watch that smooth panel of pine, for I know that I shall see on it presently, when the long slanting rays of the sun are strong enough, the shadow of the geranium plant.

It appears! A vignette! The most charming picture, blossoms, leaves, pot, and I wonder why the reflection of something that is already lovely can be still more lovely. But is it not always so? An artist's painting of a tree more beautiful than the tree itself, or a girl's face in a mirror—something is added.

And then, once, there appeared on that pine panel, hovering over the plant, a tiny hummingbird, fluttering with sudden flirts and lifts, plunging his beak in a blossom, then withdrawing, plunging again—then, unbelievably, a second hummingbird—

What a vignette—but not a story.

Sooner or later every writer evolves his own definition of a *story*.

Mine is: A reflection of life plus beginning and end (life seems not to have either) and a meaning.

Rachel is making rapid progress.

This morning I took her for a long walk with me, on a short leash, and she paced at my side in a ladylike manner, not protesting, although I held the leash pretty short.

The time came, of course, when she forgot it and lunged, and was caught by the throat. It happened just once more. The next time, starting to leap, she checked and glanced at me, as if to say, "Oh, I forgot! Excuse it, please."

It did not happen again.

When I praise her and caress her, she goes into an ecstasy. I have been keeping her alone with me as much as I can.

When the boys are assembled on the terrace or in the living room, Rachel and I are apt to be off by ourselves somewhere. Sometimes I go up to my room early, taking her with me.

I make myself comfortable against pillows in bed with a book, and Rachel lies stretched out, a ravishing figure of grace on the dark burgundy carpet. She knows there are puppy biscuits on

148

the bedside table and sometimes gets up, stretches, yawns, and comes nosing to my hand for a pat or a biscuit, then turns away; and with a deep sigh of comfort, flops. She lies with her head on her paws, her eyes flicking to me at every page I turn.

Sometimes my solitary occupations pall, and the loneliness that is inherent in human life—even more oppressive, I think, when it is in the midst of a crowd—makes my breath drag. And I find myself wishing there were some women of my own kind around so that we could chat and gossip and maybe play bridge —and I remember the early days of my marriage in Los Angeles when four of us would meet each week in the afternoon to play bridge at a quarter of a cent a point, and one of us would make a batch of fudge and there it would sit beside the table, until we had finished the game and the fudge and paid our small debts and it was time to go home to our husbands and small children and dinners.

Eugenie won't be here till the second week in August.

I find I'm waiting for her. But then, I'm always waiting. If I'm with Michael and the boys, then suddenly I must get away. And Rachel and Pompadour and I go off together. And if I'm up there on top of the world, suddenly I have to get back.

Yesterday I couldn't be alone at all. Simply could not be left to myself. I wanted the impact of happy voices or any sort of noise on my ears; the glossy hides of the horses on my eyes. I wanted to watch movement—the boys' bodies as they did their scissors and handstands, as they vaulted or tumbled off and leaped or scrambled on. (It's amazing how quickly they have learned.)

So I went down to the practice field when they were doing monkey drill and sat against a fence post to watch.

I sat with my arms around my knees, a sprig of mint between my teeth, thinking about loneliness—trying to fight it out. Since every human soul must live and die alone it is strange that from birth onward we struggle to escape this solitary confinement.

Eyes, hands, hearts, reach out, always supplicating for companionship—for its culmination and consummation in union.

All the long childhood and adolescence we wait, straining eager eyes through the mist to see that point in the road ahead

149

there—that magic point, where the miracle waits for us. Then, when we've grown up, we rush upon our destiny and cry, "Now! Now!" and, through love or through art or through religion, we receive—what? Something. A hint of union, perhaps. A moment's surcease. Then the cold fog barriers drift down again, enswathing, separating, isolating. And the anguish of disunion and loneliness is sharper than ever. Even lovers are thrust apart. Oh, the pity of it, that loving you as I do, loving me as you do, yet this abyss between us—

Shouts of laughter interrupted my thoughts.

We have one ridiculous little animal that must be called a horse since it is nothing else. A guess would make it a cross between a pony and burro with head and ears like a mule, a fat belly, short piano legs and a black stripe down its backbone. It is called Skippy and is uncannily smart. It plagues the other horses; they plague it. When we hear a barrage of squeals and kicks we know that Skippy has started something. In our school of equitation Skippy is the dunce's stool. Any boy who shirks, alibis, or fails to live up to our traditions is made to sit upon Skippy facing her tail with his arms folded.

What Skippy has to do is ignore him, go about grazing—and she never fails to do it.

It is Harry on the dunce's stool. He is thoroughly enjoying it. The boys shout and whistle, gallop around him. Skippy continues her quiet grazing. . . .

Lightning split the sky. I looked up, startled, to see black clouds, and suddenly it began to pour.

The practice troop took off for the stables and Michael galloped up to me, dismounted, and put me on Juanita, whom I am not supposed to ride because she's too much horse for me. He gave her a whack on the rump which started her off with a leap that like to unseat me.

All this rain! Hardly a day without a downpour! Wonderful for the hay. I walk through it measuring it against my body. Up to my knees, halfway up my thighs.

All the animals are filling out.

150

Chapter 21

The first big event of the summer is the covered-wagon trip across the plains to attend "Frontier Days," the rodeo that is held the last week of July.

It is a western summer festival on a large scale and is nicknamed *The Daddy of Them All* and that's probably true.

It is a week of wild-west shows held in Frontier Park, just outside of Cheyenne. The grandstand accommodates a hundred thousand. It attracts visitors from all over this country and from across the seas too.

It features bronco-busting, bull-dogging, covered-wagon races, Indian races; any sort of western stunt that is violent, exciting, dangerous, guaranteed to break bones, spill blood, put men (and sometimes girls) into the hospital, and occasionally kill.

Two ambulances are on the grounds at every show; and not the least exciting moment of the afternoon is when the roar from the grandstands rises quickly, is suddenly broken off, and there is silence while every eye is on a still figure stretched out there on the ground; then a low, long-held moan on a questioning note, and the sudden clanging of a bell, as one of the ambulances rolls out across the arena.

Before the show, comes the Frontier Days Parade, and this, to my mind, is the best part of the whole thing.

There is a Queen attended by her lady-in-waiting, two beautiful girls dressed in white breeches, handsomely tooled white leather cowboy boots, soft white suede Indian fringed tunics, white leather gauntlets and immense white sombreros. They ride two matched Palomino horses at the head of the procession.

Soldiers and officers in uniform (from Fort Russell Warren) are everywhere and brass bands play constantly.

Lastly there are the pioneer women driven in surreys and buckboards with escorts of frontiersmen on horseback.

The women of Cheyenne ransack their attics and old trunks to find costumes that belonged to their grandmothers or great-grandmothers; flounced skirts, leg-o-mutton sleeves, poke bonnets. They wave lace-edged handkerchiefs, bestow smiles right and left, carry parasols; are driven in style behind slowly pacing teams. Costumed cavaliers prance beside them.

During the week of the festival there are many parties and both men and women wear a sort of fancy dress. The men have evolved a dashing half-military outfit; snug, tan gabardine trousers, a matching pleated shirt, Mexican string tie, flat sombrero. They shine with polish and look very handsome. The women are not so uniform. At a cocktail party at the Governor's mansion I saw brilliant colored tights with braided tunics, numbers of "squaw" costumes—silver-spangled pleated skirts in turquoise, yellow, or red; I saw one storybook vision in palest pink tights and sweater with long golden hair flowing down her back.

To get from our ranch to Cheyenne is only thirty miles. But Michael has plotted a route across the plains which is about twice that distance. They have to camp out one night and are accompanied by a chuck wagon with the traditional white canvas cover of the old prairie schooners. They arrive at their allotted camping place in Frontier Park on a Saturday and spend the whole week there. When they get back to the ranch I always have to put one or two to bed with an indisposition, which we call Frontier Fever.

All the strenuous horse-backing of the first three weeks of our camp term is to prepare for this trip. Each boy has to know not only how to ride but how to care for his mount and equipment.

The date for this expedition is approaching and already it is practically the only topic of conversation.

What horses will be ridden? What colts will be along? For if Mamma goes, baby must go too. How much money has each boy saved up to spend at the rodeo?

Harry Brimmer, it appears, has had it in his head ever since he arrived to ride in the bull-dogging contest at the show.

He and Michael have hour-long arguments about it to which

we all listen. For some reason this makes me frantic. Will Michael let him or not? Harry wants an animal to practice on. Ham suggested the Roamer, which I vetoed. Michael finally agreed to bring in a well-grown yearling heifer and stable it in the cow barn so that Harry can practice.

Now, every evening after supper, we go down and lean against the corral fence, waiting for Harry to explode out of the barn door on this white heifer. She throws him immediately, whirls to face him, nose down, all four feet braced, and waits for him to get up and mount her so she can throw him again.

Frederick Martin's horse, Shag (so called because he's good at shagging polo balls), has sprained his shoulder, as he does every so often. And Fred is almost ill with anxiety lest the horse will not be able to go to Frontier.

This Frederick is another boy I cannot understand. (Billy Allenger was the first.) If there is anything Fred wants he becomes white with passion. His eyelids widen until you can see white all around the pupil. And this is over nothing at all—his desire to have a certain place in line, his wish to have the boys call him Rick instead of Fred—such *intensity*. Puzzling, but interesting.

To save the lame shoulder, Shag is not allowed to take part in afternoon monkey drill. Like an old fire horse when he sees the engine going to a fire without him, Shag whinnies wildly, runs down to the field riderless, gets into line and performs with the other horses.

All the boys roar, "Look at Shag! He doesn't want to be left out!"

Fred goes to Shag, draws him out of the crowd and stands apart holding his head, caressing him, whispering secrets to him. Then goes around to all the boys and asks each one individually to be sure not to jump on Shag, or call him, or in any way interfere with him. And I notice that strange look on the boy's face, almost beside himself.

Riley is excited about driving the chuck wagon, and has a brand-new ten-gallon hat, new blue jeans that are turned up to his bandy knees, and cowboy boots so high-heeled that he minces from bunkhouse to barn when he carries the pails down for milking.

Hilda and Fumiko are getting ready for holidays in town, for I give them plenty of time off during Rodeo week.

Old George and I will keep the ranch. We will do the milking, morning and evening. If there is anything we cannot manage, Rube Haygood will ride over from his ranch and lend us a hand.

Often George and I have been here alone together. He comes down into my kitchen and gets a meal for me now and then. He is slow, exact, scrupulously clean; accustomed, from many lonely winters as caretaker on western ranches, to all departments of housekeeping.

He is supposed to work with the horses, too, but Michael says he is afraid of them. Perhaps so.

Michael has been to town and chosen the place in Frontier Park where he will camp with his "troop." He has ordered bales of hay to be set down there in a long row. Near it a picket line will be stretched to which the horses can be tied.

The chuck wagon has been mended, spruced up, greased, properly equipped. It will carry bedrolls and cooking utensils besides supplies of all kinds.

Most of the boys will be riding geldings, but there is Red's young stallion, Rheingold. Michael had some doubts about this and thought of giving Red a different horse for the trip. But Red was brokenhearted, so he relented. There will be several dry mares and four with foals at foot—Juanita, Falla, Bonnie and Glory.

Heretofore the old work team, Fanny and Captain, have always made the trip, but Michael wants the young team to have the experience, so this year it will be Ginger and Jock.

An extra horse will be taken, tied behind the wagon. This will be Baby, who is either light work or saddle.

The boys are always asking how the horses get their names and cannot see why such a big husky is called Baby. I tell them that her whole name is *Poor Baby*. This is worse yet, so I explain that when she was a month old she lost her mother; and the

154

first time I put the nursing bottle in her mouth I exclaimed, *"Poor Baby."*

"I bet I know how Bonnie got her name—from the song 'My Bonnie Lies Over the Ocean,' wasn't it?"

"Wrong. We had been waiting for that birth a long time. And when at last the colt came I said *à la bonheur*. Now if you know French, you know what that means—"

"You could have called her Ala. Can I name a foal Ala?"

Usually when I let the boys name foals they come up with something from the race track—Madame X and Fraidy Cat. But Ala sounds quite smart.

There has been another near accident. Again—it might have been so serious yet turned out to be nothing.

Ham and Harry, after a long ride the other afternoon, were down in the pasture doing stunts. They were feeling their oats and made their horses rear. As they were bareback it was not too easy to stick on. Jazz went up on his hind legs obligingly, but it wasn't high enough to suit Ham. Ham pulled him higher. Jazz went higher—Ham gripped tight—Jazz went over backward. Ham stuck on and the horse fell on him.

I have seen Michael pull a horse over backward to discipline him—slide out of the saddle, be standing on the ground when the horse lit, and mount him again as he scrambled to his feet.

The first I knew of the accident I saw Michael walking up from the meadow carrying a boy over his shoulder.

Ham couldn't walk; one leg would not work. The backbone of the horse had come down exactly on the right groin.

If it had come down an inch or two to the left, the doctor said, the bladder would have been ruptured. As it is, the violent blow was received by the big thigh muscle, which would be paralyzed for a few days, but would gradually recover tone and be as good as ever.

Ham can stand, putting weight on the leg, but cannot lift it to take a step. He can, however, progress backward, dragging it. So at present that is his method of locomotion.

I can stand only so much of that world made up of the horses,

155

Michael, the boys, the noise and violence—like a big dust cloud just off there near me—then I have to find a retreat.

I take long rides alone with Pom and Rachel. I think of Music. I think of Reese.

Reese has always been caught into the same things that take possession of me. When I was seven and he was nine, he would hear me playing those deep fifths and come running and sit on the bench beside me. We would look into each other's eyes and listen and wonder while the whole afternoon passed. We were knocking on a door—where did it lead?

This has not changed. When, after ten years of absence in Los Angeles, I returned to New York, I met him first at a dinner party. There was talk of some south African rhythms and I asked him, down the length of the table, "Did you by any chance, a few years ago, see a moving-picture travelogue in which there was a tribe of savages moving through the jungle, singing a war chant?"

Reese exclaimed, "I did indeed!" In unison, we broke into that strange and disturbing chant.

There was something else that we would do when we were children. I would play a simple piece as it is written. Then Reese would cry, "Now play it big!"

And, as I had done with the little teaching piece *When the Wind Blows,* I would cut loose, play it with all my fingers, with all my passion—as big as I could.

Then there was the *Wind Harp*.

I composed this years ago when we had not been long at the ranch. I was lying up there one day on the top of the world lost in the skies and the wilderness and I apprehended wind moving all around me. I could hear it singing and yet there was no movement, not a blade of grass, not a cloud. And I thought, But it is a harp—this place! And I imagined the bank of filaments slanting down across the world. And shoulders of wind like immense angel's wings thrusting, making this faint twanging, this sighing—a sound so full of beauty, so full of doom—so potent to lift you and yet crush you, cradle you and drink all your tears—

Two long melodic lines came to me for that piece and when

they did I suffered a sort of shock. I could hardly move or speak for several days. I felt the ecstatic quality.

Well, what is ecstasy? It is the thirst and the drink together; and how put that into music?

Simultaneously it flowed out and drew in.

I looked up *wind harp* in the encyclopedia and found under the long dissertation these beautiful lines: "It is said that King David had a wind harp suspended over his couch; and in the long watches of the night it would sound with ravishing harmonies when the north wind blew."

I was playing this one morning early in Reese's apartment when suddenly I heard a shout and the thud of his feet as he leaped out of the shower. He and a bath towel arrived at the door of the drawing room.

"Play that again! Again! Do it again! Don't stop! Go right on!"

How long did I keep playing it? He wouldn't let me stop.

For Vernon Spencer perhaps even more than for Reese, this piece had deep significance. He seemed stunned by it. He read it again and again, slowly, pausing now and then to drop his hands in his lap and stare at the music, in deep thought.

"How ever did you get those two melodies?"

He played them slowly, one note at a time, dropped his hands in his lap again and thought again.

Finally he turned to look at me with brows drawn down.

"It's love!" He exclaimed this suddenly as if surprised. "It's just—so—full—of—*love*."

This I had not known or particularly intended, but why not? Have I not been in love with love all my life? ("All but love," wrote the French author, François Mauriac, "is torment.") And all that is symbolic of love. Of all flowers, *roses*. Of all colors, *pink*. Of all musical intervals, *the major third*. Goetschius speaks of this interval—its piercing sweetness; and says, "Use it sparingly." Yes, yes, always use love sparingly. "The fierce joy of loving too much, it is a terrible thing," wrote James Barrie.

Spencer forgot my piece, sat with hands in his lap, fingers curled inward a little, staring past me out the glass wall of the room. Cruelly sharp-edged hills stared back at him.

"I sit here," he said in an odd, strangled voice, "day after

157

day, week after week, year after year, working like a gopher!"

It shocked me. I had seen too many gophers.

He went on in the same estranged way. "There is a verse by Dowson." He recited it:

"They are not long, the weeping and the laughter,
    Love and desire and hate:
I think they have no portion in us after
    We pass the gate.

"They are not long, the days of wine and roses:
    Out of a misty dream
Our path emerges for a while, then closes
    Within a dream."

He took off his glasses, shook his head suddenly and with the heel of his hand wiped the tears from his cheek. "I'm sorry. Those lines always make me cry."

He stood up, went to the end of the room and threw logs on the fire. The doorbell rang. That meant the next pupil was there. He paid no attention but pointed to the sofa.

"Sit down. I'd like to talk to you a little."

Words poured forth. A torrent. He told me his life from infancy to the present moment. Every hour the doorbell rang again and another pupil arrived. They accumulated in the anteroom.

At five he dismissed them all.

I was wrung out. I slowly rose from the sofa. With his customary bright smile he patted my cheek. "You don't mind, do you? Some other day we'll go on with your piece. Today it broke me up. I just felt I had to tell you everything."

What has stayed with me out of all that long tale is the picture of a little boy fourteen years old who stood in short trousers, long black woolen stockings held up by round red garters, pleading with his father. Since he had won the contest and had been appointed to be the organist of the church, could he not please have a pair of long trousers?

When *Wind Harp* reached Sam Fox in New York and he sat listening to the record (Spencer had had one of his finest pianists play and record it) he too sat staring out the window, and said, "It sounds like the wind."

He published it, because, he said, people would like to hear those two long melodies.

The Dutch piano virtuoso who had played *Twilight and Birdcalls* played *Wind Harp* too. And when I asked the friend who had brought this about, "Oh! He liked it?"

"He *loved* it. He said he found it *very moving*. And not at all easy. Because of the two rhythms. The going and coming together."

Now they have left for Frontier.

Chapter 22

Riley was resplendent on the seat of the covered wagon.

The two broncs, Ginger and Jock, were in harness, Baby on a lead rope behind the wagon.

When I see the confusion of getting this little group into action—hear the noise and shouting—I marvel how armies can be moved.

There was trouble with the team.

The road down from the stables has been cut into the gentle slope between the back of the house and the pine grove where the boys' cabins are.

Riley, trying to steer them down the hill in the midst of the milling group of mounted boys, was on his feet, his bandy legs braced apart, his big hat on the back of his head, his arms almost wrenched out of their sockets by the pulling broncs.

Suddenly they were out of hand, plunging and rearing.

The wagon careened this way and that. Baby, jerked to and fro on her lead rope, began to plunge too—came down across her rope and went crazy.

George and I, on the ground, were spectators.

What a roar! Riley, George, the boys. But suddenly Michael's voice, from his saddle on Juanita, rose above the others.

"George! Get to their heads! You blasted—g—o—s—g—e—n!"

(Michael was back in the war again.)

George was terrified of the horses, but still more of Michael, and he ran toward the upended beasts.

Fortune favored him. Riley's hat blew off. George conceived it to be his first duty to retrieve Riley's hat and ran after it.

It was a moment of real danger—a runaway, an upset wagon,

the barbed wire that fenced the road a little farther down—so I moved to the horses' heads. After all, I've known those broncs since birth, and they know me.

I was indignant that they should behave so badly on an important occasion like this.

"Ginger! Jock! You stop that! Behave yourselves!"

They know my voice and are accustomed to obey me. I managed to get hold of the reins under their chins, but then they went up in the air again, taking me with them.

Michael's voice rose above all the noise. "Mary! Get away from them! Mary!"

Suddenly there was comparative peace. The broncs descended to eight prancing feet. George presented Riley with his hat. I stood away. Michael led the boys down the hill, turning in his saddle to tell George just what he thought of him; the wagon rolled smoothly—Baby, the temperamental, the only one protesting.

Hilda and Fumiko, from outside the back door of the kitchen, waved a last goodby and went inside.

Slightly winded from my struggle with the broncs, I stood watching the cavalcade as it wound down the slope and across the pasture, and at the same time began to think of all the things I would have to do during this week.

I must carry the mail to the campers, do errands for them in the car, fetch and carry provisions, carry them our fresh spring water and big cans of milk.

Michael had explained just where tonight's campsite would be, drawing a map to show me how I could get there by short cuts across the plains which would link up with some old dirt roads.

They would make camp at about five. I could reach them in an hour's driving. I would take Hilda and Fumiko with me as far as Granite Canyon, drop them off there, pick up the mail; they would catch the evening bus into town. George would get Rube Haygood to help him with the evening milking.

Baby was still acting up. Before they reached the curve in the road which would hide them from my sight her determination not to go to Frontier culminated in furious action. She leaped,

161

plunged, wig-wagged, galloped a few yards, then began the performance all over again.

But the team, once under way and with Riley urging them on, took no notice of what was going on behind the wagon.

Her last inspiration was to sit down on the ground and see how they liked *that*. So she sat down like a big dog. It made no difference. The wagon and the broncs continued smoothly on their way.

The last I saw of them, Baby was going around the bend of the hill on her fanny.

I stood there a good five minutes more, not moving, watching the dust settle, letting the din fade out of my ears. Then I went to the piano.

It was a little after ten. I would have five hours to work.

The *Bonde Danse,* so far, was only one theme, and I knew it would have to have a second part.

Reese's voice: "Play it big, Mary!"

I played it big. I improvised on it freely. Seeing in my mind's eye that crowd of girls and boys dancing in the birch grove, I saw one little girl run out and do a solo dance. Instantly there came a delightful running theme, and I improvised on that.

Consulting the Goetschius book, *Lessons in Form,* I discovered that the *Bonde Danse* was now in a classical form. The first theme, (A); then the second theme, (B); then the return to the first. A-B-A form. Or Simple Song Form. Or Sonata-Allegro Form.

I was ready to write it.

Fumiko's voice, "Lunch, Mrs. Bergwin."

"Take it out to the terrace, Fumiko."

After lunch I would rule the measures and periods on manuscript paper and block it out.

I had expected to sleep comfortably in my own bed that night, but I slept instead on a horsehide, laid out on the prairie.

Most horsehides do not have names, but this one was called Musetta.

The short cuts across the plains which Michael had mapped for me proved not to correspond with the terrain I found as I

162

drove (and drove, and drove, and drove) across the prairie that evening, carrying mail, milk, water and provisions.

And there had evidently been a flash flood in the neighborhood, for after a long time I found myself on a wide dirt road in a sort of lowland through a wooded section and the road was covered with a slime of mud four to six inches deep.

To force myself through this I had to keep going pretty fast, and the car slid in arcs from side to side of the road—*all the way* from side to side.

And it was growing dark.

I was uneasy. I was quite miserable, for I hate being lost worse than anything. I went along that way for another long time. It seemed endless, and no way out.

So it was wonderful when I suddenly emerged and began to go upward on a dry road and heard voices and whinnies and then saw lights ahead of me and the silhouette of the covered wagon up there against the red afterglow of the western sky.

That horsehide!

When we first came to the ranch we became acquainted with and finally good friends with the Charlie Careys, one of the old families in Wyoming, originally from Virginia. They had a house in Cheyenne and a large ranch out of town. They took us under their wing. They would come out and spend whole days with us, and Charlie would persuade me to the piano bench, sit down beside me, and I must give a command performance of every opera aria I could remember—especially the Musetta aria from *Bohème*. He would keep time by pounding with his boot and exclaiming "Boom! Boom!" He could do that all day long.

The first job he ever had, he told me, was riding around to different ranches fixing windmills. He had a sorrel pony. In time the pony died. Charlie felt sentimental about him and had the hide cured and used it as a carriage robe in the car, or spread on the ground for a picnic or a nap or a night's sleep, and he finally gave it to me as a Christmas present.

Michael had thrown this into the chuck wagon with all the other bedrolls, rubber ponchos and blankets.

I slept that night rolled up warm in blankets with Musetta between me and the ground. I slept like the dead.

163

When I got back to the ranch the next afternoon George greeted me with a long face. The Roamer was missing.

"But he's got the long chain on."

"No, Missus. The Boss took it off before he left. He's gone up to that Burt Langley's ranch again. Sure as you're born he'll cut him. He said he would if he showed up there again. You'll never get no more calves out of *that* bull, Missus. W'en you see him again he'll have blood running down his legs, or he might shoot him—"

"George!" I yelled. "Will you shut up? Go saddle Pom for me while I change my clothes."

On the run, I stopped to call back, "And get me the wire cutters. There'll be fences down."

I ran upstairs, tore into my riding things and remembered that I could take the car, go out the back way onto the county road and then around to Langley's ranch—good roads all the way and it would be quicker than riding. But no—I'd have to bring the Roamer back over the plains. I couldn't herd him along with an automobile.

All this time my heart was pounding because I was afraid.

Afraid of even going to that ranch where Langley lives with all his henchmen—the very men, I felt sure, who had deviled me so with that red bull.

And achingly afraid that this time it would be too late to save the Roamer. George said he missed him first yesterday at milking time—that gave him twenty-four hours' start.

Afraid most of all of the trouble there'd be between Michael and Langley if Langley had done it.

I did not enjoy that ride. I saw no beauties of nature. I saw only what was in my mind's eye. Langley's corrals—and me marching in there demanding my bull; and, too, I couldn't help seeing the Roamer just as George had described him; standing over there in the corner, bloody and vanquished. When he saw me he would give that low moan.

I came to Langley's boundary fence, slowed up and rode along it, looking for the place Roamer had been through before and we had mended. He would be likely to break through the same place again.

164

I came to the place, but there was no break. I rode on.

Then I saw another rider coming on the other side of the fence. We approached each other at a walk.

From my first glimpse of the heavy rider, saddle and horse, all the typical western accoutrements, I recognized Burt Langley.

I wondered if he would be in a rage and offensive.

Or he might be polite, admitting nothing.

Or he might blame it on someone else and pretend to be sympathetic.

We came abreast of each other and pulled up.

I nodded. "Hello, Mr. Langley."

"Howdy, Miz Bergwin." He was expressionless, chewing his cud.

We sat looking at each other. He spoke first.

"Lost that bull o' yourn again?"

"Well—er—a couple of my yearling colts strayed out of the band—"

That long stare. That swinging jaw.

"They ain't over here."

"No—they wouldn't break through wire—well—thank you—" I touched my heel to Pom and we started off at a walk. He did the same.

I glanced back. He glanced back. And suddenly he put on that show again; made his horse buck; yelled, spurred him, raised his sombrero and flourished it, whacking his horse, neck, flanks, head; and I could do nothing but sit there and watch while that horse practically turned inside out, crow-hopping, cork-screwing, sun-fishing.

With one last flourish Langley pulled him up into a perpendicular rear, held his sombrero out toward me in a gesture of farewell, and galloped away.

As soon as he was out of sight I cut back to the ranch, thinking, Then if Roamer isn't at Langley's ranch, or Haygood's (Rube would just have brought him back to us and mended the fence himself) it must be Pomroy's. And Pomroy's ranch was way north. All our meadows were between us. That meant four fences broken through. And the light was waning.

165

As I rode down through our gorge to get to the meadows, George met me, shame-faced.

"He's here, Missus. He was hidin' out all the time down in that little draw in Section Sixteen. The son-of-a-gun. He didn't come in for his grain ration at milking time yesterday, dod blast that bull. Nor this morning neither. That's why I figured he was gone—"

I slipped off Pom and threw him the reins.

"Take her up to the corral and unsaddle her. Give her a good rubdown—she's hot."

"Could I get your supper, Missus?"

"I wish you would, George. That'll give me time for a hot bath."

George and I sat for dinner at the drop-leaf cherry table in the corner of my kitchen. The table was covered with a red and white checked cloth.

The kitchen is almost my favorite room.

It is fairly large and white-washed, with two French windows opening onto the terrace and Green.

It has a big black iron stove set into an alcove at one end. Doors, cupboards and spice closet are of dark stained wood, all made by Michael and very quaint. The floor is painted apple green and protected at strategic points by small oval hooked rugs, made by Pat, hooked rugs being her specialty. She likes to put red and pink roses on a cream background with green leaves and black and tan borders.

In the morning, the room is flooded with sunshine.

At night, like this, lit with kerosene lamps, it is cosy, full of the smell of good food and warm with human fellowship.

George has one specialty. Raisin and pecan pie. He knows I love it. This was his peace offering tonight. We sat long over the table, the dogs asleep near the stove.

And before he left I told him to put the long chain back on the Roamer. "Get Rube to help you."

166

Chapter 23

I have ridden in the Frontier Parade.

I wore a pioneer costume lent me by one of the Careys—an embroidered basque bodice, a long, flounced, full skirt and a poke bonnet.

Newspaper photographers were waiting for us when we descended from our carriages.

The IZ outfit, namely our troop, was also in the parade. Michael led on Juanita, the boys on their well-groomed horses behind him, then Riley driving the chuck wagon and Baby on the lead behind.

The four foals got the biggest hand of any. Whinnying with astonishment, their lifted heads and sharply pricked ears just one big question mark, bouncing along on their springy pasterns, astounded by the brass bands, the milling crowds, now and then a head down and a hind leg poked out in defiance, they kept their places and stole the show. Occasionally one would rush to his mother, thrust his head underneath her belly and get a few gulps of milk. The crowd would roar, Mamma continue on her way, baby bounce off, twist up his sharp head and squeal angrily. What's going on here anyway?

The weather is exquisite.

I have been standing at the end of the terrace just soaking it up. The dogs sleeping on the warm dry grass in the sunlight. The radio playing a beautiful program of Schumann pieces. Just, passively, to receive the pulsations of that color—the blue, green, gold, our red roofs, the lovely medley of the flower borders— makes one feel as if one were doing something important.

That mysterious "movement of the soul" which we call happiness—what is it? And how is it to be won? Pursue it and it is nonexistent; forget it and suddenly it is there.

If you saw a person standing there, entranced with bliss—would you know it by his look? I have read these words "rapt away."

When Pat was ten she fell in love with wisteria. There was an arbor hung and festooned with it. She picked a great cluster of blue bloom and took it in her arms.

"I held it to my heart and wondered why I was so happy," she told me.

Was it the color—the blue? Was it the perfume? Or was it the utter purity of the love that flooded her?

When in my grandmother's house at Deercreek, in the summertime, the fingerbowls were brought in and set on the table—the ruby red, and sapphire blue, and emerald green—and Grandma May with that sweet, quizzical smile, looked at me, touched her finger to the water, then moved it around the edge of the bowl—it sang! It emitted a musical sound of such pure beauty that I felt stabbed with ecstasy, which has never left me.

And one year when we were quite small she took us to Switzerland and there we were told about the edelweiss, the small, star-shaped white velvet flower that grows in the snow; how rare it was; how hard to find; and always we could be thinking of that, and looking for that, and trying to accomplish a supreme thing —the finding of an edelweiss in the snow.

And we climbed the Dolomites, and played in the snow in the summertime and I looked and looked for the edelweiss. I would murmur the word over and over to myself. (It still thrills me.) We found a few during the summer and brought them home. One I saw and thought the most beautiful of all, but I could not touch it, for it grew on the other side of a crevasse on the mountainside, just too wide a crevasse for me to dare to leap. I knelt down in the snow and looked at the unattainable flower. I strained, I longed, I anguished for it.

If children come into the world "trailing clouds of glory," perhaps it is this intensity of desire.

Sometimes, as a child, I discovered beauty in a mere word. I

168

would lie in bed at night filled with excitement and joy whispering the word over and over—*silver—silver*. I felt as if I possessed a secret treasure all my own. No one could take it from me or even know about it. I went under the bedclothes, I doubled up hugging myself, I choked with sobbing laughter.

But this is the ancient teaching, ancient wisdom. Repeat a word over and over and it "lets you in." Certain psychic centers have been touched and awakened. In India, students are told to repeat the word *Om*.

It is said that when one is ready to study Yoga a guru appears.

This happened to me in California and to Reese in New York. Though we were not in communication (we seldom wrote letters) yet we found our way to the same path. Soon he was reading and listening to lectures by P. D. Ouspensky. And I was deep in the Sacred Books of the East.

East and West were exchanging cultures. We carried to the old world our techniques for a better material life; they sent to us a stream of powerful thought to mitigate our materialism and teach us control of the mind, which, in turn, controls the body.

My guru was not Indian but Irish, with a dark Italian face that could have been the face of Savonarola. He lectured in an oblique, sardonic manner that left you hunting for the meaning of fables. But face to face he was a seer whose understanding never failed, and a friend whose hands could lift mountains.

Even when I first saw him he was old with silver hair above luminous dark eyes.

I paid him the last visit, knowing it would be the last, for I had been told he had not long to live.

One does not often—in a whole life—stand in the presence of greatness.

He always sat in a comfortable armchair to receive his students, in front of him a table, and all around, high book cases at all angles, which made the immense room into a maze and darkened it, so that only a dim diffused light flooded in above them.

As I stood beside him I knew that I hardly had a right to be there, for at first there was no change on that dark almost frowning face. The upright back of the chair supported his head, which was slightly tilted forward. His two hands rested on the arms of the chair. I laid my hand on his. His eyeballs rolled up and I knew he saw me . . . and loved me.

I removed my hand, and after a moment, his lips moved.

"Pretty pink dress."

It was not exactly pink but a soft light red silk printed all over with tiny sprigs of white which lightened it. It was made with soft pleats and a small black velvet collar.

We stayed so a while, I standing beside his chair, he not looking at me, his eyes half-lidded, weary.

At last I knew the visit was over and I must leave. I lifted his hand and put the back of it against my cheek and held it so for quite a while before I laid it down, smiled at him and turned to go. Then he spoke once again.

"Pretty pink dress."

At the Granite Canyon Post Office today, on my way back from town, I was handed a telegram addressed to Hilda and told that I must open it and deliver her the news verbally, for it contained the notice of a death.

It is her father who is dead. What will this mean to her? I headed back to town immediately and found Hilda at her hotel. She burst into tears and never stopped weeping. She must go home, she said, go immediately.

I brought her back to the ranch and packed her suitcase while she wept. Dressed her while she wept. Took her again to town, bought her ticket, stowed her in the bus and stood outside the window while she wept.

"I'm sorry, Mrs. Bergwin," she sobbed, "whatever will you do? The boys will be home in three days."

"I'll get along. Don't bother about me."

"But what'll you *do*—Fumiko can't lift a finger in the kitchen."

Her distress about me, added to her distress about her father, had her almost in hysterics.

"I'll get someone."

"There isn't anyone in this town."

"All aboard!"

170

The door slammed. The engine started.

"Goodby, Hilda. Write me."

"Goodby, Mrs. Bergwin."

I have been to the employment office, but there is no one there who wants a job in the country. Here in the west, people go *to* town, not away from it, in vacation time.

I drove slowly through the streets toward Frontier Park.

The town is jammed.

Banners are strung across the streets announcing that the greatest Rodeo in the world is in progress.

Scores of youngsters on buckskin or piebald ponies gallop up and down the streets, interfering with automobile traffic as much as possible.

Visitors are dressed with ultra chic; scarlet or purple or yellow silk shirts, with large white poppies patterned in the silk (very pretty, these), bright bandana kerchiefs, tight breeches, embroidered boots—and no distinction in dress between men and women.

When I reached our campsite my heart lifted at the sight of the long, neat picket line of horses, the rampart of baled hay, the saddles strung neatly along the fence with the "officer of the day" guarding them.

Michael told me three more boys had joined our group. Ham Park's older brother and two friends had driven from New York to see the Rodeo, and wanted to be with us for the remainder of the camp term.

Michael and I talked over the domestic disaster and looked at each other.

"Alice?" he suggested.

"I was just thinking of her. Do you think there's any chance of her being sober?"

"Not likely," he admitted, "during Rodeo week."

"Unless," I suggested hopefully, "she got too drunk and is in jail."

This offered hope to Michael too and he decided to go scouting.

I sat in a comfortable crook of baled hay and chatted with the boys and enjoyed myself until Michael returned.

171

Alice had been located, was moderately sober; would be delighted to come to the ranch to cook for the rest of the summer (we've had her before) but could not think of leaving town until the Rodeo was over. And it would take her one day after that to get her stuff together and finish up some little things she had to do. She would come out Monday.

"Think you can manage it?" Michael asked.

"No trouble till you get back with the boys Saturday, but then there'll be eighteen of you for two or three days. I don't know—"

"Remember old Harvey?" suggested Michael. "I ran into him. He's a pretty good cook. We might get him today and keep him till Alice comes. At least he could do chores for you."

"But he's always drunk too," I objected.

"On the wagon now," said Michael cheerfully. "Told me so. Says he has realized at last that it really doesn't agree with him. He wanted to know if you wouldn't try him on the ranch again some time."

I pondered. "I did want him to corn a cow for me. I'd like to know how that's done. And everyone says Harvey knows. But he couldn't do that now. No—I'll make out alone till Alice comes."

I bought enough supplies to last until Monday and drove back to the ranch, feeling a sweet cool peace descend on my soul as I saw the ribbon of road winding westward into the sunset, and thought of the quiet empty house, the dogs, my piano, the long evening, and the *Bonde Danse*.

My father once showed some of my compositions to Josef Hofmann, whom he knew slightly, and Hofmann said, "Too much thematic material."

Critics say this about many young composers who come to their work with more inspiration than training. It was said of Gershwin.

Gershwin answered spiritedly (in print) that if a composer had a wealth of musical ideas, why be stingy with them?

I wondered if he was right. Or the critics?

I have always believed there is such a thing as Universal Technique. You can do *this* because you know how to do *that*.

172

I quickly learned how to write scenarios because I had been made to analyze and dissect sermons. And when I came to the building of a house I knew something about it because I could build a scenario.

That house, on North Rossmore Avenue in Hollywood—I engaged the best architect I knew and then disagreed with the plan he made. "If you go right from the front door into the big living room there is no suspense."

Eventually we turned three corners, each with its particular revelation. Each turn increased the expectation. The same method would be used in a scenario if you wanted to lead the audience up to the point where they would say, "Oh!"

One had to get way into the living room and then turn around before one caught, through the tall glass doors at the back, the lovely vista of long narrow green garden walled with poplars—a deep well—and then you would say, "Oh!"

Applying such techniques as these, with which I already have had experience, I see that of course there can be too much thematic material in a composition, for there certainly can be in a play. And if there is, it will be confusing and boring. Audiences must know what you are talking about, recognize your themes, get to know them by heart.

The audience reaction, in music, as in a play, is emotion. Tension, relaxation, hope, suspense, aversion, dread, fear—all the rest of it. The pulse beat, hurrying, slowing, almost stopping at times, makes an embroidery. And if you are expert in your construction, you provide the pattern for it. You decree exactly how the audience will feel.

I once played a new piece for Mr. Spencer and he suddenly yelled, "You can't do that!" (I had introduced a rather effective figure in the bass.)

"Why can't I?"

"It's thematic!"

At the time, I felt as Gershwin did. The more the better. But now I see that I had dragged a red herring across the trail. It would have thrown the hearer into confusion, and he would perhaps have begun to listen for the new theme rather than the old.

173

So I teach myself with meditations on Universal Technique, and with Lussy on Rhythm, de Lavignac on Music, and Goetschius on Form.

Many composers have been self-taught—many of the greatest. By great gulps I am absorbing Thematic Development.

Chapter 24

Coming back from Cheyenne—they do it in a day, taking the shortest possible route across the plains and coming in the back way from the county road. This leads directly into the corral and stables. The chuck wagon trails in hours later.

The boys are ravenous of course and there is always a specially good dinner prepared for seven-thirty, to be kept over till nine if necessary.

Without Hilda, this dinner was a test of efficiency for me, particularly as I wanted to preside at the foot of the table, say the grace, and give the usual air of ease to the meal.

Fumiko is accustomed to serve. These last few days I've been coaching her in the rites of dishing up. The hours of work preparing vegetables and cooking—this I did myself, with a tub full of cool water waiting for me upstairs and a fresh slip and dress laid out ready to be pulled over my head at the last minute.

I made Plum Duff for dessert.

When Fumiko rang the first bell I was in that tub and the boys were gathering on the terrace. At the second bell, five minutes later, I entered the dining room and Scotty pulled out my chair.

Tomorrow one or more of the boys will look a bit peaked, perhaps have a temperature; and I will put him to bed in the spare room and arrange a little table with a tumbler of water holding a thermometer, a pitcher of fruit juice; and will sit beside him and plump his pillows and take his pulse. They quite enjoy it.

When dinner was over we all sat on the terrace.

Our overhead cloud was there above us—larger than usual and

175

filled with electricity. The light would blaze on, the cloud would shudder and blink, glow ruddily, then go dark. Then it would begin over.

Day was turning to dusk. *Enchantment of Dusk.* Here it was —a soft magical indigo blue, and the nightbirds beginning to make their sudden, dramatic announcements.

If you are quiet you can watch this change come over the world. The boys were quiet. The big cloud was moving eastward. Finally, mumbling and growling, flashing on and off, it slid over the hill. Then a few stars appeared, pale and far apart. More and more appeared until the whole sky was blazing and brilliant.

The boys went to bed early.

It is Harry Brimmer I have in bed today. He actually did enter the bull-dogging contest, shot out of the chute on a very lively animal, clung for about ten seconds before he was tossed off. He is covered with bruises; I apply Sloan's liniment and the whole house smells.

On my way to the stables, I passed Bobbie sitting on the stone coping of the fountain doing his washing. He slapped his blue chambray shirt in the water, his eyes dreaming off to the horizon.

"This is fun," he said slowly, smiling at me. "I'm glad we're back."

Seems to me Bobbie's face is a little rounder.

The boys have found where Missy has hidden her kittens. What a place! Under an outcropping ledge on the hillside that, you would think, hardly a mouse could get under.

But the dogs sit stubbornly in front of it barking. Missy sits nearby, unconcerned, washing herself. There's nothing there— how could there be?

But I heard those infinitesimal cries—and suddenly Missy made herself thin as a weasel and vanished underneath.

Now she has moved them again.

Michael went to town today to do the marketing for me, as I cannot leave the kitchen. He would bring Alice back, too. This is my last day! But he came back without her. Those "few little

176

things" she had had to do before leaving town were such that she had been arrested and put in jail.

The judge told Michael that he would let her out if Michael wanted her, but Michael thought it wiser to let her do her sobering up in jail.

So I have three more days to go with nineteen to feed and the thermometer suddenly and unaccountably soaring.

All is well.

Alice is here, slender, quick, meek, quiet, efficient. Definitely, she has charm.

She looks to be about fifty-five years old. She has short, tightly curled hair, more green than gray, is never without a cigarette stuck to her lower lip. She slip-slaps around in old felt slippers, her mottled gray legs bare. She always promises not to drink while she is working for us at the ranch. If she gets nervous and simply has to have it, she is supposed to ask us.

She comes gliding into the living room. "Mrs. Bergwin?"

She is balm to my spirit and I have forgotten the hot and hectic days in the kitchen and need think of nothing now but the *Bonde Danse,* which in its larger form is to be called *Svenska.*

That second theme of *Svenska* which I have invented—it has a program, a story. One little girl—one gay, wild child—darts out from the group, her red, whirling skirt standing out from her body, and begins to run in and out the crowd, pausing now and then for a turn and whirl and kick, then runs again—the music runs, pauses, whirls, kicks—a second solo dancer joins her, and the two pursue each other while the rest invent their own wild movements as chorus—everything goes faster and wilder—at last chaotic and out of rhythm—then this dies down and becomes steady and sustained—and so to the end.

Have I done this properly?

You have to develop a theme according to its very own character and potentialities, coordinating it to the program. This bit at the end—grotesque and crazy—I don't feel that I made it up—it just went inevitably to that sort of music there. As if those fellows had all had a little too much to drink, or the music and

177

the girls and the dance went to their heads, and they just broke loose. And what a clown a man is when he breaks loose! So here, at the end, the men are clowning. The girls are squealing. Wild shrieks!

The question I am wrestling with is: Is it Swedish? The first theme is, I know. Well—what is Swedish? Sweden's basic culture—that complex of habits bearing on art, business, daily living, racial psychology? The thing you could remember the nation by, the race; as you remember the French by food and clothes; the Dutch by their phenomenal cleanliness, the Germans by the goose-step, and so on.

I cannot answer this question, so I fall back on the original rhythm and melody of the little *Bonde Danse* and the remembered picture I have of a Swede dancing to it in the bunkhouse, and tell myself that if the second theme provides contrast but no disunity, then, musically speaking, it is correct.

I work on it at night when everyone else is asleep. No one hears. Sometimes I go out of doors and wander around. At times the music lets go its grip on me and I stand and listen.

I am not the only night prowler. Oftener than not I hear the close or distant yapping of coyotes. When they do that, they are in a group, sitting down, noses pointed up, and I remember how the dictionary defines them: small wolves; prairie wolves. There is a bounty on them. They are ferocious, carnivorous little beasts who hunt in packs. They gang up on some helpless little bunny, arrange a relay race—post runners at intervals all around a long meadow. They could run anything down. The sounds they make fill you with a primitive terror.

Several times I have heard the scream of a wildcat, once quite close. I think it came from up there on top of the cliff. It sounds like the last long screech of a woman who, just about to be murdered, catches sight of the murderer and the uplifted ax.

Sometimes, as I wander around on the Green, or sit on the steps of the terrace, I see that the stars are fading. The sky lightens, and a delicate apricot color appears behind the cliff top in the east. The night is gone.

Alice has a boy friend who comes to visit her, a sad-eyed and

178

bedraggled old man. He has a little ramshackle car and appears and disappears. I don't know where he goes. Now and then I find him sitting in the kitchen. Has he— Oh, has he brought her a bottle? it seemed to me, when I was giving the orders this morning that she was slightly kittenish. This is a sure sign. Her usual smooth gliding walk changes to a rhythmic step, almost dancy, and her eyes watch me in an alarmed questioning way: —? —?

No. He has not. All is well. After all, Alice promised.

Perhaps he is one of her husbands. There has been a procession of them. She is ingenious at explaining just how and why the last one—though she married him with all regularity and in good faith—proved to be, just by the breadth of an eyelash, not quite a husband after all.

The short heat wave is over and suddenly it is cool with a smell of autumn in the early mornings.

They say, "Come summer, then comes the Rodeo, then comes winter."

The boys talk of fall plans. What time school opens; whether they shall return east by train, plane or car. The ones that are going to college for the first time are excited.

They look brown, robust, an inch or two taller and many pounds heavier. Bobbie has gained six pounds. He continues to eat his heroic breakfasts.

We all know each other much better, and there is much more talk and discussion. A good deal about religion.

They have seen on my bookshelves my set of the Sacred Books of the East. On another shelf I have the massive tomes of the Early Christian Fathers. They want to know which I adhere to and I tell them, "Both."

"I don't see any disagreement—perhaps a different point of view. But it is instructive to know all different points of view. I have another, too, you remember—"

"Your father?"

"Yes. My early Protestant and *very biblical* training."

"When you had to learn all those Bible texts?"

"Yes."

"But how did you ever memorize them?"

I tell them then of the Sundays of my childhood; in the

179

mornings, Sunday School and Church and *real* listening to sermons and dissection and discussion of them at the dinner table afterward; and the late afternoon when we would all gather around the piano for family group singing of hymns; but the early part of the afternoons was spent in our rooms, under orders to memorize one text out of the Bible. Each of us one whole text. And in our frantic search for the very shortest text there was, we practically memorized the Book.

"How short a text did you find?"

"Two words."

"What were they?"

"There's a Bible in there on the bookshelf—find it yourself!" Groans and laughter. "Oh, Mrs. Bergwin! That's no fair."

What they are particularly concerned with is whether or not they ought to, or can, believe in God. So many friends, members of family, schoolmasters, do not.

I am in something of a quandary. I would like to give them something to hold on to, for all the rest of their lives. I would like to give the certainty I have myself; and the enduring thrill of the mystic's vision. But I do not want to seem sanctimonious, or too pious, or too anything that has become old-fashioned and boring to them. But not too erratic either. Not too much of a Yogi. I fall back on words (and of course the Bible texts):

"Do you know what the word *apprehend* means?"

They begin to guess and argue. Sometimes, merely by starting a search for the meaning of a word they get into a lively discussion that lasts an evening.

"Everyone has to apprehend God in his own way. Some apprehend Him as Order. Some as Light."

"How do you?"

"As Life."

They always come back to, "But is this religion? Doesn't sound like it."

"Well, what is religion? What does the word mean? We know what *ligature* means. And *re* always means repeat. So it means, *tie again*. Unite. Or reunite. I think of it as meaning a handclasp. A human being reaches up a hand. And there comes down the hand of God to clasp it. That's religion. Not hard to remember, is it?" And continuing the improvisation I visualize a man drowning in mid-ocean—only the upreaching, desperate hand above the water. Then the response. The handclasp.

"Do you think the world can be saved?"

"Why, of course."

"How? Don't tell me. I bet I know. By Communism."

"No."

"Socialism, then."

"No."

"How then?"

"Just by saving every soul in it—one by one."

A groan went around the table. "How long would that take?"

"Not so long. It's catching. One soul catches it from another."

"Is this in the Bible?"

"Everything's in the Bible."

"Tell us."

"Well—*I, if I be lifted up, will draw all others unto me—*"

At dinner I am sometimes asked, "Mrs. Bergwin, will you ride this afternoon?"

"Yes, I think I shall."

"May I ride with you?"

"You certainly may."

"Shall I saddle Pompadour for you after monkey drill?"

"Yes, please do."

This is probably Fred. As I am lying there in the hammock after monkey drill I hear him coming with the two horses.

"Mrs. Bergwin, your spurs fascinate me. They are so tiny."

"The General got them for me in Paris a few years ago. You see they are set right into the heel of the boot. Give me a leg up, Fred, Pom is so tall."

"I've been meaning to ask you if you would show me exactly how to give a leg up?"

This is in the department of manners, to which we pay much attention. It is mentioned in our advertising circular along with equitation; the parents comment on it with surprise—"Manners! In such primitive surroundings!"

But even our horses have to be mannerly. When Michael holds

181

out a pail of oats for them they are forced to take turns, not crowd, not kick each other. The dogs and cats too. All of them accept and seem to enjoy behavior that is almost ritualistic.

Bobbie decides to join us, and we go riding along the westerly ranges, away from Blazes and his mares.

Occasionally we pull up our horses and look around, scanning the mountains, drinking that soft steady westerly wind, losing ourselves in the sky.

I saw, far to the south, a tiny shape that looked like a horse— only it stood so still. It was black, and I thought of Trombone. Trombone is unique. Someday when I have time I'll go up there and try to make friends with him.

Rachel goes with us and is beside my horse oftener than she used to be. Already, half of her daily mileage has been eliminated. From a quiet evening spent with me in my room, she goes *on the leash* to the tool shed and is locked in for the night with Bunny.

They sleep the night through. There is no barking unless in the line of duty (coyotes or other marauders).

In the morning George lets them out, they take a snack of breakfast, then play and run about but do not go far because of the imminent excitement of saying good morning to everybody.

After that, the hour of brushing and practice with me on the terrace (also those delicious raw eggs); and then, though the wide world calls, yet music calls too; and often she drops on the mat outside the door while I am at the piano and spends the morning there.

Already she looks like a different dog. Not only are her bones better fleshed, but she is alert and proud. Proud of her obedience, proud of belonging. Proud of knowing that there is a right and wrong about things; that it gives a grand feeling to be right; that she can always get a glance of approval from me if she tries.

Less and less does she go cringing around to others. And when she stands on the bench and I brush her, Michael glances at her critically and says, "She's almost in show-dog condition. Her muscles are wonderful."

Her running—the kind of running that is definitely running away—is done in the afternoon and early evening; but much less of it than before. I do not bother about it.

182

Before we got home from our ride there was a light shower and a rainbow, quite perfect, stretching from hill to hill across the valley.

And a smell of frying chicken on the air—and how hungry we were. Fried chicken, lettuce, baked beans, apple sauce and thick yellow Guernsey cream. Whatever shall I do with it all when the boys leave?

Trombone is out there on the farthest range behind the saddleback.

This morning I took the car and drove as far as I could, then left it, and with a bucket of oats on my arm and my binoculars hung around my neck, began to climb to that plateau.

The pasture is a couple of miles square. Rocks and crags jut up out of it, there are little dells with juniper and currant bushes, plenty of hiding places if he didn't want me to find him.

I knew it would take time. But Trombone knows what oats are. He knows a bucket. He was handled and halter-broken during his first year. If this had not been so, there would have been no chance of my getting anywhere near him.

So I stood out there in the middle and began to call him the way I call Rachel, on that A above middle C and then the F sharp. It makes a long, steady, ringing cry.

I did that over and over in all that emptiness and wildness and was pretty sure that if he was within two or three miles of me he would hear; and if he heard he'd become curious; and if he once became curious, he'd come to investigate.

An hour passed—seemed like a day. The clouds sailed slowly over me. When I got tired of calling I took the binoculars and went over the landscape inch by inch. Not a sign of him. Then I sat down and rested for a long time—thought about *Svenska* and did a little work on it—then got up and repeated my performance.

I saw hawks, I saw antelope, innumerable rockchucks; and quite near me an ermine came up out of his hole. His snakelike head, turning like a periscope, watched me for quite a while, then disappeared down the hole.

I stood against a low wall of rock and looked all around and thought, "If I should fall I'd fall into the sky."

183

That is what makes this country so different. Usually the sky is just the ceiling of the world and you don't see it unless you look up; but here it's all around you, as if you were held in the middle of an immense blue bubble.

The whole morning passed and I began to feel hungry. I continued my routine. When I stood out there calling I sometimes swung the bucket of oats. Sometimes I called, "Oats, Trombone! Oats!"

There was not a sign of him.

The sun was past the zenith and began to slide down the western sky.

Then I saw a black speck on a mile-away rock and thought it had not been there before. It could be a hawk. I took the binoculars. No, not a hawk, that was Trombone's head, the rest of his body was behind the rock. He was looking at me, and I could not help laughing—that irrepressible curiosity, his ears so pricked, his head so astonished and alert.

It became a game then. I walked forward, calling, swinging the bucket. He came out from behind the rock and circled, trotting magnificently. He went up on the rock again, fully exposed now, high-held, gazing at me; then disappeared; came back again. Circled again, a little nearer. Finally we stood facing each other a mile apart. Without the glasses he looked like a child's toy charger.

Now I knew he would come, and probably fast. I began to be nervous and wondered if I would be safer with my back to the rock or right out in the open. I thought he might actually run me down. But the rock—I'd be squeezed between the rock and the stallion—

I decided on the rock—I was afraid of his pushing me over—and as I backed up, he *came*.

This was really an exciting moment. To look at him in action with his head up and all that hair blowing about him was simply thrilling. He did not canter, never broke out of the trot—but what a trot! By the time he got near me he was small no longer, but the most immense horse I had ever been close to.

I talked to him, holding out the bucket. "Here, Trombone! Oats, boy! Come, Trombone!" But I didn't need to coax him.

184

He was headed for that bucket in spite of being terrified himself —I could see that by his wild, white-ringed eyes.

Then he was there, about six feet from me. He stopped short, his legs braced, his weight back. I reached the bucket out—and reached—reached. He stretched his head forward, stretched, lipped the edge of the tin—still taut to leap aside or whirl and kick. He drew his head back, his weight came forward, his legs eased. He poured over me great snorts and breathings, then took a step forward bringing the wild ferocious face close to my face for a second before it dipped into the bucket.

This of course was the dramatic climax to all the morning's maneuvering and it created an explosion of fear in him. As he jerked his head out, he leaped! (Something to see! that great body in the air and the whirling hair!) This took him a good many yards away from the dangerous bucket, and he trotted off, mouthing what he had in his mouth. He circled several times, head up and ears sharply pricked, watching me every second in his figure eights, his legs lifted high in that marvelous floating action— Then he was back for more—dipped again—leaped and rushed off again.

He finished the bucket, but there was nothing peaceful about it from first to last.

My arm ached as I lowered the bucket. I reached out to him— I wanted to get my hand on him, to pat him, to feel my flesh on his, before I left. Just one pat on the face or the side of the head. But he did not allow it.

When I turned to leave that spot he followed me. He butted the empty bucket with his nose, then whirled away and trotted off. Circled back, came after me again.

Following me close, he bit my arm. This, I knew, was for interest and affection, but it hurt. I turned and brandished the bucket.

"Hi! Get away there!" I made as if to bash him. He leaped away with a brassy grunt, circled off, came back again.

At last I felt him take that big smell of me—his hot breath in my nape. Then the snort. Finally the strong shove in the middle of my back. He followed me so close he was almost stepping on my heels. I went faster. He stopped a few yards from the car watching me get in. What a pose! That twist in his body, the thrust-out legs, the head way up and chin down and in, the ears like spears, the terrified and terrifying white-ringed eyes— and all that hair. Sometimes women's hair grows abnormally. One used to see them on the vaudeville stage with hair dragging on the floor, making a great mantle all around the body—

After I had driven away and he was out of sight, I heard half a dozen ringing whinnies—all on a questioning note. No doubt he was trotting up and down there where the car had been—pacing the floor as it were. But now he would never forget me.

What was going to become of this horse? If he were turned loose on the range, he could gather up a band of mares and go wild again. If we did this, we would be dispossessing ourselves of one of the finest animals we had ever bred. Fine business for horse breeders!

If we kept him on the ranch ungelded, we would have this to think about: There can never be two kings.

Long live the king! means that a king is dead.

He would kill Blazes.

Chapter 25

Eugenie and Jeannie came—and went.

"Just for a week," she cried, as I met them at the station in Cheyenne. "Ed is simply furious." And it *was* just for a week, but that week she spent at the hospital.

She wanted to ride and Michael put her on Bonnie, that old good-natured mare. But mares do not always behave well toward each other. Fat Pink, who has a colt, objected to Bonnie's place against the corral fence, turned and tried to kick her out of it.

Eugenie said, "Ouch!" It was not much of a smack on her shinbone, but of course it was sore that evening. And in the morning she told me it had hurt her so during the night that if the sheet touched it, she would wake up. That worried me.

She was going to Cheyenne next day and I made her promise that she would go to see the doctor. But she didn't. When she got back, she made a face at me and said it would be all right.

This was just dinner time, and I heaved a big sigh. I must take her in. I expected trouble, and it came.

A special nurse on the job that night in the hospital—hot compresses on the leg changed every twenty minutes—a possibility of osteomyelitis—Ed telegraphed for—

I think Eugenie had rather a pleasant time at the hospital. She was no longer in pain; everyone visited her; her nurses were very nice; everything was being taken care of and the doctor was a knockout. The leg began to mend.

Ed arrived, satisfied himself that all was going well, spent a day with us at the ranch, and left.

Jeannie always loves to be at the ranch; she kept up with the boys in all their riding and, as usual, would be at the cattle guard

187

to meet the car in the late afternoon, all ready to announce the disaster of the day.

"Some fishermen left the gates open and there are a lot of somebody else's white-faced cows in our meadow, trampling the grass—"

"Shag is lame. He can hardly walk. George thinks his leg is broken."

"Bunny's got his nose full of porcupine quills."

We call her Calamity.

During this sixth week of the camp term the boys' work becomes more exciting. It is the branding of the spring colts, the breaking of a few three-year-olds, the halter-breaking of some two-year-olds.

For days before it begins, Michael keeps them on tenterhooks.

"When are we going to brand the colts, General?"

This question, at breakfast, causes all the boys to freeze, staring at Michael.

As if he had not heard the question, his eyes wander down the table and he asks Jerome to pass the honey.

They try another tack. "Wouldn't you like me to ride up on the range, General, and bring down Blazes and the brood mares and colts?"

This, from Harry, brings a laugh all around.

As day after day passes even I begin to feel the suspense. "Tell them, Michael. They are just bursting. So am I."

Michael would rather bring the band of horses down from the range all by himself—ride out quietly, so dressed and accoutered that any westerner would call him a dude, find the band, call them to him with whistle and a can of oats hanging over his arm, lead them down to the county road gate; dismount, set the can on the ground to keep them there while he opens the gate, mount again, deploy and do a bit of rounding up of a few of the wildest ones, and finally get them all through the gate; then dismount and close it, then, mounting again, walking his horse, keeping at some distance from the band, he would reach the corral, open the gates and leave it to the horses to find their way in.

But if the boys "assist," they manage to have the gates closed just when they should be open; some boy's head pops up unexpectedly at the exact moment to stampede the mares; or, getting mixed up in their team work, two boys from opposite directions drive at the horses, so that they scatter and take off for ten miles across country. Every order Michael gives them they manage to misunderstand.

"But General, you *said* get behind them—"

"Exactly. And you got to the side of them—"

"No, I didn't—you said behind them, and I was standing here and you there, and behind means the opposite from where you were—"

"It does not. It means at their tail-ends—"

Six others join in, and this interesting discussion on relativity takes place at the top of their lungs.

The most difficult thing is to get the mare away from the foal when the foal has to be put through the gate into the little round corral, where he will be lassoed, thrown, and branded.

Dam and foal seem united by an invisible umbilical cord—no matter how fast she gallops, wheels and turns, hounded here and there by the yelling boys with their lariats, the foal sticks to her side, gallops, wheels and turns beside her.

Well—it is done.

There was one casualty. Fraidy Cat's little black colt, running in the round corral, rearing against the bars as they all do, suddenly was running on three legs. One foot dangled loose as a tassel.

Michael shot it and the boys dragged it out on to the grass. Michael brought the car. They dragged it up to the old mine shaft and pushed it in.

Tonight the band is out on the hills again, each colt looking smart and tailored with the IZ branded on his shoulder, and the year of his birth on his foreleg. The best and most promising colts have also the Jewish A on the cheek.

Blazes has them in charge again, the mares grazing quietly on the slopes below him, starlight flooding over them. But one mother has no long-legged little boy at her side. Now and then she lifts her head, looks around, sniffs the wind, whinnies.

Almost from birth the little foals indulge in a daily "recreation hour." This is apt to be at sunset time. They leave their mothers, forget all about obeying signals or even being hungry, seek each other out, and begin to play games.

There is the thunder of small hoofs. Sudden rushes and runs—they rear at each other, whirl and kick, now and then there's a sharp smack as tiny rear hoofs thud on the side of a taut belly; they squeal and race each other, jam to a stop, whirl, rush off again.

For whom is this superlatively entertaining show staged? For the sun setting off there in the west in an orgy of purple and scarlet, or the hawks wheeling slowly overhead, or the evening star, which has just come out, smiling, bathing itself in golden light.

I have ridden up there with the boys. It is something I would like them to remember.

Right now is when the foals learn those fighting strokes; as they rush past each other the quick rear and hammer stroke on kidneys; or the teeth raking the haunch; or, facing each other, the down-snaking head, forward thrust and crunch of foreleg; or, both upreared, the two heads weaving and intertwining, all the teeth bared, front hoofs flailing. But it is all in play—just shadowboxing.

Out walking after supper I came upon the Roamer standing motionless, his nose at the root of a small pine tree. I stopped at a discreet distance, puzzled by his attitude and the fact that he was so absolutely still. I circled a little; without moving he rolled his eyes at me and it seemed to me it was a look of pleading. I went closer, and then saw that his long chain was wound around the trunk of the tree, so that he was a prisoner. He could not budge an inch without tearing at the sensitive membranes of his nostrils.

Silently he begged me to help him, but I took to my heels and brought Michael. To tell Michael that an animal is in distress gets the same sort of response from him that you would get from a mother if you told her her children were asleep in a burning building.

190

The Roamer did not reproach me. He rolled his eyes at me again (where I stood safely behind Michael) while Michael unwound the chain, and it was as if he said, Well, at least you brought help; I hold nothing against you.

Silently, eyes glinting angrily, Michael removed the chain from the nose ring and stood back. "There, old fellow—"

The Roamer felt his freedom, walked off a few paces, stood in a magnificent attitude, head high, eyes alert, scanning the pasture, the trees by the creek, the low pine-covered hills of Section Sixteen, and suddenly trotted off into the gathering darkness.

Michael took the long chain up to Riley, told him to put the short chain on Roamer tomorrow at milking time.

We have today a stalwart horse, suitable for saddle or light work, whose name is Jinx.

His life began in a calamitous manner. He was a late summer colt and experienced his first winter storm when he was only three months old. It was a fierce storm, and the mare was very old.

I have thought of her standing there in that last storm of her life, turned tail to the driving wind and snow as all horses do, and of the way the colt, bewildered and terrified, pressed to her side.

When he nuzzled for the warm milk, she would turn her big shock head over his haunches, her lips touching him; and they would lean together, bracing themselves against the driving force of the storm.

She knew every tree, cliff, valley on the ranch. Why did she not seek shelter and take him with her? Either she had not the strength, or the colt had not, or her senses were leaving her and her eyes growing dim.

They stood in the middle of Section Nineteen where the wind arrives from a two-hundred-mile open sweep, and for the first time the colt heard that long, high, singing whine of a blizzard and felt the lash and sting of the frozen fog, moving at eighty miles an hour.

In these storms all the animals take refuge in a profound

191

stoical endurance. For the most part, they take their positions, strategically calculated, then do not move.

The long hours passed. It would have been at about two in the morning that the heat in the mare's body began to diminish, her blood run slower.

In a last instinctive effort for life, did she summon her vestiges of strength and plunge in the direction of the hills? Did she stumble, fall to her knees, and gratefully feel the earth coming up to meet her? Did she lay herself down upon the snow and yield herself?

Sometimes a horse gives a deep sigh.

Next day when the storm had blown itself out, a neighbor stopped in at the ranch and said, "Do you know there is a small colt of yours out all alone in Section Nineteen?"

We never expected to raise him.

I have raised lambs and calves and other motherless colts on the bottle. (Clean sterilized bottles.) But this baby would have nothing to do with rubber or glass.

He did show a slight interest in oats, but the veterinarian warned me that no three-month-old colt had the digestive apparatus to assimilate oats; it would just make him ill, and that would end him.

But this baby said, Just try me.

Michael felt that real mother love and cherishing from one of his own kind would do more for him than anything else. So he presented the colt to our work team, old Fanny and Captain, and told them this small creature had come to comfort them in their old age.

They adopted him with enthusiasm. He went everywhere with them. In pasture he was between the two, or close to them. In harness, about to start off to work, Fanny would turn her head and nicker for the colt. And he would run, kick his heels, go along with them on the job.

He grew and thrived on love and oats.

But bad luck followed him. He had his first tangle with barbed wire. This happens to nearly all the horses and the experience is so frightening and horrible to them, they will never even step over a piece of barbed wire again. Possibly they carry one or two scars from the first encounter, but usually there are no serious results. Not so with Jinx. His wounds became infected, and again I had to play nurse and nearly lost him.

He was a yearling when Michael built the little swimming pool the other side of Crooked Meadow.

This delicious little cup of water—one hundred by one hundred and fifty feet—was made by damming up a small stream in one of the hilly pastures. Michael thought he would experiment and see if he could store trout in it. If not, it would be a fine swimming pool for summer.

He made an excavation two or three feet deep. Earthen retaining walls were lifted another three feet all around it. This took six weeks of work with several men helping. It cost a good deal of money.

Then the water was let in. It filled up to the top in one night, and the water began to trickle over the spillway.

Michael and I went down to look at it and stood bursting with pride. What fun it would be for all of us—the boys too.

There was something astonishing about it. Nowhere else on the ranch could just this charming picture be seen—blue sky at your feet! Clouds sailing across it, birds cutting across the clouds, color and movement—I marveled again at the miracle of reflection.

We cheered and rejoiced as we did when the windmill made its first feeble efforts.

Then, even as we stood rejoicing, came Jinx—awkward, overgrown yearling—who elected to run across the three-foot-wide earthen causeway that was the retaining wall at the lower end. In the center, he gallantly leaped over the cement spillway. Then turned and did it all over again.

I saw an anxious look appear on Michael's face.

At the lip of the bank, a few clods of earth had broken off and dropped into the water.

"Get off there, Jinx!" he shouted.

He might as well have said, "Run back and forth across that causeway, Jinx!" For that is precisely what Jinx proceeded to do.

More clods broke off, and more and more. Finally we stood in dead silence, watching the whole bank dissolve, become riddled with holes, the waters curdle and foam, cross currents boil and shoot up in the middle. At last, with a roar, the whole body of water tore out the causeway and hurled itself into the stream bed below.

One last big jump took Jinx out of danger's way, and he trotted off into the pasture with a gay whinny.

In five minutes the scene before us was placid and quiet, the little stream below meandering gently as it has for centuries, the hole in front of us like the empty socket of a tooth that has been pulled, oozing moisture.

"I knew it!" cursed Michael, blaming himself. "I knew it all the time. I should have let it settle. It should have settled for a year before I let the water in! The waste! The work! The stupid ass!—"

I should know by now that Michael's quick-flaring rage is his way of throwing off a disaster, and yet it always surprises me.

I had it myself as a child. I remember a scene in the nursery when I was not more than five or six years old. I had been left alone to put my shoes on. The shoes had been wet, then were dried, and now were stiff. The shoe I had got on did not feel like my own shoe. I tried again. I tried both of them. The sensation was horrible. I took them off. But I could not go downstairs without my shoes. Rage rose and exploded in me with drenching tears. Since there was nothing I could do but wear them, this was utter defeat. But before accepting the ignominy of this, I could at least punish them, and I carried those shoes around the nursery, whamming them on the floor, pounding them with everything I could find heavy enough, howling, sobbing, calling them every bad name I could think of.

This was one of the most intense emotional experiences of my early childhood, never forgotten. But the hammerlike blows—disappointment, frustration, disillusion—fell so thick and fast that, soon, looking around I saw that everyone suffered them—I saw, indeed, that this was life; and if ever a wave of rosy expectation swelled within me, it was as if something behind me plucked at my skirt and warned—

Some people keep this childlike red-hot anger all their lives. I think they are lucky.

194

Michael built the pool again and let it settle for a year.

Now it is always flush with the banks. There is a constant flow over the spillway and a springboard at the deep end. The boys ride over, hot mornings or afternoons, tie their horses in the bushes, strip and plunge in. They stretch out on the banks and springboard and sun themselves.

I like to bathe there all alone. I swim, then lie on my back and float and feel as if I were at the bottom of a bowl—the sky curving over me close, the big clouds drifting, soft green hills rising from the level of my face to meet the sky.

Then I drop my head far, far back and see the sky as if it were down and the plains as if they were up and it is so beautiful and so strange I almost lose myself in it.

Painters like to put their canvases upside down against the wall and study them.

Yesterday, after my swim, I walked home through the meadow in my wet bathing suit, a towel slung over my shoulder.

Jerome came hurrying to meet me. There had been an accident. Michael had sent him to find me because I must take Fred to the doctor right away.

I found Fred, rather white, sitting in my hammock ready to be taken to town. His arm was bandaged and in a sling.

Michael announced with suitable cheerfulness that it was probably just a sprain, but there was a look in his eye.

"It doesn't hurt," Fred said. "It was such a simple fall. Not half as bad a spill as we all take every day."

He was riding down in the pasture after monkey drill, and on a quick turn just slid off, put out his hand and caught himself on it. That was it—his weight on that slender wrist.

I ran upstairs to dress and Michael followed me.

"His hand was turned right around."

I made time on the highway. It was Saturday afternoon. Every doctor in town would probably be off fishing or playing golf.

It took two hours to round up Dr. Phelps and the doctor to take the X rays. We couldn't find a nurse anywhere, or an anesthetist.

The X rays confirmed what one glance told—a compound fracture of the wrist.

Fred went on the table in the operating room. Dr. Phelps administered the anesthetic himself, then gave me the cone to hold while he set the arm.

Fred screamed and writhed (which made me sweat and shake), but he remembered nothing about it when, a little later, he was conscious again.

Another X ray showed that it was properly set, it went into a plaster cast, and I telegraphed his family.

Except for the time my collarbone was broken last year when a bronc bucked me off, this is the first broken bone in six years.

All is well. No complications. Fred riding again one-handed. I have had him in the house with me at night since the accident, but he is asking to go back to his cabin.

We have never had so many wildflowers. I stand in a little glen hardly able to believe my eyes. There are two-foot-high bushes of something that might be Giant Sweet Alyssum—very fragrant, a small dainty blossom, and pure white. Larkspur of blue, lavender, pink and white; wild delphinium of a wonderful rich, dark blue, tall Scotch bluebells on stalks as fine as hairs, with rows of bells hanging from them; Mariposa lilies that always look to me like a bride.

I keep the house full of flowers and spend hours arranging and replenishing them. They don't last very long, but they are irresistible.

Walking through the meadow I notice that the hay is very thick and nearly waist high.

"If nothing spoils the hay," says Michael, "it will be the best crop we've ever had."

"And prices are good, too, aren't they?"

He looked at me with a big grin and nodded.

And immediately I see Betty Bedford's Connecticut house in the east, the two big brick chimneys, the old oak trees shading it, the lawns and terraces; and there we are, Michael and I, with

196

a few boys. Not to mention some horses grazing in the paddock, Rachel and Bunny.

These next few weeks, then, will be a crucial time for us. Either it will be this year, or something will happen as it always has before; and it will be just the two tumbleweeds again, separated and waiting—aimless—drifting—

(Second thoughts; if hay is to be sold it must be baled. We have no baler. Well then, buy or rent one—)

Chapter 26

It is just dawn. I did not sleep much—*Svenska* keeps me restless at night. Waking, I heard again the high wind in the pines. I know the windmill is spinning fast.

I looked out of my window to the northeast where the pine cliff curves down into a gentle bare hill—the night pasture. I saw the cows standing there quietly, waiting for the morning milking. I saw a big coyote standing near them. They paid no attention to him. This surprised me for a moment, till I realized that a coyote is more familiar to them—more a part of nature— than a human being.

I saw the sunrise beyond the hill. There were long horizontal bands of deep rose and golden pink, with dark blue sky between. There was a mass of mauve and violet cloud above.

Yesterday there was a feeling of autumn in the air. And on my walk I noticed different flowers. Not so much larkspur and delphinium and bluebells. Instead, feathery goldenrod; black-eyed Susans; asters. Everything gold and purple now, for fall, instead of blue and pink and white.

The sun has just come up and is sitting on the farthest hill to the northeast. Long fingers of light streak out, touching the pines and rolling hills, the yearling colts over there, the cows in the pasture (the coyote has disappeared) and then, when that blazing ball of molten fire slides up a little higher, the light is a flood, filling hollows, pouring warmth everywhere, barn, Green, the house—all the animals turn their bodies to take it broadside, sinking their heads, completely relaxed so that the healing bath of ultraviolet can fill every cranny of them.

I put my face out the window, and it burns in my eyes and

makes me blink, and suddenly I find myself with tears on my cheeks for love and gratitude and my dear ones and all the beauty and dearness of life—life like a flower vendor, with a tray full of posies, the boutonniere of pansies, or will you have this pink carnation? Or the violets? Or the little foals at play? Or the rainbow, lady? Two, three rainbows? Something to give you a sweet perfume, lady, to carry with you all day long?

Riley is milking the cows.

In the corral Juanita is having her oats; beside her, her smart, dapper little sorrel colt of this spring. And there is Gold Coin, the big sorrel. How his coat shines. He probably thinks he is the papa of the colt, but he isn't. Way out on the range, over the hump-backed hill beyond the county road, Blazes is standing alert over his band of brood mares, eyes in every direction at once, ready in an instant to drop his head, undulate his snaky neck and round them up. Blazes is the Papa.

I noticed Roamer standing outside the corral and not far from him the little heifer, Domino. The cows all pick on her; the bull is her only friend. I asked Michael the other day if he had noticed it and he said, "Oh, yes. He loves her. And you can't blame him, can you? She's such a gentle and intelligent little thing. Just a pet, really. In the bull world, she must rate pretty high."

I wonder if this is the reason the Roamer hasn't been running away lately.

Soon, now, there will be the smell of coffee in the house.

I shall spend the morning working on *Svenska*.

This is a week of sight-seeing, for boys must not come west and fail to see the famous scenic spots, Yellowstone Park, the Tetons, Jackson Hole. They left right after breakfast, and once again I am alone with my animals.

Three cars were needed to accommodate the crowd. The Parks boys offered theirs and we rented one from Cheyenne. I will be without transportation for a week. If I want the mail I must ride horseback to Granite Canyon.

199

I am letting Alice go to town today. Riley will drive her in the pick-up out to the Lincoln Highway where she will catch the nine o'clock bus. She will have a permanent, she says, and will bring me back some manuscript paper and a roll of film for my camera. I want a picture of Juanita with her handsome colt. He is not named yet.

Late last night, before I went to bed, I was standing on the terrace and it seemed to me that from very far away on the upper ranges, there came to me the sound of galloping hoofs and a man shouting. On that range there is not supposed to be anything but Blazes and his band of brood mares. Could anyone be running them? It made me a little uneasy. This afternoon I shall ride up there to see if they are all right. Probably they are— Blazes will come trotting out of the band to talk to Pom, nicker and neigh and ask her what she is doing away from the band. And Pom will answer that it's none of his business, but she will be restless.

Here now, in *Svenska,* this B flat and E flat. As I play it over and over I think of Reese—for this is it—

It has let me in! Yes, it is Shinar, so quickly gained today. Sometimes I enter as easily as one slides into a dream—and I move through a mountain. The walls are held apart, not because I am making any effort of concentration, but because I am collected into a wholeness—no part of me left behind (this in itself is bliss). I go forward to bathe in air that is purest joy—how can music do this to me? I swing on the groundswells of it. I fall into troughs of anguish which are also delight. If I were sobbing I would not know it. It is all bliss and I am helpless.

. . . I have played those four measures for two hours . . . I will just keep playing them . . . why should I ever stop?

It was after two before I walked up to the stable to saddle my horse. Shinar had shut me out.

I had known it would, of course. It would fade, as if doors and windows were being closed, and even though I strained to listen even more intensely, I would hear less and less and finally

200

be numb to everything. Just playing E flat and B flat over and over on the piano—silly—

Then comes the dry grief of dislocation. Loneliness. Nostalgia.

Rachel and Bunny were leaping beside me—the bliss of the day was just beginning for them.

There had been a light shower at lunch time and then it had cleared again, but the air had the storm smell, and I wore a raincoat and was prepared for weather.

The saddle horses had all been turned out into the Stable Pasture, so I took the whistle and stood at the open corral gate, blowing long blasts. Rachel stood beside me, watching, trembling and whimpering.

Presently two mares and one colt came cantering toward me —Pom and Juanita. I suddenly determined to ride Juanita. She's too much horse for me, as Michael says, but her gaits are wonderful, she gives me a grand ride, and I love to ride her.

While I saddled her in the corral Rachel lay at her heels, crying piteously through sheer anguish of anticipation.

I am able, now, to call Rachel to me from a long way off.

I have been working at this, accustoming her to the special sound, "Ray—chelle," loud and ringing on first A then F sharp.

First I let her become accustomed to it by singing it to her softly at such times as she is close to me. Then, a little farther away, then, at last, when she was nearly out of sight and I wanted to call her back.

When she first heard this, she stopped, turned, stood looking at me, then dashed away and disappeared. This happened several times.

But one day she decided she was going to come; and came like a streak, ears laid back, tongue flapping, grinning from ear to ear and with a look of utter love and happiness on her face.

She was welcomed, of course, with puppy biscuit, and much petting; then had a little walk on the leash beside me before I turned her loose again.

And now it never fails. Her education is complete and she's by way of being a perfectly behaved little lady, although I still have to watch that she does not overdo.

Of course, Juanita's colt accompanied us. Now and then he

201

would put his head down, flirt his heels, and chase Rachel. Rachel would dash away, come back, he'd go for her, she'd dodge, leap up at his nose— This is something dogs always do; I wonder if it's to nip or just touch noses—a doggy kiss. Bunny is so small, it's hard for him to reach. The horse often accommodates him by lowering his nose until a kiss is possible. Particularly Gold Coin. There is quite a crush between Gold Coin and Bunny. They never omit the kiss of greeting.

It is glorious riding on a day of late summer when the season is changing and all the sights and scenes and skies are different.

Up on the high ridge behind the saddleback, the air was so clear it gave me glimpses of the very farthest ranges, not only covered with snow, but a fresh fall, so that the white mantle was solid and came to a low line on the foothills. Between me and them were those long undulating lines of other ranges, each line a different color—blue, mauve, or brownish.

Way off in the west a storm was gathering, or lurking—quite apart from the rest of the scene. I wondered if this was the storm that had drenched the ranch at lunch time. If so, the wind had changed, for, watching the coiling of the clouds and the way the storm was moving, I saw it was coming toward me. It was very low, close to the earth, rolling along.

We enjoyed ourselves up there, cantering briskly, keeping an eye out for the mares, but there was no sign of them. The storm, meanwhile, was gathering force and speed. It seemed to be coming at me with sinister intention and I realized that if I didn't find the mares soon, I would get a good soaking.

The wind was rising. So far, I had avoided heading directly into it, but now I became convinced that Blazes had found shelter for his band somewhere in that direction, and I swung Juanita around to face it. She flinched but I forced her, and we bored in.

Now there was a steady moaning sound. Here and there a jack rabbit leaped up and sailed away like something blown on the wind. The prairie grass lay down, quivering.

There was a sudden darkening, an immense smother of gray which blotted out the light, and then came rain—long, slanting sheets that lashed my face and beat down the grass. I pulled my linen hat lower over my eyes, and when Juanita quailed, and turned her head away, I put my spurs against her, squeezed my leg against her and talked to her encouragingly.

Then I came upon Blazes and his harem, tails and manes blown forward, backs to the storm. When they stand this way their chins are drawn in and down, their forelocks blow over their eyes, and their faces have the look of children with eyes half-hidden under too long a bang.

I stopped Juanita and started to count the mares.

Blazes came trotting out to meet us; there was much nickering. Our little foal ran into the band, smelled the other colts, talked to them.

The count was right, mares and colts all there. Wind and rain stung my eyes and I turned Juanita, touched my spur to her, and we ran before the wind.

The colt squealed protest at leaving his pals, but then came galloping after.

Way down in front of us, many miles away, the upland fell to a lower level, and then a still lower—gigantic steps. One of these lower levels lay in bright sunshine. Over it was blue sky with a line of white clouds, level on the bottom, puffy and pointed on top like curling surf on a blue sea; a calm and smiling scene. But that storm which was chasing me was one of the electrical infernos that explode on the ranch every so often. The thunder crashed with reports like cannon. The colt would leap, squeal, look wildly here and there, rush to Juanita's side, then have to bounce away again. I told Juanita with my body, my voice and my hands and heels to run her hardest. And how she ran!

But the storm raced us, and suddenly encompassed us. Day grew darker, rain more blinding, lightning was incessant—sheets of flame that made the whole world quiver, then great golden forks stabbing down into the earth. We were right in the core of it.

It was moving slightly south of east. I was aiming to get out of it in a northerly direction, where a not-too-steep slope would curve down toward that sunny sea, and suddenly we were over the crest and in the lee.

A few minutes more and we were in fair weather.

Here the colt expressed his relief by running in front of us and leaping joyously into the air, doing a perfect little jack-knife dive, for all the world like a trout flipping out of the water and back in again.

Juanita whinnied in passionate maternal admiration and I laughed out loud at the handsome and conceited little fellow.

Handsome and conceited—what did the words remind me of? Why, Eitel Fritz, of course—one of the sons of Kaiser Wilhelm; and I immediately saw the picture of the royal children of Germany during that summer when Grandma May took us there—a row of boys in sailor suits, more or less alike except this particular one whom the German people had lovingly nicknamed Eitel Fritz, because he was so handsome and conceited.

So Juanita's colt came home well baptized and well named. I was already calling him *Eitel* for short.

While I changed into dry clothes I looked out the window and saw the rainbow, a blazing, sizzling arc, complete from end to end. . . . I must look again . . . now there are two . . . in a minute I'll look again for the third—yes. The three rainbows—and off there in the sky hangs a blur of fire like a torch. . . .

To my surprise Billy Allenger showed up for supper.

He had got a ride back from Yellowstone and had decided to leave for the east tomorrow.

Chapter 27

Billy and I had the long evening alone together. It was chilly enough to have a fire and I sat on the sofa with an ambitious sewing project spread out all around me, the making and quilting of a cherry-red silk winter housecoat, snug around the body and flaring voluminously down to my insteps, made in fact like a coachman's coat, and vividly lined with a silk patterned in crimson, yellow and lavender. A light interlining of lamb's wool made this the last word in luxury and I enjoyed every stitch I drew.

I think it was Grandma May who first kindled in me this delight in clothes, for she would bring us, from her visits abroad, such exquisite things—little fur pelisses from Wiesbaden in Germany, and Roman-striped brocade sashes from Sorrento in Italy, and the loveliest dresses from Liberty's in London—I remember one of pale blue silk, smocked across the shoulders. And nothing would content me till I had copied the dress for my doll. I remember something of my struggles, for to cut the pattern down to doll size, and then smock the silk—this would be no easy undertaking for even an accomplished dressmaker. From doll clothes I graduated to my own shirtwaists, and I can still see the exasperated face of a schoolmate who exclaimed, "Oh, you make me so mad! You have such pretty shirtwaists!"

I have never given this up. I have even had a "Betty" made to my own exact measurement. Sometimes it is put away in the closet, but mostly it stands in the corner of my room with something half made on it, and the first thing Elma says when she comes to visit me is, "Let's see what's on the Betty—"

Billy opened up and talked to me, and little by little it became an immense unbosoming; and as I realized that this "sad young man," this blasé thirty-year-old businessman, was the most naive child imaginable, I began to be amused. I might have known it. I got laughing. Billy laughed too.

And while I stitched and cut and snipped he told me how, tired of being treated as a child by his parents, when he was so sure, within himself, that he was a man grown and well able to take care of himself, he demanded freedom.

He pestered his parents. At length they gave in. On his sixteenth birthday, just a year ago, they had stuffed his wallet full of bills, had given him a month of time and their blessing, and turned him loose.

There followed the tale of his spending the money, and when he got to the double brandies I interrupted him.

"But why a *double* brandy, Billy? Why couldn't you have just said a brandy?"

"I dunno. When the waiter said, 'What'll it be sir?' I just thought I'd have to say a double brandy—and I kept saying it wherever I went. I kept going from one night club way in the north of town to another night club way in the south, and then it'd be the same thing over again. But of course I was *trying* to get drunk—I never had been before, and this was my last night—by tomorrow night I'd be home again—but I got worried because the taxi drivers kept taking so much of my money and I was running out—"

"Where was this, Billy?"

"Chicago."

"Chicago! Why on earth would you be in Chicago in summertime?"

"Well, first I had gone to this dude ranch in Colorado, and they didn't like me much there so I had to leave—"

"Why?"

"Well, I just did everything I had seen done in western movies, chase the cows and steers, and whoop it up, and always keep galloping—so when they told me to get out I went to Chicago for my last night—"

"To get drunk."

"Yep."

"Did you?"

"Stinking. It was good in a way, because every drink I took made me feel richer! The money I had left was to pay my bill at the Congress Hotel and feed me till I got to New York, and it wasn't any too much. But I had my return ticket. . . .

"I liked the music . . . I play the clarinet myself and I sat close up to the orchestra and I turned my chair around and kept time . . ."

Billy's long slender hand tapped out the rhythm of a swing piece on his bony knee.

"Say, do you know, that when I tried to say anything to the waiter I'd stutter? I've never stuttered before. And I couldn't really sit still—I'd sort of writhe all the time—and rub my hands along my legs—and look around the room, and if I saw anyone watching me I'd nearly go under the table."

"So you kept on with double brandies—"

"Yes. And whiskey and gin—didn't matter what. . . . I went to Winona Gardens and Sadie's Shack and Quick and Dirty—some other joints—I forget the names. I'd fall asleep in the taxis going from one place to the other. There was a Lobster House somewhere—no orchestra, but a Negro who was a wizard at the piano—I watched him a long time—close up. There was just one thing that spoiled the whole evening for me. My trousers. It was the only pair I had and I'd worn them out at the Dude Ranch. They were gray slacks, torn and dirty and snagged—why every time I stood up I almost went through the floor. Well, I got really mad at those trousers—it got to be I couldn't think of another thing. So when I got back to my room at the Congress Hotel I figured I'd just get even with them. So before I went to bed I drew the tub full of water and eased those disgusting trousers down into the water."

"Billy!"

"Yep. That'd show them."

His face, as he remembered about this, was rather pitiful.

". . . the next morning was awful . . . Oh, my head! I never knew a head could feel like that. I couldn't think. And my train left at three. And my only trousers were in the tub. I tried and tried to think, but I couldn't. I just sat in the chair with my head

207

in my hands. It took me the most awful struggle to get it figured out that I just *had* to get sober, get to Marshall Field's, buy another pair of slacks, and make that train. I had to count my money. I could hardly do that. When I did I could hardly believe it. If I bought the trousers, I wouldn't be able to eat unless they'd let me pay the hotel bill with a check.

"So I put on those wet, dirty, holey trousers and went down in the elevator and through the streets to Marshall Field's. . . ."

Billy was silent quite a while. I saw by the misery on his face he was reliving that awful walk through the streets—his wet foot-steps—people looking at him, smiling—

"Mrs. Bergwin, life can be pretty awful, can't it?"

"It certainly can—did you get the slacks?"

"Yes."

"And did they take a check at the hotel?"

"They said, 'Certainly, Mr. Allenger, if you can identify your-self.'"

"And could you?"

"I told them just to call up the *Long and Fisher* general offices. They are my father's Chicago associates. I told them to ask for Mr. Fisher. He's the one who knows me personally. So then I thought my troubles were over and I began to feel pretty good; but the man came back from telephoning and said Mr. Fisher wasn't there—wouldn't be there until later. This floored me and I tried to figure out what to do and my head was killing me, and then the manager said, 'I think we must ask you to pay your bill in cash, Mr. Allenger.'"

There was another silence, then Billy continued. "I just began to shake. Nothing made sense in my head. I felt like a steam roller had gone over me. I wondered how people get along in the world when things like this are always happening. I began to turn my pockets out, and the bills and the change fell out. He picked it up and counted it. There was enough, with a little change left over—not really enough change for tips . . . a boy grabbed my suitcase and carried it out—I took it from him and gave him all the change I had left. Anyway, I wasn't leaving a wet puddle on the street every step I took—do you know what I wanted?"

"What?"

"Just one nickel! *Just one nickel!*"

"What for?"

"For a Bromo Seltzer. But I hadn't one. Not a cent. And I'd be on the train twenty-four hours without anything to eat. And I had no money for a taxi to take me to the station—"

"So you walked?"

"Yes—and at the station they told me my return ticket had expired ten days ago. It was a student ticket. The man said, 'You'll have to pay almost fifteen dollars more to get to New York.'

"I thought maybe I could find someone higher up and talk them into it, but then I began to feel nauseated; anyway, they wouldn't, and when I walked away from that last window, I thought I was just going to curl over and pass out. I didn't know where to go. Then I saw a telephone booth and I went into it and shut the door tight, sat down on that stool and set my suitcase on the floor, and put my face in my hands and began to cry.

"I just went on and on and on crying—there didn't seem anything else to do . . . it made my head worse, but somehow comforted me too—I guess I cried steady for about a quarter of an hour, then I hunted through my pockets for a handkerchief so I could blow my nose, but I didn't have one, then I opened the suitcase and hunted and I thought this would be it, really, if I can't even blow my nose—and I looked in the pocket of an old cardigan and I found a handkerchief and a nickel.

"First I thought of the Bromo Seltzer—then I thought of another telephone call to the offices of *Long and Fisher*."

I took a few stitches, waiting for Billy to continue, then glanced up at him and saw that his face was beaming.

He took his eyeglasses off and wiped them. He ran his hand through his hair. I began to smile myself. I saw there was going to be a happy ending to this sad tale and I prepared to rejoice with him. I laid down my handful of sewing. I was thinking it was a little story all readymade and it could be named, "He Couldn't Blow His Nose."

"Well!" I burst out, *"Tell!"*

He grinned. "Mr. Fisher had got back, and of course that was all there was to it. I took a taxi—he met me and paid for it—he took me up to the office—I just sat in a daze and they telephoned and made out checks and sent the office boys around, and they brought a lot of money, and filled my wallet and gave me an airplane ticket, and put me in another taxi and sent me off."

After a long silence, he added, "That's all. . . . I got the Bromo Seltzer at the airport. But on the way home, I kept wondering and puzzling about how to get along in this world. I can see how easy it is for grown-up people, and I used to think that's all you'd have to do—just grow up—but that's not all, is it?"

"No—not quite all—"

So then we said good night and I went up to bed—pretty tired really with the long ride and the long evening; but while I was undressing I couldn't help smiling with the thrill of such a happy ending, especially when I thought of that father pouring out good things for that lost boy—and of course as I got into bed I thought of a text: *Try me now and see if I will not pour you such a blessing that there shall not be room to receive it.* . . .

Chapter 28

Michael got back with the boys.

Alice never got back.

I took the wheel of the car almost out of Michael's hands as he arrived, drove into town, and at the door of the employment office ran into Etta Biggs—again looking for a job.

I brought her back with me. We will be haying soon, and I must have a cook for the haying crew.

Returning to the ranch I found the boys chattering and excited.

"Suicide ride tomorrow, Mrs. Bergwin!"

This, which at first was just "the last ride," has evolved into a heroic affair led by Michael in person. It is talked about all summer, vividly described to intrigue, not to say terrify, the new boys. It is all that really holds them here now. There are always falls. If half the boys come back on their horses, that is doing well.

When this is over they'll not really be here any more—just crowding forward to the future.

(Well—is there any *present*? It's just a razor edge between past and future.)

I seldom see much of the Suicide Ride. See them start perhaps, and fifteen minutes or so later catch sight of them silhouetted on a rocky hill far away, then turning and coming down lickety split. Or they suddenly shoot out from the trees onto the fields, jumping the brook one after the other, their horses looping over easily; then turn, double back, make a longer loop this time at a wider place; suddenly disappear entirely; and all is quiet again but for the dust swirling.

Today Jerome was the hero of the ride—in reverse.

I had seen them about half a mile away, streaming along the mesa above the Swimming Pool Pasture. And as I watched, one figure left his horse, curved in an astonishingly extended parabola through the air and merged with a bush.

At supper I said, "I saw someone take quite a spill near those rocks in the Swimming Pool Pasture. Who was that?"

"Me, of course," said Jerome, chagrined, but grinning bravely. (The summer has shown that there are still a few weak spots in Jerome's horsemanship.)

"He passed a bush, Mrs. Bergwin, and of course he had to fall into it."

Jerome could not learn to jump until Michael had the boys dig up and remove a bush that stood to the right of the jump. Every time he passed it, some horrible power reached out from it to him, seized him and made him hurl himself into it.

"For no *reason*," said Michael to me, weak with laughter; "no reason at all." He wiped his eyes.

And of course the cruel leprechauns tormented him. Out riding, they would yell, "There's a bush, Jerome! See! Over there!"

At which a fixed stare comes over Jerome's face. His horse, apparently of its own accord, leaves the band and heads for the bush. Passing it, the horse is riderless and Jerome is in the bush.

The boys hate to say goodby to their horses. Particularly certain ones. There is a very close bond between Fred and Shag; and Red Brewster and Rheingold.

Early in the summer Red taught his horse to follow him. He would knot the reins, throw them over the horse's head, walk away, giving the command, and Rheingold would follow so close he'd almost be stepping on Red's heels.

I saw them, the last day, saying goodby. It was the duty of each boy to assemble the tack, put everything away in the tack room, then lead the horse to the open corral gate and turn him loose. Red hesitated at the gate. I stroked Rheingold's nose.

"If my Dad would buy him for me, Mrs. Bergwin, do you think the General would sell him?"

Red lives in a suburb of Boston.

"We've got plenty of ground. We could convert a garage into a stable for him—"

"But Red, Rheingold is a stallion."

"I know—" he muttered.

Now the boys have gone and in their place a crowd of dark-browed men are moving around the ranch; the haying crew.

All our thoughts are on the haying now, and after all, there will be no need either to buy or rent a baler. For Michael has made arrangements with a contractor to cut, bale and store the entire crop in our barn.

The good weather holds. The good luck holds. It is hot summer again.

Sanski, the contractor, uses our teams, Captain and Fanny, Ginger and Jock. The horses look at his men with surprise and suspicion, turn their heads to listen to these so strange and different voices.

The men are everywhere. They live in the bunkhouse but take their meals in our large kitchen. Michael eats with them because, he says, it helps in planning the work. I don't see much of him.

Etta Biggs is in her element. She provides them with thin fried steaks, thick flap jacks, thick floury gravies with plenty of lumps in them.

She has a sudden, loud, unexpected laugh that I can hear all over the place. Every evening, after supper, I see a big, black-haired fellow waiting at the kitchen door while she finishes the dishes. When she is through, they walk off together into the darkness.

When it's haying time in Wyoming the sweet smell of it is on the wind for hundreds of miles.

But Sanski, with his crew of men, mowing machines, rakes, and big gasoline baler, has altered the ranch beyond recognition. An uneasiness pervades it.

Once again I am just outside of a noisy world that moves like a dust cloud over there. I shut myself up in *Svenska*. I take long rides on Pom with Rachel.

213

We went up there today.

In spite of these hot days the snow is still deep on the Never-summer Range and the wind smells of it.

Up on the top I dismounted and sat on a rock, the reins over my arm. Rachel crouched between my knees, shivering with excitement and tension just because she is up there, because there is endless strange enticement offered to her eyes; because the wind fills her nostrils with one strong scent after the other so that she does not know which to follow but starts, pricks her ears, trembles, turns, is motionless, staring, then trembles and twists again; until I put my hands on her ears, smoothing them down and say, "What is it, Rachel? What is it, little girl?"

Then her body relaxes, her ears drop, she writhes around to give my face a few frantic licks, then turns and sits down again between my knees, again listening, again sniffing, again trembling.

The reins over my arm are loose. Pom stands close beside me, an upthrust statue of a horse with lifted alert head, as taut and wild as Rachel. It is as if they are both filled with a potent wine.

Svenska! Svenska! My nails are broken to stubs and there is a little bloody hole at the corner of my little fingernail. It really gets very noisy when the boys and girls are dancing in the birch grove.

I took out a lot of the screams—too many. It began to sound tame. So I put some back.

When I practice the part where the little girl runs out and dances alone, I think of the word *flicka* which, in Swedish, is little girl.

I have named one of the yearling fillies Flicka. Perhaps, in another incarnation, she will be a little Swedish peasant girl with red ballooning skirt and white, lace-trimmed drawers.

Why should this little filly not be the heroine of the horse story I am going to write? I saw her when she had just been born. It was by chance—the mares usually find secret hideaways when they are about to give birth. Out walking one day, I decided on a shortcut from one of the meadows upward through a draw thick with bushes and rocks. I came upon the mare planted there, head down, ears pricked, eyeing me. She blocked my way and would not move as I advanced. Then I saw why. The foal was behind her, on its feet probably for the first time, and waveringly feeling for the teat. I moved back slowly and silently and left them alone and in peace for their great moment.

This filly has developed into a beauty with the same coloring Floss had—golden coat and cream-colored mane and tail. She skims the uplands like a swallow.

I shall write this story. *Flicka* is a good name for it.

I've been in a good deal of trouble with this piece—my usual difficulty. I fall in love with some particular bit and lose proportion with the whole.

There's always this rivalry between the whole and the part. When I begin a story or music it is because I have a vision of the whole, but when I am working on the detailed scenes, I lose the whole. I stop writing, go away, find *the whole* again. But sometimes, working at detail so long (because after all you have to put notes or words on paper—thousands of them), I have so completely lost the whole that I cannot recapture it. I even forget it. Then I come staggering to myself and say, "Why am I doing this? Where am I going? Was there not something that started me? Something *wonderful* that led me on? That will tell me when it is finished?" But can you really see the whole until it is finished? For the whole includes the end—must include the end—and if you are creating not a story but a life (our own), how can you know whether this immediate detail—this new adventure you are just embarking on (this eastern school)—is part of the whole, until you have seen the end?

Well—you cannot. We embark on the adventure. We hope it will turn out to be part of the lifeline, but it may be just a detour. It may, after all, be a mistake.

Going east will be for me, going home. It completes a circle. And perhaps it is time for me to do this. But I have written that wrong. I should say, going east *would be* for me a going home. For of course we do not yet know.

We watch the skies. Heavy rains right now could ruin the hay crop.

And Michael said, "Do you think there's any chance that Betty might renege?"

"Renege?"

"On her offer of the country house—for our school, you know."

I gave some thought to this. "Well—of course she'd renege if she wanted to use it herself."

"You haven't written her yet?"

"No. I thought I'd wait—just until we're sure of the hay, you know—"

Michael took several puffs on his pipe, his brows drawn down. "I think you'd better write her."

"All right."

I've written Betty. The letter is on its way, airmail.

There's a very heavy cloud bank over Cheyenne today. It does not move perceptibly, but it has pushed up somewhat. It is east and south of us. Just a solid, sullen curtain of leaden gray.

But we are in sunshine. Our luck holds.

When Sanski finishes mowing and baling one field, his men move to the next and our men move in to glean.

We shall keep about fifteen or twenty tons of hay unbaled for the use of our stock during the winter. It will be stacked in the square tower at the far end of the cowshed, convenient for feeding out.

I ride through the meadow where our men are gleaning. With just our teams, no gasoline machines, no black-browed strangers, it looks and feels and smells like our own ranch again. And I move around there, on Pom, enjoying myself, and dismount and lie down against a pile of hay holding Pom loosely by the end of the reins. And she digs her head into the hay, pulls out long, fragrant tufts, dropping half of it on me, and munches, turning her eyes off to the distance, her head almost directly over me.

The men were stacking. By cocking an eye I could see Michael's blue shirt, brown throat; bare, bronzed arms swinging the fork.

How sweet the wind. Mint, pine, hay, the freshness of running water—I tilted my head back until I could see nothing but sky and clouds—and suddenly I remembered Della and a talk we had had about happiness last year in Los Angeles (I burst out laughing so suddenly that Pom gave a start):

Della: Are you happy?

Mary: Sinfully happy!

Della: Tell! Explain! Give! This about sinful happiness I have to hear!

Mary: Well, going to bed at night I know I have only to wait till morning and then the wonderful moment of five o'clock when the birds begin to sing and I can lie there listening. I can jump up and see the light through the trees. And I can step out on the balcony and see the mountains just pushing their shapes through the mists. The wonderful mountains! The wonderful birds! The wonderful five o'clock! And we laughed like two small girls.

Della: Go on! What else is wonderful?

Mary: The piano! No one can hear me! Or if they do they are so used to it they do not notice. So for an hour or two I revel!

Della: More! More revels!

Mary: I am thinking I shall presently hear martial steps, doors banging and slamming, then see that charming face of my husband advancing toward me across the room!

Della: Oh, please! More charm!

Mary: And then we will say the most wonderful things to each other!

Della: Such as? Oh, this I must hear—

Mary: Such as, "It looks like a nice day." (This doubles us up.)

Mary: It might even be, "Shall we have breakfast in the patio?"

So now, lying in the scented hay, watching the men gleaning, I see the wonderfuls and charmings and I revel.

Particularly those wonderful blue clothes.

It must be that blue is the cheapest dye there is, for all over the world, the heavy cotton and denim clothes manufactured for

217

workmen, farmers, peasants, are blue. Dark blue to begin with, and as it fades with wind and sun and weather and washing, it turns a soft but vivid shade, not unlike the blue of a deep summer sky.

Elma told me of the donkey girls of Japan dressed in tight blue cotton trousers of this lovely shade, a tunic blouse coming down over the trousers, and belted with a wide scarlet sash. The perfect little costume topped by their thick smooth straight hair cut in bangs across their foreheads—black and sleek.

The sudden impudent song of a red-winged blackbird brought me back from Los Angeles and Japan to the meadow and haypile. Pom lifted her head and pricked her ears. She took a step, making the saddle creak (her big hoofs so close to my ribs), tore out another big mouthful of hay, showering me again.

Way down the field I heard the men calling to each other.

There's a good name for a foal—perhaps the one Pom is carrying right now. *Redwing.*

The leaden bank of cloud has slid down again so that we can only see the rim of it over Cheyenne. I try to push it back and down. Oh, just *stay* there until we have the hay in!

Michael is uneasy too. Sanski has finished about three quarters.

Michael is in a jam with Sanski.

Sanski, who contracted to cut and put up the hay for a stated amount, keeps asking Michael for advances with which to pay his men.

It is not incumbent upon Michael to accede, but we are in funds after the summer school, so he gives Sanski a check every few days when he asks for one.

I have warned Michael that the money is being paid out more rapidly than the hay got in.

I showed Michael the figures—Michael was surprised. (One always is.) Now he's told Sanski he wouldn't pay him any more until he had completed the job.

Sanski is mad. He says the hay is much thicker than he had

218

estimated; couldn't be cut for the amount he had named; he would have to have more money. Michael said to hell with him. Sanski said he would quit. Michael said quit and be damned.

Sanski has left with part of the last meadow unbaled. Michael and Riley are hauling the loose hay in to stack in the little tower stack. Sanski is going to sue Michael; Michael is going to sue Sanski.

I think Sanski came out ahead. Anyway, we have spent an awful lot of money on the job.

Every fall when the haying is finished, we give the cows the run of the meadows so that they can share in the general sense of celebration. A nice change for them after the summer pasture, which begins to get a bit skimpy by September. And every fall they behave in the same way, like a lot of frisky children on a lark. Instead of staying in the Home Meadow, they follow the men and the teams through the gates, which are left open for the hay wagons. They charge the piles of hay, toss it with their horns, kick up their heels, stay close to the gang. Their glossy yellow and white coats, their long intelligent faces always watching us humans in a puzzled questioning way—

The hay. I can hardly believe it. None of it spoiled! Hundreds of tons *baled*! Well, maybe two hundred. It's already stored in the barn.

It is a treasure. Prices, even now, when there's plenty of feed everywhere, are good; later when feed is scarce, they'll double. We have never felt so rich. We stand in the barn and it is dark and cool, and there is a feeling of wealth in it, like an underground vault in which ingots of gold are crisscrossed.

I climb around in it.

Missy's kittens are somewhere here, I am sure. She is there most of the time. But she gives us no inkling. The boys and the haying crew have been too much for her this year and she's playing safe.

If we go east, it will only be for the winters. I wouldn't want to lose what we have here. I want the largeness and the wideness never to leave me. I want to keep it and to give it, too. I wish I could go about and say, See here, do you know what's up there? On the top? Do you know that size and that emptiness and that blazing incredible beauty? Do you know that you can draw a deep breath and take it into yourself and be swept clean of small crawling miseries?

But you can't live in it all the time. It's too big, too epic, and much too lonely.

Chapter 29

I am going to have a quarrel with Michael. I am sorry, but it has to be. I am going to start it by saying, "Michael, you do not co-operate with me about the cows."

If he would base his answer on rational grounds I would be ready with my arguments, but knowing this, he avoids reason; he switches the issues, introduces emotional elements and drags red herrings across the trail. All this renders me helpless and speechless.

The reason that so mild an accusation on my part will start a quarrel is that Michael's dignity does not suffer any accusations whatsoever. I rack my brains to find some way of correcting this situation without making an accusation but can't think of any.

Here is the trouble. The care of the cows is my province, but Michael permits no one but himself to give orders to Riley and George. If I want the cow feed changed, a certain cow bred or not bred, calves weaned, I must tell Michael. Michael will then tell Riley and Riley will get it wrong.

I suspect Michael's is the blame. At the moment of relaying my order to Riley, some other idea occurs to him as better and thus he instructs Riley; I find fault with Riley; Riley refers me to the boss; I ask Michael, but Michael has forgotten or denies or is too impatient or busy to listen.

So I will start a quarrel and I have planned what to say and I shall say it.

But not today.

Today he is in a particularly sweet humor and I'd hate to spoil it. I'll say it tomorrow. I *have* to say it because one of the cows is coming in heat and I don't want her bred until October so that she will freshen just when camp opens next July. She must be locked up.

Last year, when I wanted a cow locked up and told Michael to tell Riley, Michael—at the last moment of relaying the order—thought it would be a pity to lock her up in such nice weather and told Riley, instead, to put her in a certain distant pasture. There happened to be a Hereford bull on the other side of the fence; so, in due time, we not only had a cow coming fresh when there was no one at the ranch to use the milk, but the calf was red with a white face.

No, I can't say it today either because some people are coming to dinner. Besides, Michael is very busy. And besides, there must be time to go all through with it and time enough after to get over it and make up.

This is going to be *quite* a quarrel. I can't see that, in this argument, he'll have a leg to stand on. I wonder what on earth he'll say? I wish I knew, so that I could get ready some good answers.

He's avoiding me. He knows something is up. Sometimes this goes on for weeks. A lot of women know about that. Sometimes, when they have something important to say and have been evaded too long, they catch their husbands when they are taking baths—which puts the husbands at a slight disadvantage.

"Michael, you don't cooperate with me about the cows."

"You don't cooperate with me about the horses." This whipped back at me swiftly and upset me as much as if I had not been rehearsing the scene for days.

"Why!— Why!— How can you! Why, Michael, you know perfectly well—"

He began to shout. (He knows I can't stand this.) He yelled without a break between words into which I could thrust an answer.

"I can't run the ranch with constant interference."

"I can't run the dairy unless the men follow my orders."

222

"Oh, I'm always wrong! I never do anything right! I'm just a nitwit—"

I burst out crying. "But Michael! If you'd just—now you know —listen! If you'd only *listen*—"

Though I had foreseen all this and deliberately brought it about, it reduced me to a nervous wreck and I fled to my room and carried on in a most juvenile manner, walking the floor, sobbing, wringing my hands and muttering maledictions. But all the time I was congratulating myself inwardly, for I had done it. The worst was over, and in the end I would get that cow locked up. She would freshen at the proper time next July and we would have the milk for the boys.

And now I must hurry and get my eyes dried and my face in order for the next installment, which will be this:

Michael will summon Riley and me and say to me coldly in the voice of a patient man tried past all bearing, "Now what is it you want?"

"I want Bouquet locked up till she's out of heat."

And he will relay the order to Riley, glaring at him ferociously, and Riley will say, "Yes, Boss," very pleasantly, and I will run away again and sit down at the piano and play *Svenska* with tears dropping on the keys—

—and so that's what happened.

Then I proceeded to get angrier and angrier. Michael's displeasure was thick. The atmosphere was unbearable. He was punishing me.

I announced that I was going to town; got myself ready and was in the car, releasing the brake to start down the hill when I heard a shout behind me.

Glancing back, I saw Michael flying down the hill toward me, every white tooth showing. He leaped on the running board, leaned in, flung an arm around my head, pulled me over, said, "Forgive me," and was off the running board. I straightened my hat.

I was not mollified. I went to town determined to forget him, to forget the ranch, to forget our struggles, forget everything.

The way to do this is to go to a movie.

When Reese and I met again after having been on opposite

223

sides of the continent for many years, each of us, now, parents of children, and having an ex-spouse and a present spouse—it was as if we had to get to know each other all over again, and discover what our mature tastes were. So we probed and questioned.

"Do you like movies?" he asked me.

I said, "Oh, yes! You go into that dark place—people sitting all around—so quiet—and a soft carpet under your feet—everything silent except that dreamy music—and you look at the screen—"

Reese finished for me, "—and forget everything!"

We said the words together and smiled into each other's eyes. That was it! A long, long way we had both come from those dreams of our childhood when in the middle of the night we would tiptoe to the window seat in my room (the Brooklyn house) wrap ourselves in eiderdown quilts and sit and listen to the boat whistles out on the bay; and think of the great ships coming into that harbor from all over the world—or sailing forth to distant, exotic lands—and wondering to what *life* they were going—and to what *life* we would so soon be going—and draw our breaths with difficulty because we were so bursting with hope and wonder and expectation—

And now we had reached the distant lands—and all that hope and wonder and expectation. We had come the long voyage.

And though we had been four thousand miles apart, it seemed our feet had walked the same path and reached the same goal— *to forget everything!*

So now, in Cheyenne, I would go to a movie and forget everything.

I did. It was a screenplay in which Fred Astaire and Ginger Rogers danced divinely.

The music and the smooth happy swoops and glides and taps put me back to childhood and immersed me in a blissful dancing experience of my own.

This was when Elma and I, aged about eleven and seven, were at dancing school, and were called upon to do a solo dance.

First I must make a picture of these two small girls. They are pretty, resemble each other, and are dressed identically in white

224

organdy guimpes, and silk poplin dresses of the Stuart plaid. The skirts stand out stiffly, the tiny bodices with straps over the shoulders are tight. The little girls have pale peaked faces with swift smiles that come and go, and eagerness in their large dark eyes. Their hair is a warm brown, brushed in glossy smoothness over their heads. It is cut in a thick bang across the eyebrows. Behind, it falls in heavy curls to the waist.

The dancing class had learned the Schottische together. Then came the order to choose partners. Elma and I chose each other. The music began, the large room filled with the small revolving, kicking figures. Suddenly the clack on the palm of Mr. Dodsworth's hand. Children and music stopped. "Take your seats— all of you. You, Elma and Mary, stand still." The other children sat down on the long seat that ran all around the walls of the room. Elma and I stood alone in the center. The master signaled to the musician. The music began. Then to us, "Dance."

We danced alone in that ballroom with Mr. Dodsworth and all the children watching. We were applauded. We received the medal.

We danced together all over Europe.

So I drove home after the show (arriving about ten-thirty), quite mollified, smiling and happy as if the medal were pinned upon my shoulder.

Michael was sitting in his pompous chair by the radio, absorbed by a playlet.

"Do you mind if I hear this out?" he said politely. So I went up to bed.

And that's how I got Bouquet locked up.

Seems rather complicated.

We are now entirely without help.

Riley has left for the winter. Old George went too, wanting a little vacation, but will return as soon as we need him.

Michael had thought Etta could stay on and cook for us until I go to Los Angeles and he goes to Washington, but I didn't want her and she saved me the trouble of firing her.

I almost collided with her at the kitchen door. She had a

225

visitor—the big fellow with the black hair who had been on Sanski's haying crew. He stood leaning with one arm propped against the wall watching us in a silent, inscrutable fashion, as she said to me belligerently, "I'm leaving, Mrs. Bergwin."

"OK, Etta," I answered. "I'll take you to town in the morning with George."

On the way in I stopped at Granite Canyon for the mail and picked up a big square envelope with the unmistakable writing of Sheer Genius on it and realized with a throb of excitement that here was the report on *Joy in the Morning*. (No answer yet from Betty. There could have been by this time.)

I read Spencer's letter in town, as soon as I had a moment to myself. It was a blast. He could say nothing favorable about the piece. His words reminded me of part of a prayer we had been taught in Sunday School—"We have left undone those things which we ought to have done; And we have done those things which we ought not to have done; And there is no health in us."

". . . you have failed to write in one style and one degree of difficulty throughout . . . a person who could play the difficult passages would not be interested in the simple parts . . . whole piece inconsistent. Either make a concert waltz of it or a child's piece. The material is fine for the latter, but you will have to throw away most of it. It is, in short, mongrel."

I thought about this all the way home. I see exactly what he means—I take some rather simple music, simple thematically, the type of music that would be popular just because of its simplicity and tunefulness and singability, and then I *play it big*. And whoever hears, particularly unsophisticated listeners, like the baggage man and Elma and Michael and all the hired hands, is enchanted with it.

This confirms me in the opinion that most of my music is really for the musical comedy stage. But not all. There is the *Wind Harp,* and *Twilight,* and the Schirmer pieces. I see that *Joy in the Morning* must go into the *box* and wait for *The Catch Colt*.

When I got home I sat down at the piano with his letter and

played the piece over several times, checking it against his criticism.

Of course, he is right.

I felt an inevitable depression. This was mitigated somewhat by the fact that my latest-born (and of course most-loved) was no longer this piece, but *Svenska*. Wait till he sees *Svenska*!

Also, we have the hay!

I could not be depressed long.

I decided to say nothing to Michael about this. He would feel badly for me. Also would be bolstered in his general feeling that I had better stick to stories and forget about music. Besides, I want to play *Svenska* for him as soon as I have completely mastered the technique. It takes playing. I have really finished the composing—finished it several times, but keep going back, trying for a better climax. I have already begun to make the ink copy of the first part.

I had taken Rachel and gone up to my room early the other night when Michael came in and stood in the doorway, smoking.

"Seems odd Betty hasn't answered your letter. Where did you send it?"

"Newport. She's always there this time of year. And Alan mentioned it, too. She's going to Europe the end of this month."

Rachel, who had risen from her place beside my bed to greet Michael, was standing in front of him, looking up, her brush waving gently. His hand dropped to fondle her ears.

"I shall have to go to Washington in any case."

"Yes. And I'll have to go to Los Angeles."

Michael looked at his pipe, which had gone out. He used both hands to relight it, and Rachel returned to her place beside my bed.

I pulled up my knees and propped my open book against them.

"I was thinking," said Michael when his pipe was going again, "do we have to depend on her? Could we do it anyway?"

"I've been wondering the same thing." We discussed this.

What we need is a large country house, plenty of bedrooms and baths; stables, barn and grounds. There are many such places going begging in New England, more or less abandoned because they are too large to keep up and no one wants to buy or rent them. They are being taken over by institutions—academies, convents, schools, rest homes, etc.

"The difficulty would be to find it."

"When I've finished in Washington, I might drive on up there to New England and scout around."

We were both quiet then, thinking of the cost of scouting—just cruising here and there, sleeping in motels or hotels, eating three meals a day in restaurants—and there was the matter of time, too—if we were to start this winter we would have to be ready to open by mid-year.

And this money would have to be spent (and probably borrowed first) before we had sold the hay—or knew what it was going to bring.

Everything was so uncertain. . . .

Next day I wrote again to Betty. She might be away visiting.

Of course, now, we have much more milk and cream than we need; more young ducklings just the age to eat; more mushrooms in the meadows.

I am drying off all the cows except two—I am the milker now.

Michael cannot milk. When we started the dairy, I said, "Someone in this family has got to know how to milk."

Michael appreciated the necessity. I could tell by the way he looked at me. Then he said, "It's not going to be me."

He is the one who does everything. Builds houses and bridges, repairs plumbing, cleans stables, breaks horses; no matter how arduous or difficult or unpleasant the job is, he is the one who does it. If he knew how to milk, the daily chore—four o'clock in the morning, four o'clock in the afternoon—would be added to his duties. This would not be so planned, but would be sure to come about. So I understood.

There is another good reason. He just *can't* milk. Those big fingers that can do everything else, are completely incompatible to a cow's udder. She turns to look at him in surprise. Who is doing *that* to my underparts? And his face is the contorted face of a concert pianist playing impossibly difficult technical passages.

228

When I was a small child at Deercreek, I was allowed to go to the barn at milking time and milk a cow. Try to milk, I should say. Joe put my little hands on the udder, showed me how to grasp the teat, and pull. I never quite forgot the feeling. And when I tried again at the ranch, it was easy to learn.

Lucky that I could, for the time came when I had to.

It was when I was running the dairy. We had two young boys as milkers who were, in a way, wards of the ranch, having been placed in the care of Michael by his good friend, John Pickett, the district attorney of Cheyenne.

The boys had committed a serious crime.

They had gone out into the country one day with their twenty-twos to shoot rabbits, but instead had shot a man, and not altogether without intention.

"How did it happen?" asked John Pickett when he found them in the woods a couple of hours later, still rabbit-hunting.

"We saw a freight train coming along over there, very slow. And there was a hobo standing on top of one of the cars. And I said, See if you can hit that bum. We both shot. And he fell off."

"Well—you killed that man."

"Aw—"

"I've got to take you back to town with me."

"Aw—"

"And put you in jail."

"Aw—we ain't got even one rabbit yet."

"Come on."

"Say, couldn't you let us hunt a little longer? We bin plannin' for this hunting trip a long time."

"Well—a little while then."

John sat down on a log and smoked.

The boys were put on probation. John asked Michael to give them jobs and keep his eye on them.

They were fine milkers. One of them could strip a cow in four minutes. One day, in their noon hour off, they thought it would be fun to start walking down the railroad track.

They never came back.

Fortunately I had at that time a man cook in the bunkhouse who, twenty years before, had milked in a dairy.

There were eighteen cows to be milked. Tim and I milked them at four in the afternoon and at four next morning in sub-zero weather.

Tim woke me in the early morning, tapping at my window. Michael woke too and came to my room. He was miserable; said he would come with me. This I thought unnecessarily heroic, but he insisted. And stood beside me, in the dark barn, holding the lantern as I went down my line of cows. And cheered me on when my strength was used up and I could summon no more. And took my hands in his and chafed and warmed them when they were in such anguishing cramps that they would no longer do what I bid them.

Twenty-four hours later our two milking boys came back, hungry, weeping, promising.

And now I shall bake some bread.

When I first came to the ranch I expected to be shamed by my country neighbors in all such matters as curing hams, smoking tongues, baking bread.

I found instead that the ranchers consider stuff bought in town at the A & P or the Safeway much more *chic*.

I like bread of smooth, solid texture, not too light; slightly creamy in color (which is achieved by adding whole wheat flour in proportion of one to five) and made with water rather than milk. Is not the classic bread made of flour and water, yeast and salt? And I like it with a taste—something of nuts, or meat, or cheese, or egg yolk.

I experimented endlessly.

My best results came from a recipe out of a newspaper purporting to be a family recipe of Teddy Roosevelt's.

One makes the yeast by combining a little corn meal, *new* milk, and a dash of sugar and dash of salt, and setting it to ferment all night long in an even warm temperature.

In the morning, if it has *come alive,* you proceed to add flour, knead, and set-to-rise as you would any dough. You do this several times.

The result is the most superb rich, smooth bread with the faintest taste of cheese.

Whether or not the yeast has come alive can be known by the way the house smells when you come downstairs in the morning.

The first time, I was simply bowled over. I exclaimed that something must have died in the walls! Then I remembered the yeast, rushed to smell it, rushed away again holding my nose, then rushed back to take another sniff and see if it really did—*if anything could*—smell as bad as that!

So, when you first open your eyes in the morning, sit up and sniff—sniff—you'll know immediately. Most often, sad to say, you can fall back on your pillows and take another snooze. But now and then— And you can leap out of bed and hurry to dress—

I would rather eat this bread—cut not too thin, toasted on top of an iron stove, spread with fresh unsalted butter—than anything else in the world.

Chapter 30

Before the boys left there was to have been the breaking of the last three broncs.

It turned out to be two, for Cinder, the little gray roan, had got into the Stable Pasture and could not be found.

Cinder is a two-year-old filly, fleet as the wind, with a delicate, airy style. All her life she has run with a little gang of six colts of her own vintage. They spend their winters on one of the sheltered sections of the ranch and the summers up on the hilly range. Out riding I have often seen this group—wild as deer. At the slightest sound they are off! Cinder, the wildest, the lightest, the fastest of the bunch. She sails over the ravines without a leap, merely by folding back and under those slim forelegs. She seems free of gravity.

Michael had to find her and break her before this summer was over.

The day before Riley left they scoured the Stable Pasture on Gold Coin and Diabolo, found Cinder and got her into the corral and went through the routine of breaking her.

Cinder turned out to be one of those horses who would rather die than give in.

She would not cease to hurl herself, to fight, to rear and go over backward. Twilight came and still she was unyielding. Michael left her tied to the post when he came down to dinner, planning to untie her before he went to bed and give her the freedom of the corral for the night.

He was worn out, frowning, morose. He would hardly speak.

I went up to look at her at eight o'clock. In the dim light I could see her delicate silhouette. When I got close I saw she was

232

bleeding from a dozen places. Her eyes were wild and terrified. I spoke soothingly to her and took her the bucket of oats. But at my close approach she began that frenzied plunging again. So I left her.

At ten Michael went out to untie her. He stayed longer than I expected and when he returned, said, "Well, I'm afraid that little mare is finished."

He had found her unconscious, hanging by her head to the post, legs limp. He had freed her, but she lay on the ground without moving. He said he thought in her wild plunging she had somehow twisted her head between the rope and the post and broken her neck.

But I hoped—I hoped—

And so it was. In the morning she was on her feet.

Michael let her out. She grazed a little, but her neck was still badly twisted and there was a great swelling on it. Though she could put her head down and reach grass and water, she could not lift it, nor straighten her neck.

Michael put her out on Number Seven where she can be entirely alone. Of course she shuns the other horses. All horses are ashamed when they are ill and must be alone. (I agree.)

I saw her once or twice at first, standing motionless, her head down. She was in a little secret dell. The next time I looked there, she was gone.

"She'll either pull out of it or die," Michael said.

I have a rather bad abrasion on my hand. Pom jammed me against the branch of a tree. It bothers me, playing the piano, but I haven't much time anyhow, with the cooking and the milking.

Soon I shall have fresh slipcovers on all the furniture of the living room.

All summer they have been sat upon by blue jeans of different degrees of griminess. Every fall, when the boys leave, I take them off and send them to the laundry. Then in the spring before the boys come, I have them tinted a different color. Pale yellow. Light gray. Soft blue-gray. This summer they have been white.

They are at the laundry now. They will come back rough dry, and then I must iron them, and the living room will look all fresh and clean. I hope my hand will be well enough.

Salt-rising bread again; and again it "took" and I almost staggered when I came downstairs in the morning.

Michael is intensely interested in the process. It takes nearly the whole day—the smell abating gradually until the bread emerges from the oven, so delicately and richly flavored and scented that when I wrap the loaves in clean cloths and stack them on the kitchen table, Michael comes sniffing to the door.

"Is that ready yet?"

When he sees the stack, he comes in, gets the bread knife, cuts off the end pieces of one loaf—all hot and crusty—spreads them thick with fresh butter, and eats them.

While I was working with it this morning, he suddenly called to me from the terrace where he was sitting with an after-breakfast cup of coffee.

"What is it?" I shouted.

"I want to show you something."

"What?"

"It's a drop of water hanging on the tip of a lilac leaf."

"But I'm busy."

"The sun is shining on it. You never saw such color—blue, red, orange—"

I stirred my yeast.

"You've *got* to come," he shouted.

I went out in my kitchen apron, long-handled spoon in my hand.

So that I should get his exact line of vision he pulled me down on his knee, and stretched out his arm. I perched there, craning my head.

What a miracle! All the colors of the rainbow played through it.

We watched it for ten minutes. It was never for five seconds the same. Orange, crimson, violet, green—

"Like a diamond," I said at last, getting up.

Michael putting his hand over his eyes, for the blazing light

234

of the drop hurt them, answered, "That is what they must mean when they say, A diamond of the first water."

He hustles me; bustles me.

Although he accepts the fact that I must work at my music, and wants me to, yet now, with no one else to boss, he can't help storming around, doing unnecessary things himself, as a reproach to me.

I am accustomed, at a moment's notice, to abandon a dinner I am preparing to cook, because he comes out of the pantry with materials for a totally different meal.

I want the dish towel—look around, see it slung over his shoulder. Fortunate that I don't mind. I finally slip away and leave it all to him. If I get indirect reproaches later, I say nothing.

When my slipcovers came home from the laundry and I stood in the kitchen at the ironing board, working at the little box-pleated ruffles, he stopped to watch me.

"Do you have to iron those things? Won't they smooth out when you put them on the furniture?"

"All but the ruffles."

"Well, let the ruffles stay rough."

"But it seems to me that to have all the little box pleats neatly ironed is the thing that makes them look fresh and tailored."

"That's true," he said promptly, and still stood watching. "I could do that for you—save your sore hand—"

"Oh, it isn't bad—" I knew he found those exactly measured little pleats seductive.

I finished one piece, dampened the others and left them piled on the kitchen sideboard.

Sure enough, in the middle of the afternoon, I found Michael, in his usual riding outfit (which looks like parade regalia), standing over the ironing board, ironing the pleats.

"Thought I would spare your sore hand," he explained.

"Oh, thank you ever so much!"

I've been riding a mare called Pink. Jerome told me she has good gaits and is fast. You don't expect it from an animal that looks like that. A strawberry roan, cross between saddle and work. Thick, ungainly build. And now she has a colt, also un-gainly, ungracious and perverse, with a long awkward body, an ugly hammer head, and ears flatter back than any equine ears I ever saw. He bares his teeth and bites everything in sight—his mamma, when she doesn't stop and let him nurse the minute he wants it—or her rider.

Michael said she wasn't the proper horse for me but I prom-ised him to take it easy. Jerome was right—she is one of the fastest horses on the ranch. Unfortunately she has a hard mouth and if she takes it into her head to run, she runs. But I figured, with the colt along, she wouldn't run, and she didn't.

I keep looking for Cinder. I saw a horse the other day, quite far away, holding her head strangely—she was just flying along. I'm sure it was Cinder . . .

. . . now Michael has seen her and says it *is* Cinder— If we could just get her in without frightening her—

Yesterday, walking over in Sixteen, I came upon the yearlings grazing in a little dell. They gathered around me, clustered be-hind and followed me.

They look stunning. Smooth and sleek—their little hides so full and taut they look as if they would burst.

It has got much colder.

Late last evening, when we were reading in the living room, suddenly Michael raised his head, listening; he had heard some-thing outside.

I had heard it too, but subconsciously, without being dis-tracted from my harmony book. He strode out and came back with one of Missy's kittens cuddled under his chin.

"Bad Missy. She brought him out into the cold. Poor baby. There, there, Papa's holding you—bad Mamma—" He stood be-fore me, displaying the wee thing poking its pretty head out of his cupped hands like a little jack-in-the-pulpit. His eyes shone tenderly.

Presently, after we had both held it and played with it and quieted its crying, he carried it back down to the barn, and told

Missy sharply that she was to leave her babies down there, that they were not to be brought out into the cold.

We spent the evening picking fleas off ourselves.

No sooner had we gone up to bed than we heard the tiny sharp cries again. She had brought him back.

Then another and another. As fast as we carried them down, she carried them back. She wants them inside the house now that all intruders have gone and cold weather is coming.

But Michael says no. We closed all doors, hardened our hearts and went to bed.

This morning early, Michael left to go to the government Remount Station in Nebraska. They have a new stallion over there he wants to see. We might have some of our mares bred.

Not long after he left, a team of county men arrived to inspect our cows. They have a program of thinning out the Wyoming dairy herds.

Any cow that does not come up to a certain standard in weight, condition, age and milk production, they shoot on the spot, give the rancher a check for the specified amount (very small) and depart, leaving the rancher to dispose of the carcass.

In the bunch of dry cows, they spotted Moon, and said she would have to be shot.

I had a soft spot in my heart for Moon, for she is the cow who had her udder so badly torn by barbed wire that she could not stand the rough hands of the boys milking her. I milked her myself, most carefully and gently, taking a long time to empty her udder, and while I did this, she would stand quietly, with her head turned all the way around, watching me, relieved to have the milk drawn out of the bursting udder, and sure that with me on the milking stool, it would be done without pain to her.

I did this every morning after breakfast when the barn was empty, all the other cows out in the corral, very likely lying down, chewing their cuds, and waiting to go out to pasture.

When I would go down to the barn to do this, Moon would always be out in the corral with the other cows.

I would call her name—just stand at the door, saying Come, Moon! and she would slowly turn her head to look at me, then get deliberately to her feet, then come into the barn and into her own stall.

And now this thing of just shooting her and letting her lie where she falls—

There's no use in arguing with government men—in fact, the program is a wise one and will benefit the state.

To tell them I was alone on the ranch is the kind of plea I don't like to make. But what a welcome for Michael! To come in late tonight with that dead animal waiting to be dragged up to the mine shaft—

I could see the men were sorry.

I asked them at last if they could take time enough to let me lead the cow up to the mine shaft and do the deed there?

They agreed, but seemed to doubt whether I could lead the cow—said they could not undertake a long struggle.

But I had only to call her.

She came to me immediately from where she was grazing in the Calf Pasture, looking at me trustingly out of her big brown eyes.

In fact, I did not have to lead her. I said those same words, "Come, Moon," and she followed a foot behind me, the two men bringing up the rear.

We climbed the long gentle slope of Sixteen, till we came to that shaft. When she stood on the edge of it, they shot her; she careened forward; disappeared.

We stood silent, waiting, until we heard the thud.

. . . nearly midnight, and Michael not home yet.

As so often, when I am alone here at night, I begin to feel nervous and constricted in the house and go out and wander around. The sky looked stormy. There were thick clouds, torn and patchy, with light streaks between. Now and then the moon glared out for a few seconds, then was covered again.

Michael on the road, I thought, driving out. Hope he's all right. At times the danger of life on the ranch, on the highways, oppresses me—danger of life everywhere—something can always happen— I stood listening intently. I heard the trains out on the track, one after the other. I heard some cars way off there on the Lincoln Highway, heard the gears grinding and a horn—probably the big transcontinental buses. I heard the Roamer moaning, I heard a cow bell tinkling. But no car coming in on the ranch road—

So I came indoors again and got to work on the ink copy of *Svenska*.

I finished it. I will mail it to Vernon Spencer tomorrow.

Summing up the music—what have I accomplished in the past year? The four pieces sold to Schirmer (out of eighteen written); *Joy in the Morning* (with a bad mark from Spencer, but it can wait for *The Catch Colt*) and a great deal of serious study. A great deal *mastered*, actually, and a *summa cum laude* from Spencer for *Invention in G Minor*.

Now *Svenska*. Verdict still unknown.

I fell asleep on the sofa and Michael came in at three.

The fire had gone out. He built it up and got himself a drink from the kitchen.

He sat down and we chatted about the government stud for a while, then I asked, "I don't suppose you were able to get the mail?"

(We've almost given up expecting Betty Bedford's reply, but still we hope; and every day there's suspense when we pick up the mail.)

"No. When I passed Granite this morning the mail train hadn't come in yet."

"And tonight it wasn't open."

"No."

We were silent. Our thoughts were traveling the same path, and arrived at the same point—the bank.

"I stopped at the bank on my way through Cheyenne this morning."

"You did? About a loan?"

"Yes. Before I leave for Washington I have to know what I'm going to do."

"Of course. What did they say?"

"They'll give us what we need all right—"

239

There was doubt in his voice as he ended. Because this is what we've had to do so often. Mortgage the earnings of the coming year to meet the necessities of the moment.

"The only other thing we could do is sell the hay right away at present prices."

"We won't do that."

"Or," he continued, "give up the school for this year—"

"Well—we can't tell yet—"

"I saw old Harvey in town," he went on. "He's still asking when he can come out to corn a cow for you. How about getting him now? Till George comes back. Save you the milking and the housework."

"Is he really sober?"

"Sober as a judge. On the wagon, he tells me, for good and all."

"That's a laugh—"

"Don't be such a doubter."

"Who else did you see?"

"No one else this morning, but I got back to Cheyenne about six and ran into Jessie Reid when I took my car to the garage to have it oiled, and she asked me up to the house for dinner. There was a big party at the Post for General Todhunter. We went on to that afterward."

"Oh, is he back?"

"Just came yesterday. Then we all went down to the hotel. Lieutenant Guffey and I got talking. We ended up with scrambled eggs at old Joe's. I just loafed coming out. Beautiful moonlight."

"Oh, the weather's cleared then? It was overcast a few hours ago."

"Yes. The moon's out. And there was a Beethoven Symphony on the radio."

"Which one?"

"I forget the number. The one with the thunderstorm in it."

"Oh, the Pastoral."

"I guess that's it. Anything happen here?"

I was silent so long, thinking about Moon, wondering whether to tell him now or wait till morning, that he looked up sharply.

240

"Well?"

"I've finished that piece I've been working on. The one I call *Svenska*."

He knocked the ashes out of his pipe, put it in his pocket and stood up. Beginning to blow out the lamps and setting the screen up in front of the fire he said, "You must play it to me."

"Not till I can really play it."

"Thought you said you'd finished it."

"Finished the composing and the notation. Playing it is something else again."

I've been working at it steadily but it's rough yet.

Wonderful weather today. We've caught glimpses of Cinder, near the cows. Michael thinks she's lonesome, feeling better and wanting company.

Michael said when I went out riding today that I might go out on Section Seven and see if she would come up to me. She might even follow along with me. If she did, bring her in.

I chose a circular route that would almost comb the north range, including Seven. I saw no sign of her.

I was riding Pink, and the colt was a nuisance. Every time it got near enough it bit my leg, whirled and kicked at us, laid its ears back, gave mean little squeals. It was furious because I was in some horrid way attached to its mother.

I decided Cinder must be at the other end of the section and went all the way down there.

Suddenly Pink and the colt startled and pricked their ears. They turned their heads and I was sure Cinder was near. I looked all around, still could not see her, but then, with a rush, she came down on us at a gallop.

I rejoiced to see her! Not damaged then, not maimed—really just her old quick, slender, beautiful self.

Pink whinnied. Cinder whinnied. The colt rushed to Cinder— then braced, stopped, rushed back to us—then back to Cinder.

Deciding to lose no time, I turned and headed back to the ranch, the colt and Cinder following.

241

Without slowing up I led them all the way home, through the pasture and right into the corral.

Michael was there. He got a bucket of oats, offered it first to Pink who guzzled greedily, Cinder watching wistfully from a little distance. Then he presented it to her. She circled about, excited, anxious, afraid, ran back and forth before him. Finally, soothed by his voice and quietness, she stopped. Not quite near enough, she stretched out her little head, almost reached the bucket, then a little more, a little more, and finally had her head in for one good big mouthful. Scared at her own daring, she leaped to a safe distance and stood munching.

The gate was still open. When I led Pink out to pasture, Cinder followed, and there she is now. Juanita and Eitel Fritz, Gold Coin, Pink and her little goblin boy, and Baby—all there together. A lot of quiet old stand-bys who will calm her down and tell her all about us people, and that we are her friends, and that she need not be afraid of us.

While I had been out on Pink, Michael was riding Rheingold on the saddleback. Suddenly Rheingold saw some of the saddle mares scattered around, grazing, and decided it was his duty to round them up and bring them to the corral. You might say, Rheingold suddenly came of age and became aware of his rights and duties as a stallion.

A stallion rounding up mares simply cannot be ridden, but Michael was on him and stayed till the end of the run. There was no possibility of controlling the horse. Down went that undulating neck close to the ground, and Rheingold followed it at top speed—a rough, driving gallop that shook Michael's very teeth. Down hill, through rocks and stones, across ditches and gullies, circling, swerving here and there, he gathered them up and swept them through the Stable Pasture and into the corral. The run whipped and tore the muscles of Michael's back. He walks stiffly and with pain. But there is a look on his face that is not exactly like anything I have ever seen before. He was carried away, and not only physically. Perhaps a sort of Shinar for him.

242

Chapter 31

If it's an adventure, then, this life at the ranch—and there was the Hollywood adventure before, and there is another coming— then after that will there be another? And another and another? And all life turns out to be an adventure? I think so. How then could life be taken seriously?

Not too seriously. One couldn't bear it.

Winter is bearing down on us.

The high wind in the tops of the pines, a continual soft roaring—it makes me restless.

It is mysterious and dramatic that I must change in my feelings with the changing seasons. Now, with autumn, I want to do different things, think different thoughts, make different plans, wear different clothes.

There's an extremely good military tailor in Cheyenne. He makes women's suits too. So Michael and I are each going to get a new suit. His will be Oxford gray. He likes very conservative clothes. It will be just right for Washington.

Mine, I have decided, will be green. A rough green wool, not too heavy. This I can wear in Los Angeles, and also in New York when I get there, but it will really be a country suit. I can wear it all through the Connecticut winter.

I stand at the end of the terrace and wonder where, just overnight, the luscious greens and reds and blues have gone.

The sky has faded; the meadows, the Green, the house, my flowers are all dull.

It is bitter cold; some of the geraniums in my blue boxes have been nipped. Word came from Laramie that it has snowed there.

The hedges are full of elderberries and I have picked quarts and quarts. Rube Haygood has given me a recipe for making elderberry wine. He says it just can't be beat and that if you stick to the recipe you can't fail. It was his mother's recipe. It takes several weeks, from first to last.

It's down in a keg in the cellar now, and it smells. Not so bad as the salt-rising bread, but still pretty bad.

To really *master Svenska* so that I can play it for Michael with confidence and perfection—this is what I am striving for at present.

Sometimes I play very well.

This is usually when I have been composing something new, working day and night with all my power, and it's just beginning to get into my fingers. At such a time my technique is suddenly adequate, in fact, astonishing.

Sometimes, at about midnight, with no one else within earshot of me, I become a virtuoso. I do things that I simply cannot do, and do them with ease.

George tells the hired hands who come and go, "You wait till you hear the Missus play. There ain't nothing like it on the radio."

There is a long bench across the outside of the bunkhouse, and there they sit, evenings, and smoke and listen.

I must play well when I play *Svenska* for Michael, so I am practicing all the time.

It really is a gorgeous piece.

I heard Michael stamping into the kitchen.

I came to with a start; it was almost dark.

"Are the cows milked?" he roared.

"Gosh, no! Is it milking time?"

"It's five-thirty."

"I'll go down right away." I started out the door. He came too.

"Where are they?" he asked. (Of course I am supposed to bring the cows in if they haven't come in by themselves.)

"Aren't they down by the barn?"

"Not a sign of them."

I felt sure he knew where they were. "Have you looked around?" I asked.

He nodded. "Yes. Someone must have left the gates into the meadow open, and they got through." (This always makes him mad.) "Come on. I'll take you in the car."

On the terrace, I stopped, looking at the darkening sky. "It's going to pour," I said, and ran back to get my raincoat and beret.

No sign of the cows in the first meadow, or the second, and when we reached Castle Rock Meadow, a veritable cloudburst hit us.

The cows had found shelter in the aspen grove at the far end. To make cows move, you have to yell in a certain way, and it helps to have a stick in your hand. They were on both sides of the creek.

While Michael waited in the car with the engine running I yelled and waved my stick and jumped back and forth across the stream and finally got them started for home. Then I got in the car and we drove the rest of the way slowly, herding them along. I milked in my wet clothes.

Michael was furious about the open gates. All the horses are mixed up again.

So I got mad too, and didn't care whether I ever played *Svenska* to him or not . . . had to change all my clothes . . . hunting for something in my dark room I tripped over my riding boots and got still madder. Then, hunting for my book before I went downstairs, I tipped over the ink bottle, which was uncorked. The ink drenched my desk and hands.

With icy self-control I lit a lamp, got a rag and mopped up the mess.

Michael saw my hands, exclaimed in horror, led me firmly to the kitchen sink, presented me with his can of Skat, and helped me to get them clean.

I did not sleep well. Woke about midnight. Then went through all the foolish motions, foolish thoughts, that come when one lies awake after midnight. Paroxysms of coughing. Was sure I heard a car coming. Got up and prowled around, looked out every window. No car, no riders. I went back to bed and decided I was terribly unhappy. I sank away from everything, terribly alone. . . .

Everyone is alone and lonely from birth to death. Is the diary-writing habit a defense against loneliness then? It may be, for here I am today, writing it all out.

I have been thinking about the famous diaries of famous authors. Kafka's, and Gide's and Katherine Mansfield's and George Moore's—especially George Moore whose diaries continue from year to year, from place to place.

Katherine Mansfield speaks of her "huge complaining diaries." Do mine complain? Well—why not? Weeping is good—it comforted Billy Allenger in the telephone booth, it comforted Vernon Spencer—

And in the translation of a French diarist I read, ". . . I find in these outpourings such solace! . . . as I sit scribbling pages no one will ever read, I get the feeling of an invisible presence which surely could not be God—rather a friend made in my image, although distinct from me . . . and I caught myself turning my head toward this listener, with a longing to weep that shamed me. . . ."

Even animals must, I think, now and then weep to someone—pour out a tale of desperate sadness.

I remember when Michael and I came home one afternoon in Los Angeles and found Hitchie, our little bull terrier, dragging himself around, crying pitifully. We thought immediately of an automobile accident. (Hitchie had had one before.) We saw no injury on him, but thought it might be internal. So we gathered him up carefully and took him to the vet.

He yielded thankfully to the doctor's examination, still whimpering and trembling.

When the doctor pronounced him unhurt, and we changed our tone, exclaiming, "Why, you little scamp! There's nothing the matter with you at all!" he changed his tone too, leaped joyfully from the table and pranced about with happy barks, wagging his tail.

The explanation was given us later by a neighbor. There *had* been an accident that afternoon which Hitchie had witnessed. A little dog was run over and killed. But it was Hitchie who

246

threw himself down, howling, and would not be comforted until we came home to hear his story.

And another case—that stray dog who came to the ranch once. He was without physical injury, but his mind or his heart had been broken and he hid away and was terrified if anyone approached him.

We put out food for him, but he remained deep under one of the old wagons and would not emerge till we had gone.

After days, I determined to really get to him, and went and sat down near the wagon, and talked to him, called to him, waited for him to come. I sat there waiting for hours. He came at last, crawling inch by inch and crying piteously as he came. I made no movement but kept reassuring him as he came nearer and nearer. At last he was on my lap, in my arms, his head on my breast, and then he told me the whole thing— What a tale of despair and loss and fear and horror!

He just had to tell that story.

But there are other tears than the tears of grief. Wonderful tears, when the sight, the sound, the thought is too noble to be borne. In all the great books about the great beings one reads of such tears.

And the least of us too, when the deeps are touched. I myself, with music. And Michael . . .

Once when we had been to a concert by Paderewski and at the end he was receiving a standing ovation from the house, I saw tears on Michael's face. He wiped them away unashamedly. "He always makes me cry. He is such a great soul."

But diaries are not only catharsis. There is something else about them. Something else that makes people undertake to keep them. It is a passion that begins very early in life to turn everything that happens to you into literature. You see something beautiful. What will it be like in words? And you immediately attempt the translation.

This amounts to a very strong inborn bent toward authorship.

It began with me as soon as I could write, aged about seven. The books were brown manila blank books that I brought from school.

When I got to be ten years old my allowance was raised and I could afford nicer books. These had soft black leather covers, smooth thick white paper and gilt edges.

I have always been aware of the importance of thoughts and feelings, and discovered early that words were a clue to these, provided it was *the very words*. It became my habit to demand not only, What did she say? but, *What were the very words?* so that I was tabbed with it—here's Mary wanting to know the very words. Add to the words the expression of the face, the tone of voice, and the gesture, and the whole inner life is revealed—the movement of the soul.

All of this, written into my diary, not only gave the page a lively look but, if read aloud, made the stuff into a story. Everyone wanted to read my diaries.

I also invented tales out of whole cloth, telling exactly what she said and how she looked when she said it. These stories were told, mostly, to my younger sister, Bess. We endured the whole long ennui of a tour through Europe, by means of a continued story told by me to her, which began on the boat going over and lasted till the return home.

Whatever part of the older continent we were traversing—the Austrian Tyrol, the Dolomites, Sicily, Germany, Algiers—she would sidle to me, slip her little hand in mine, say softly, *Go on!* and I would take up the tale where I had left it the day before. We would even walk through the art galleries doing this—so quiet by ourselves, so well behaved, our deceitful eyes so quick to pretend we were looking at paintings, that whatever person was herding us would be hoodwinked, and we would succeed in escaping all those advantages for which we had been taken abroad.

So my life was made up of stories. Invented and told to other people, read out of books (my bed was full of books for the forbidden hours) and the story of my own life filling diaries that filled shelves that were gradually filling my closet.

Now I shall quote from an old diary:

"Don't you want to see Mary's diaries?" asked my sisters of the Family (the Family being our Father and our stepmother whom we called Matrigna).

There was everywhere a morbid interest in my diaries that kept me on my toes, guarding them. I locked doors of chests and closets upon them. Bess was insistently curious. She wanted to know how I could possibly think up words enough to fill them.

When the Family said, yes, they would very much like to see Mary's diaries, I was wildly excited and intensely protective. It was to be only the outside of them that anyone should get a glimpse of.

The Family lived on the second floor, we girls on the third. My sisters carried the diaries in armfuls down the flight of stairs to the Family's sitting room while I hovered like an excited hen. They piled them up on the floor into a high tower.

Father and Matrigna looked at them with the greatest interest. Matrigna teased to read one of them but I was so violent in my threats as to what I would do to anyone who opened a single page that no one dared try.

Truth was, I was ashamed of a good deal that was in them. I feared it was juvenile.

What was in them? Well . . . *life* interested me—I had Thoughts, Reflections, Wonderings about it. *People* interested me—I had Thoughts about them too. And much Abstract Speculation—the purpose and end of life, happiness, unhappiness, love, grief—all these filled many pages.

There was also, of course, the thread of my own existence as it unwound itself year by year. Where we girls went—off to a country place in summer, back to Brooklyn in winter; a feud between my father and grandmother as to whether or not one of us could live permanently in New York with her; the schools we went to; serious illness of any member of the family; my girl friends, my boy friends—but we did not call them that. We spoke of them seriously as 'the men I know.' These men were perhaps almost in college—going there soon; or actually in Yale, Harvard or Princeton. They paraded the streets of Brooklyn in tremendous overcoats in the cold winter holidays. We also paraded—myself and a girl friend or two, alert to catch sight of them. We were swathed in winter furs. I had black fox skins that reached

249

the hem of my skirt in front, and an immense muff; the muff was the really dramatic part of the set, for it could be lifted to hide the tip of a nose which was so cold it must surely be an unbecoming red; or lifted to hide an indiscreet smile; or just to conceal embarrassment. If we saw them approaching and thought we knew them, there was the long suspense of walking to meet them and then the smile and bow at exactly the right moment—he would sweep his hat off, incline his head with the slightest formal smile, and pass by; and we would maintain absolute silence until we had gone far enough so that he could not possibly hear, then we would turn our heads to look at each other, raise our muffs to our faces and burst out laughing. If we did not know them, the tension was even greater. For it was absolutely necessary to pass them as if they did not exist. One might glance at them—it really wouldn't be much fun if one did not—one might even meet their eyes, but this must be done as if one was glancing at a lamp post, or a door knob. Positively not the slightest recognition of their existence.

To these "men" we had given the names of animals. We populated Brooklyn with a fauna. There was the Bear, the Bull, the Rabbit, the Weasel, the Stag, the Rat. I am embarrassed to admit that my particular love was the Bull. Did he know that even to pass him on the street made my heart beat?

All this was in the diaries. Also many *And ifs, I wonders, Supposings—*

Inconceivable to let the Family see any of it!

Of the five characters (counting myself) enacting this scene, one stands out, unforgettable in my memory—my father.

For while everyone else was chattering and exploding with shrieks, he sat with brows drawn together over his brilliant dark eyes, glancing from the tower of diaries to me and back again.

He was searching my future, and I knew it; and as his eyes lost focus, glimpsing the adventures-to-come of his second daughter, I saw a shadow fall upon him, and on his face; and as I looked at him, wondering, it fell on me too. I felt the pang.

The memory keeps a better record than a tower of diaries. Nowhere in those diaries will be found the description of my father's Sunday-afternoon naps, but it is a vivid vignette within me.

Aged eight, I am standing beside the large couch in my father's study. The couch is covered with an oriental rug—a Shiraz (now in my ranch living room)—and on the couch he has arranged himself for sleep, neatly upon his back, eyes closed, hands clasped on his chest. The shade of the window has been drawn and not a word is spoken. The rhythm of the moment is already one of sleep, and this she perfectly understands. She deftly folds a large black silk handkerchief, lays it around her father's head over his eyes, tucks it in behind. He remains motionless.

The final step of the ceremony is the most important. She gently unlocks his hands, climbs onto the couch herself, curls up against him, then draws his arm around her and puts her cheek on his breast.

So she stays, guarding his unconsciousness, and is only able to endure the terrible ennui of it and the long long waiting for him to wake up by telling herself a story.

What has happened to all of those diaries? Most of them have been burned. Every so often I would take the five or ten oldest, having now outgrown such childish interests as were contained in them, and burn them up. Sometimes, in sudden disgust, I would burn them all. I would go a week or two, a month or two, perhaps a year or two without a diary. Then I would begin again.

Old Harvey has come. These "old" men of the west are quite likely in their forties. I always wonder how they can get worn out and used up so quickly.

He is slim, gentle and apologetic. He will milk the cows; feed the chickens; cook our meals; and corn a cow.

No more kitchen work for me!

It seems too good to be true.

251

Chapter 32

Michael tells me that Harvey was almost tearfully grateful when told that Mrs. Bergwin wanted him.

I have always wanted to know how to corn a cow. If an old cow has no teeth it makes no milk, no calves, no flesh for beef. Harvey says these old cows are the best to corn.

My work, now, is halved. If we take a trip anywhere, we won't have to cut it short for the milking. I shall have time to do a lot more work on music before I leave.

Tonight we'll have a dinner that I don't cook myself. Michael is going to town and probably won't be back, but I shall have roast chicken. I have told Harvey to catch and kill and pluck one of our young white hens.

Michael, dressing for town, is lighthearted and very gold and blue. When he feels festive, he shines. Came into my room and asked if *this* tie was all right? Or better wear the other?

It is a strange day. I have been standing looking at the sky, which is now sultry and overcast. The sun is a dull brown ball.

I have told Harvey to dress the chicken first, then get my lunch.

He's gone to the barn to catch the chicken.

I'm going to do some sewing.

Just saw Harvey walking from the barn, where he caught the chicken, up to the spring house, where he will pluck and dress it.

He walked very slowly, and swung the chicken in one hand— by the neck—in circles.

I stared. My needle stopped in the silk.

252

It disturbed me to see him do that. It didn't look decent. I wondered if he was drunk. They usually arrive with a bottle in the suitcase and are not sober until the bottle is finished. Then they settle down.

I shall have to go and find out—

I had to talk stiffly to myself to make myself go.

I went to the spring house.

He was very respectful, said it was a fine chicken, he'd have it ready in no time; then he'd get my lunch.

But he seemed a little funny. I couldn't be sure.

Now I hear him downstairs in my kitchen. He's been moving about, in and out of the pantry, cellar, kitchen, laundry, finding out where everything is kept, I suppose.

He's gone up to the bunkhouse now—

Two o'clock, and no sign of lunch; no sign of Harvey.

I'll have to go up to the bunkhouse. (How I hate this.)

He was sprawled on the floor at my feet as I opened the door, dead drunk.

There is something shocking about the sight of an unconscious man spread-eagled on the floor.

I was miserable and frightened. I wished Michael was there. I tried to figure out in advance what Harvey would do when he came to. Would he come to the house? I hoped not. Above all, not into the dining room.

To prevent this, I braced one of the dining room chairs against the door that led into the kitchen, so that at least he could not get into the dining room without knocking over that chair and giving me warning.

Then I came up to work at my sewing again.

At three-thirty I heard him stumbling into the kitchen, and I sat listening, very tense and frightened.

The general effect was that he knocked over every piece of furniture in the room, then struggled with the door into the dining room, and kept trying until my blockade gave way with one

253

last crash. He was now in the dining room, from which the stairs led directly up to my bedroom.

He had never been in the house before. I imagine the sight of the dining room made him feel something of an intruder and his instinct was not to stray too far away from his own domain.

He got my little silver hand bell from the sideboard, carefully replaced the chair against the kitchen door, himself seated on it, on the hither side, now, of the blockade, and rang the bell.

He was ringing *for me*. I had showed him the bell, explained how I would ring *for him* when I wanted him. This much had stuck in his mind—that when you wanted to summon a person, you rang the bell.

He rang and rang.

At last I went down and stood firmly facing him.

"Harvey, you're drunk. I'm very much surprised at you, and very much disappointed. You go right back to the bunkhouse."

"No'm. I'm a-goin' to git your lunch."

"You're going back to the bunkhouse."

"I'm a-goin' to git your lunch."

"I had my lunch two hours ago. It's almost four o'clock."

This stunned him. "You've been asleep up there all this time, and don't tell me you haven't because I saw you. You've got a bottle in your suitcase, I suppose. Now go on back there. Go on!" I raised my voice sharply. "I don't want to see you down here again until you're sober!"

I got him out, locked all the doors and sat down to sew.

My hands were shaking and I couldn't see to thread the needle.

I heard the wind rising, and looking out saw sudden little whirlpools of dust shooting up in the air, and then running along the ground. *Wind-dogs* I call them.

I was too nervous to stay in, weather or no weather.

I went out, glancing at the sky. On a ranch, one never takes a step outdoors without that quick search of the heavens.

A veritable pall hung over the eastern horizon in the direction of town. Dark clouds were piling up on the south. It might be rain; it might be just wind.

Bunny and Rachel, knowing exactly what I was going to do, came rushing at me, leaping, falling over each other.

I went up to the corral, saddled Pom, brought her down to the house and tied her to the hitching post while I changed my clothes.

I planned to go through the pines to the meadows, ride the fence and see that it was intact, count the colts; in fact, do anything that would keep me out and away from the house for the rest of the afternoon.

I was careful to lock the doors again after I left the house.

Down in the meadows I found the wind violent and surprisingly cold. It cut through the thin clothes I had on. We had come out slowly, by devious ways through the pines. Here we got the full force of the wind and it was too tough to be borne. Surely a big storm was coming. Perhaps Michael would not be able to get home at all tonight. My heart sank.

If we were in for weather, Harvey would not only be no help with the stock, he would be a positive menace to my peace of mind.

I put Pom at a fast gallop and did not stop except to dismount for gates.

Unsaddling in the corral, I suddenly heard the sound of the car. Michael was back! What a relief!

I told him what had happened and he went in search of Harvey. There was no one in the bunkhouse. He found him at last in the barn, sound asleep in the hay, and left him there.

Michael was for firing Harvey and taking him back to town the first thing in the morning, but I wanted the cow corned.

"If," I argued, "you get another man, *he'll* have a bottle in *his* suitcase too, and be drunk for the first few days, so what's the use?"

Michael agreed, so now we're waiting for Harvey to finish the bottle.

At bedtime the wind had gone down and there was an icy sleet. We struggled with the window boxes again, tucking the blankets all around the geraniums.

In the night I woke once or twice to feel a cold wind blowing in from the open window with a powdering of fine snow; and this morning, waking quite late, I saw the world all white.

Michael yelled from his room. "How do you like the snow?"

"Fine!" I cried.

I do love it. It makes me feel a child again.

It made a little business—sweeping off before the doors.

After breakfast Michael started up to the bunkhouse. I yelled out the window, "I have to get on my ski suit and go out. Where is it?"

"In the camphor box, with your winter furs," he called back. I found the box, with my furs carefully packed away in mothballs (by Michael), and labeled, in Michael's flowing hand: Mary's beaver jacket; fur-lined coat; ski suit; muff.

I had a walk and a romp with the dogs in the snow.

Back home again, Michael told me that Harvey was sober, very much ashamed of himself and felt that he ought to be fired.

But I wanted the cow corned. This was not the time for him to leave, now that he was sober and fit to go to work.

I called him down and talked to him, but he was adamant. He must go, he said, because he did not deserve to stay.

I was puzzled. "All I want to know, Harvey, is this: Have you finished the bottle you brought in your suitcase?"

"Yes'm, I've finished it. The Mister went through my suitcase this morning and he seen for himself that I've got no more liquor with me."

"Then you're going to stay, and that's all there is to it. You know you want to, Harvey. You want to show me how well you can corn a cow, don't you?"

His eyes lit up. "Yes'm. I'd like to, real well."

"And Harvey—do you know anything about making elderberry wine? Rube Haygood gave me his mother's recipe for it, and we had so many elderberries this year I thought I'd put up some wine."

"Yes, ma'am, I know how to make it. I could have told you how."

"Well, you'd better come and look at it. It's in a keg in the cellar."

256

He followed me down, and I showed it to him and explained the directions I had followed.

"The thing is," he said, "at this stage, just to leave it alone. It's supposed to set in the keg twenty-one days. Did you know that?"

"Yes. That's what the recipe said. It's been here twelve days now."

"It's just poison now, ma'am."

"Well, it's got nine more days to go. Do you think it will be good?"

"Elderberry wine is swell, ma'am. It'll be good all right."

"Well, now, let's go and take a look at the dry cows in the pasture. You can plan to start tomorrow. Today, I want you to clean the bunkhouse. It's hardly been touched since the haying crew left."

We had a peaceful day. I worked at my sewing. Michael ran down to Laramie to the fish hatchery to see about stocking our stream and pool with trout. Harvey was invisible.

But late in the afternoon, when I was just coming in from a ride, I saw Michael walking from the barn across the Green with something over his shoulders which looked like a limp scarecrow with dangling arms and legs.

"What on earth!" I cried.

"Drunk again," said Michael. "I found him in the hay. Afraid to leave him there. It's getting so cold he might freeze. He must have had another bottle hidden away somewhere. I'll take him to town the first thing in the morning."

I sighed for the corned cow. But one gets to be philosophical. . . .

Today it is clear—snow nearly all gone. Michael went to town with Harvey. He was still so drunk he could hardly sit in the car. Michael said he'd look for another man—perhaps Jack. If only he can get Jack! Jack has been in the army and knows how to be an orderly. He waits on table with quite an air—

Jack has arrived.

He's dapper, slim, handsome with a pink, dissipated face

257

and gray hair, an engaging smile and a habit of blushing. He dresses as much like Michael as he can manage.

He has been here before in various capacities, but is best in the house.

It has never occurred to him that a butler could or should be invisible. Instead, arriving in the doorway between kitchen and dining room with a tray, he is the perfect prima donna, blushing, smiling, bowing.

Jack is one of Alice's long line of "husbands."

We had the roast chicken for dinner at last, and a delicious salad.

Michael told me the tale of his day. "First thing when I got to town this morning I hunted up Jack, and Jack said he'd be glad to come. I told him about Harvey, how he kept getting drunk all the time and we couldn't figure out how he had carried so much liquor with him. Well, while I did my errands, Jack got curious about that, and found Harvey, and Harvey told him. What do you think?"

I couldn't imagine.

"The elderberry wine!"

Jack grinned as he passed me the salad and said, "Sure enough, Mrs. Bergwin, he said it was strong enough to knock an ox."

"The wretch!" I was indignant. "He kept telling me it was simply poison at this stage, and no one must touch it!"

It's a comfort to have Jack.

Oh, dear. At breakfast Jack was impertinent and Michael bawled him out.

Jack retired to the kitchen, slamming the door. Michael followed him, and I sat at the table, discouraged, my head on my hand, and listened to the rumpus.

Suddenly it seemed to me—could it be?—that Jack was crying.

I opened the door and looked in. Jack, sitting at the red-checked table, had his arms flung out on the cloth, and his head was down on them.

He was sobbing hysterically. "Don't scold me, Captain. You

know I'll do anything you want me to, but I can't bear to be scolded." His voice rose.

Michael's eyes turned to me. Light dawned on us both.

"You're drunk, Jack."

"No such thing, Captain."

"Jack, you've been at the elderberry wine yourself!"

"Captain, on my honor, I never touched it."

Michael stamped down to the cellar and came back with the keg on his shoulder.

I followed him and Jack followed me.

Michael crossed the Green and emptied the wine out in the little gully at the far side under the cliff.

Jack's face was a study—embarrassment, chagrin, sulkiness.

Michael, coming back, roared at him, "As for you, Jack, the one man I thought I could trust, I'll take you to town first thing tomorrow morning." Jack began to cry again.

Michael was really sore. I thought it was terribly funny, and when, before lunch, I saw some chickens over in the gully, pecking at the elderberries and staggering, I thought it was funnier still.

Late in the afternoon a big gray low-slung car swept up the road and stopped by the house.

Though we have many visits from the officers of the Post, and their wives and children, yet we seldom see a seven-passenger car crowded to overflowing with uniforms. This looked positively official.

"Why, General Todhunter—and Lieutenant Guffey—why didn't you bring your wives?"

They crowded into the living room, and Michael was just beginning to ask Scotch or Rye when Guffey burst out laughing and said, "What we're really interested in is a barrel of wine in your cellar. The fame of it is all over town. No one is talking about anything else."

"So you thought you'd come out and sample it?" Michael grinned.

"If it lives up to its reputation, it's something no man of enterprise should miss."

259

I held up a finger. "It's no longer in the cellar. Come. I'll show you where we've put it."

They followed me out to the gully. Here were now not only half a dozen chickens, but the whole flock. It was a disgraceful sight.

Behind us stood Jack, flirting the white apron, smiling and blushing.

When everyone had watched the reeling chickens (some of them lying motionless on their sides) long enough and we were all spent with laughter, we turned to go back to the house.

Jack said, with an air, "Scotch or Rye, gentlemen?"

When our visitors had gone I put in a plea for Jack; Michael relented; Jack could stay—"But watch your step now!" Michael roaring at Jack made him feel comfortable again—"On my honor, Captain—"

But now we have had to let Jack go because it is so cold we have to have the kitchen to live in. I am wearing socks to bed at night.

There's a small room off the back where Hilda slept. I shall sleep there now. Michael and Jack put a fresh coat of calcimine on it and oiled the dark wood floor. My bed has been moved there with the green-and-white-sprigged quilt, one of Pat's rosy hooked rugs beside it.

My rocking chair and cushion and sewing basket now stand in the kitchen between the stove and window. We saved some of the geraniums, put a few pink ones in pots, and they are on the kitchen window sills.

Missy keeps bringing her kittens to the house. There are six. Whenever we see her, there is a little furry bundle in her mouth which she drops at our feet, then looks up at us with a pleading miaow.

Michael has put them in the little shed where our surplus furniture is stored.

After breakfast, Michael and I sit for hours at the table, going back and forth to the big coffee pot on the stove; discussing the new prospects; trying to see our way; deeply affected by the melancholy of the season, the uncertainty of our lives, and the imminent change and parting.

There is a feeling of black iron in this cold.

Chapter 33

It's much warmer again.

How utterly quiet it is. How gentle and lovely and calm . . . just standing on the terrace, soaking it all up. . . . Thought I heard the sound of a saw up by the tool house and wondered where Michael was and what he was doing.

People ask me if I am not lonely at the ranch when Michael and I are alone? What do I do with myself? What fills the days for both of us?

And I wonder myself what I will remember of the life here when we have gone on to other adventures—and this adventure is indistinct in the past, like a ship with outlines that become misty and vague just before it slides over the horizon—

I will remember the little things—

I wandered up to the tool house and found him working there with boards, saws, tools. I sat down on the sawhorse and he greeted me happily.

"These two-by-fours, you see, I got them from the snow fence, and if I make these notches in them I can fit them into these other pieces for a cattle guard—horse guard, rather—cattle guard is one thing, horse guard another—"

I continued to sit, sometimes listening, sometimes just hearing the sound of his voice, smiling, letting my thoughts wander.

He is ambling along like that to keep me here.

When I got down and started away he said, "Don't go."

So I got on the sawhorse again.

After a while I got down again.

"Stick around. What's your hurry?"

262

"Well, I thought I'd take the dogs and go for a walk. I've been writing all day."

"What at?"

"Stories. I thought I'd finish up one or two and take them to Hollywood with me. I might sell something."

"You might at that."

"So I want a little exercise. I was going to the pool to see how much water there is in it."

"Well, you do that. When you come back I'll have finished here. And we can drive over to Rube's and see if he's through with my plow. On the way back we can circle around to Granite Canyon and pick up the mail. Then I'll have a glass of sherry with you on the terrace before you have to milk—"

Any one of a dozen little workaday things to do together. And with that small engagement to look forward to, we separate for an hour and are content.

And the last thing at night when he is ready for bed he comes into my room for a pipe, and sits down and we chat.

The still night folds us around. We listen to the lonely sounds that come from far off on the plains. The bark of a coyote, the moaning of the bull, the cry of a night bird—

And now I am remembering that text, *Try me now and see if I will not pour you a blessing,* for we circled around by Granite Canyon and picked up the mail and there was not only one but two pieces of good news. The letter from Betty at last. And of course we can have the house (the delay was nothing, just some visits and a session at Elizabeth Arden's rejuvenation camp— evidently Betty's getting ready for her trip to Europe) and also the big letter from Vernon Spencer with a complete report on *Svenska*. He thinks it is a masterpiece.

I did not tell Michael this. I want to let him hear it first and express his own opinion freely.

Sometimes I think I'm very silly to invite everyone's critical opinions. I just make myself into a punching bag. But I can't help it.

Michael has a real musical sense, but it baffles me. I mean, if

263

he understands as much as he does, and loves it as much, why cannot he understand more?

For instance, in later discussion about the teaching pieces that Schirmer bought, he complained again that my music starts but never goes on "up." And instanced Wagner's music, and Beethoven's. They go *up*.

"But Michael, for heaven's sake! You talk of composers like that, and great operas and symphonies! How can I go *up* in a little teaching piece? Little bits of children's things?"

"It doesn't matter what you're doing. It should go *up*. Take a bugler now, he's got just five notes. But God! What he can do with those five notes!"

He got excited and his eyes flashed. "Ti-dye, ti-dye—ti-ti-tu-dye!—ti-dye, ti-dye." Singing the bugle notes in his high, sweet, light tenor (always a surprise to me, that voice), he increased the pace until I began to fidget.

He created an extraordinary surge of musical excitement there, as he stood by the fireplace, one arm propped on the mantel, pipe in hand, and sang the bugle calls.

"Why, it was so disturbing, you'd have to call the men off—make them stop it." (He was back in the war, I saw.)

"Now I, just because I don't know a damn thing about music, had to create a drum, fife and bugle corps. We just made up the pieces."

He began to sing again. I listened closely. All the technical tricks of increasing excitement, forcing the pace, which Wagner uses in many passages, were here in these little bugle calls that he had invented; and as I listened, and in imagination added the drum and fife, it made my hair stir on my head.

"Why the drummer would get so excited, he smashed his drum. And the Colonel made me stop it— For God's sake, don't play those things, especially in review—so I had to invent something quieter."

"For instance?"

"Well, something like *this* would be perfectly safe for them to parade to. Ti-dye, dye, dye—ti-dye, dye, dye—

He finished a charming bugle invention, much quieter.

All this interested me so much I forgot my music and enjoyed his reminiscences. Also it occurred to me that piano arrangements of his drum, fife, and bugle inventions, under some such title as *War Reminiscences,* might go very well. Boys might like to play them.

The session on *Svenska* (this morning) had a bad beginning.

We had just finished breakfast, and he said, ". . . when you woke me up this morning."

"Why, Michael! I never!"

"Oh, yes, you did! You were singing while you were doing your face!"

"But that didn't need to wake you up."

"But you meant it to. You were singing, *I'm doing my little fazoo. Time to wake up! Time to wake up!* I heard it before my eyes were open. And when you came down, you played it, and it's gone into that piece you've been working on—"

"Oh, Michael, it's part of *Svenska*! Tell me—did you like it?"

"Well, it's got something. It starts. It wants to go, but it doesn't go. Just gets very complicated and doesn't go anywhere."

"Michael, will you listen to the whole thing? I want to play it to you."

He threw himself on the sofa.

When I finished, he burst out laughing.

"It's funny," he gasped.

He laughed harder, then harder. He became slightly hysterical. (Like the Schirmer pieces!) He couldn't stop.

"It's *most* amusing!" He stood up and clutched his ribs.

"Do you mean—" I hesitated. "That is—are you laughing *at* it or with it?" It had occurred to me that with those girls dancing in it and all the screams and the ballooning skirts, it really *is* funny—and ought to be—

"It's just funny," he said, quieting down. *"Most complicated.* You begin it simply, then before you finish you've got everything but the kitchen stove in it! The whole orchestra!"

This cheered me somewhat. After all, I had wanted the full orchestra and struggled to get it—a wide diversity of tone. Spencer taught me that. He would say, playing something over, Listen to the orchestra now— Here's the whine of the brass, the grunt of the bass strings—

"It is quite difficult," I said hesitantly.

This sent him into fresh hysterics, for of course there is nothing funnier than a person's finally succeeding in doing—with horrible pain and struggles—something that it is silly to do at all.

But I would not give up. To avoid all "complications," would that not be to avoid all "development"?

I asked him, "Do you remember those gypsy dances we heard over the radio last night—by a famous composer and of course fully orchestrated? Do you think *those* were complicated?"

"Certainly. Just like your pieces."

That cheered me. He went into his study to address some letters, and, relieved of his presence, I played the piece again and played it much better. He realized that I was upset, for he called out to me, "It's really very good. Intellectual, and all that. You know your stuff all right."

"Do you want to know what Sheer Genius said about it? I'll read you his letter."

Michael came back from his study, licking the envelopes of his letters. I stood up and took Spencer's letter.

"You tell me what he said," said Michael, pausing by the piano.

I examined the pages. "Well, here he says it is 'stunning' and here *'transparent'*—"

"What does he mean by that?"

"That there's not one note in it that is not necessary—and says he cannot make a single correction in it—and that it's a swell job of development—"

"And what's that mean?"

"Well—*Thematic Development*—that's what I've been working at. You take a theme and develop it—"

"And turn it inside out and upside down and all that?"

"Well, more or less—"

"That's just what's wrong with most of the music you hear—it starts out to be nice, and then just gets complicated—"

"And he says it's quite good enough for a virtuoso like Percy

266

Grainger to play as an encore—as good as some of his own arrangements—"

"When are you going to town?"

I laid down the letter. "Right away. I'm going to the tailor's to have a fitting on my suit—"

"Don't forget to take these to mail, will you?" He laid his letters on the piano, gave me a quick kiss, "And don't hurry back. I'll bring the cows in and have them waiting for you. If you milk at five it'll be plenty of time."

Driving along on the Lincoln Highway I conned over the other complimentary things Spencer had said in his letter. That if I had only studied in my youth I would have been a truly great composer.

He never ceases to bewail what he considers this neglect of my talent and blames my parents. The truth is, it was I myself who never took myself seriously. Even though I was "the musical one," this seemed to me merely a family grading; it did not occur to me that, measured with real musicians, I had anything of big caliber.

Have I? I am beginning to think so. Good ear, good musical brain, good sense of rhythm—all these of course I had. But they are fairly ordinary endowments. It is *Shinar* that is rare. If I could have been great, it is because I found a way into Shinar.

I was a little late getting back. I had hunted all over town to find some tart greenings. I learned how to make an apple pie from Hilda last summer and Michael is always asking for one.

Being late would not matter, I thought, as I turned in the ranch road. I could slip out of my dress and into my blue jeans in a jiffy and do the milking while Michael started the fire for supper in the kitchen.

As I rounded the hill and saw the ranch I was surprised to notice that the two cows were still in the pasture. Aha! Mr. Michael was remiss this time—he had promised to have them ready for me in the barn—

Then, closer to the house, I saw Jinx saddled and bridled, riderless, standing quietly on the Green.

Something felt wrong.

267

As I drove in and parked the car Jinx looked at me appealingly.

There was no sign of Michael.

The dogs were leaping about my feet.

I ran to the front of the house and called. There was no answer. How could he be far away when Jinx was there still saddled? I called again and again.

The dogs, at my feet, looked about and listened too.

I got in a panic—struggled with it; told myself how many times I have felt just such anxiety, and in the end there was some simple explanation.

But Jinx was *loose*! Michael never turns a horse loose with saddle and bridle on.

If he had been thrown and hurt, where was he? He could not have vanished, nor would Jinx have left him. Jinx would have stood right there beside him.

Perhaps someone had come. Perhaps a man to buy horses; and Michael had dismounted from Jinx and tied him up, and had driven off with the man in his car; and then Jinx had got loose.

This gave me some small comfort, although I knew perfectly well that when Michael ties a horse up, he doesn't get loose.

Anyway, my job was to get the cows milked, for if I didn't they would wander away again.

So, before I went into the house to change my clothes, I went to the barn, put the cows into their stanchions, measured out their feed.

Then I went back to the house. As I entered and closed the door behind me, I saw Michael lying unconscious on the floor.

I ran to him. Face, hair, shirt were drenched as if water had been thrown on him. His face was drawn and gray.

A small strap was fastened to his right wrist, and he was lying in a peculiar twisted position with the toe of his left boot in the loop of the strap. Impossible, inexplicable situation. It looked as though someone had attacked him, attempted to tie him up—

I straightened him out and hauled him about, and got his head and shoulders on my lap, in my arms, and cried to him,

268

"Oh, Michael! Michael! what has happened to you? Michael!"

After a good deal of this his eyes opened. At last I got him up on the couch and a good three fingers of whiskey down him.

He began to look more natural and, presently, to sound natural, too. "The damnedest thing," he said, and soon was able to tell me the tale.

He had saddled Jinx to ride out to the brood mares.

Down in the practice field Jinx had put his foot in a gopher hole and gone down.

Michael is expert at falling. Often I have seen him drop his reins, bow his head, and roll down the horse's neck in a ball, landing like a tumbler after a somersault.

Instinctively he did this today, but as he rolled, his right hand caught in the reins, and the arm was drawn back and up and finally completely out of the shoulder socket.

He hit the ground, tried to stagger to his feet, to straighten up, feeling that his whole body was being torn apart, and fainted away.

Jinx stood over him grieving.

Consciousness of terrible pain came back to him and he opened his eyes, saw his right shoulder like a big cabbage beside his cheek, and understood what had happened.

He remembered that Rube had come over that afternoon to do some work in our tool shop. He must get to his feet, get to the shop, get Rube to help him.

It would have been ordinarily a walk of seven minutes. He said he scrambled along like a spider, pulled to the earth. The sky reeled.

Every minute he had to fight to hold on to his consciousness. Jinx followed.

Arrived at the shop, he found it empty. Rube had finished his work and gone home. Michael was all alone on the ranch.

He went into the house knowing that somehow he must get his shoulder back into joint.

The engineer in him figured it out, and in the end he reset his shoulder with as much accuracy as anyone could have done.

Seeing his skis, where they stood in the corner of the living room, he noticed the strap hanging in the center; removed it, using his left hand, and strapped it around his right wrist, leaving a six-inch loop hanging down.

Then, standing on his right foot, he inserted his left toe into that loop of leather, gathered all he had of will and strength, thrust his left leg out violently, heard a report like a pistol, and again passed out.

When I found him, though he was unconscious and drenched with sweat, the shoulder was in place, and he was recovering.

"Lucky for you," said the doctor, when we had driven in, "that you got it back so quickly. It's in perfect position. If these dislocations remain for days, or even hours, they become so rigid and swollen it's most difficult to get them properly set."

It will leave no permanent injury, and soreness only for a short time.

But I can't get my balance again. Michael is very blithe, with rather triumphant smiles and bright eyes.

But I feel as if I am standing in a bog—quicksand all around me. How do we ever dare to have all these boys in the summer— put them on these wild broncs! How do we ever dare to do anything?

I remember talking about this with Eugenie one day—the dangers all around—and she said, quietly, "Yes—happiness hangs by a hair—"

270

Chapter 34

I can't work, can't do a thing. I plan to make some changes in *Joy in the Morning,* but when I sit at the piano and try to get anywhere it's like pushing a wheelbarrow with a heavy load.

I can't stand this place. Can't stand the loneliness; can't stand the intensity of the life here. To live, day after day, with solitude and mountain peaks, and rainbows and wild rides, and music and death—it's too much . . .

All the town, all the county, is grieving today over young Donnie Crane's death—that fine young boy, handsome, smart and well set up—such fine parents—

I know them both. His father, dairyman north of Cheyenne—how many times I have sat with him on the steps of his barn, arguing about cow feeds, milk production, blood lines of dairy stock. His bull "Pride," my bull "Roamer."

And Donnie's mother from an old Vermont family—she and I, both of us from New England, stood on her porch talking. I simply couldn't believe it when she told me of waiting there at the door of her house near Frontier Park, ringing the bell to bring Donnie back from where he was working in the large garage a hundred yards away, calling him to dinner—and that she had a batch of cookies fresh made for him, and how she wondered why he didn't come, and how she stood there noticing by the smell on the breeze that someone was roasting meat for dinner—she smelled it—

That was Donnie. . . .

He was lying on the floor of the garage with the electric light clasped tight in his arms, his body curled around it, convulsed and fused to it by the current that had electrocuted him when he had stepped into the puddle of water on the floor and seized hold of the drop light . . .

Well—which is worse? Disaster to the child or parent? Last winter, in that terrible blizzard early in January when little Dorothy Melvin was lost, everyone—the family, squads of men out from Cheyenne and all the neighbors—hunted her for three days and nights, beating their way through a howling hurricane of snow and ice, returning to the house now and then to ask if anyone had news, to get a hot drink, to thaw frozen fingers and toes—

They found the child when the blizzard ended and the sun came out. Found her asleep in a barn. She had been napping there when the storm began, and hadn't dared go out. Her face was tear-stained. Every time she woke up she saw it was still snowing, and she would cry, and fall asleep again. She was awful hungry, she said . . .

They carried her home, and the mother went slowly up to her own room, went to bed; to rest, she said.

But it was to die.

She never moved again.

Families come here to have a ranch and build a life and make a living and raise their children—the women hoping to get running water and live "modrun," the men hoping to send their sons to college—and they all toil from dawn to dark, and year by year the inventories run down, equipment rusts and wears out, buildings begin to lean, and suddenly when they want to renew a loan at the bank, they discover that they are bankrupt. Then the heartbreaking auction. And then what? Perhaps the whole family, as well as all of the household goods and a few animals, is packed into one ramshackle old truck or car and takes off for greener fields. Maybe in California . . .

(Waste! What waste!)

I don't intend to let myself be like this.

I have sewing to do. Usually in this little breathing spell in the fall I do the accumulated sewing of the year. New curtains for the house. Underclothes, blouses, whatever I need for my-

272

self. I have three white silk riding shirts to make for myself. They are all cut out . . . at times one must simply force oneself to keep busy . . .

The wind is rising again—wind . . . wind . . . wind . . .

If I could get into *Shinar*. Escape from this! I must escape. And I play the E flat and B flat of *Svenska*—play it over and over. But it is like the man in the Arabian Nights who wants to make the rock open to him but has forgotten the word, "Open sesame!" He knocks and pounds and shouts, but the rock won't open.

Neither does *Svenska* open to me.

My head is simply splitting . . . it's long, now, since I've had the terrible migraine that I used to have so often.

It surprises me when I remember how much I was sick as a child, for nowadays, as a rule, I have endless health and energy.

Is this my guru and the "mantras" he taught me? . . . *all is well* . . . words never to be forgotten, to be repeated constantly all through life? (I notice these words appear quite often in this diary.)

I was sick in bed once, aged about eight, for one whole long winter. I remember Grandma May, sitting beside me, smiling down at me, and how her beautiful face comforted me. And when I would fret and whimper, her soft, long-fingered hands would reach under the bedclothes and gently rub my swollen and aching knees, first one and then the other, and up and down my legs, which were stained dark with itching burning iodine.

Every afternoon she would go out for a walk with the Polish girl who had come from abroad to be her companion, and she would come back with a new toy for me. I would play with it a little while, then it would go under the bed with all the others. Under the bed was stuffed with toys.

Better than toys was the large music box, which, when I sat up, I would put across my knees, then lay my head on sideways, shutting my eyes.

Elma tells me she remembers me thus as a child. Sick in bed,

273

a bandage around my head or around my throat, the music box on my knees, my head down upon it.

When I was up and around again I was carefully watched. Were there dark circles around my eyes? A white ring around my mouth?

When the family furniture and heirlooms were distributed, I chose the small walnut bed-table that bridged my knees and stood sturdily on four short legs on the bed, and carried as well as trays from the kitchen, my fairy books, paintboxes, blocks and cut-out books—the daily companions of a sick child.

Those underground tides have pulled me so far down I can smell the refuse of life—like sulfur. Brimstone, I suppose—I've smelled that before and I've read of it in novels and religious writings, so I know it's something that really comes to people. It makes it hard to breathe. Whatever my eyes fall upon is horrible and frightening; all sounds are so sad they cannot be borne . . . it makes me want to run away screaming.

I sit beside the brown pools of the stream, clasp my hands about my knees, watch the trout darting here and there in the clear water and talk aloud in desperation.

The dogs play about me, circling, following scents, coming to rest beside me.

Animals help, when it's like this. They are really healing. And their innocence and mindlessness is, somehow, a support. I keep Rachel close to me.

And the cats—Michael has given away all Missy's kittens except one. I begged to keep the one with long gray hair and blue eyes. Michael said he's the worst cry-baby of all and has an ear-splitting shriek, like a chicken, but we kept him.

I've named him Poco, and put a square of folded blanket in the corner of the kitchen near the stove for him. He took possession of it immediately.

I went up to the stable, into Pom's stall and stood beside her, leaning my head against her, my arms stretched over her back . . . *all is well* . . . it's awfully cold . . . or I'd go for a ride . . .

I went for a ride anyway.

We went up there beyond the saddleback and galloped for miles. Maybe this will be the last ride, for when it's snow-covered I don't like it. We ran into the brood mares, and then, beyond them, the yearlings.

I drew rein on that high place where Pom and I have so often stood. I remembered some of the rides last summer when I could see so far. Sometimes I would see half a dozen storms, one just coming, then turning tail and running away, then another riding up on the horizon from an opposite direction, about to collide, then sliding past each other, lightning forking in several places far removed from each other. But today no storms. The air is not clear. No color, no light, just that gray leaden look that usually means weather is brewing.

So awfully cold—Pom didn't want to stand . . . tears streaming down my face, just streaming like Spencer's . . . she kept stamping and tossing her head pulling in one direction then the other . . . we galloped all the way home. Her breath was like steam when I unsaddled her in the stable.

There is a technique for pulling oneself out of the undertow.

Yes, *words* (one repeats the healing mantras), thoughts (one seeks the small pockets of treasure, the singing finger bowl, the edelweiss), prayer (one prays the prayer of desperation which never fails of an answer, *God help me*). And there are things *to do*. They seem like empty motions, performed without heart, but one makes oneself go through those motions.

The three silk riding shirts.

Some time ago we promised the Benzigers that we would go over and see them when our camp was over. We must do that.

I must do some music. I am sick of all I was working at last summer, so I will do those three songs that I sketched last winter: *Long Ago and Far Away, Oh, Lovely Star!* and *The Big Hill*. These will be for the musical, *The Catch Colt*.

And now I'm sick in bed. I might have known. You can't get as sick in soul as I have been without the body going under too. So strange to be feeling like this—so feverish; coughing. But almost a relief. . . . Michael had to get Rube to come over to milk. . . . Michael cooks and fixes trays and brings them to me —they sit on that little walnut table that bridges my knees—a child again . . . *where is the music box?*

And suddenly it's over, and I can breathe again and look around and see that everything is all right and wonder whatever was the matter.

Chapter 35

My green suit is finished.

I tried it on for Michael last night and he likes it very much.

It converts from just a lightweight coat and skirt for cool weather into an outfit for all but the coldest winter days by a rolled mink collar (which goes on with invisible snappers) and a green cashmere sweater underneath. There will be a mink cap, too, though this isn't ready yet. For the very coldest weather, take off the mink collar and wear the beaver jacket over the suit.

The three songs are done. They went very easily.

When I write a song, first I know the mood and emotion of it; feel it, merge with it; then a rhythm grows out of it and I begin to beat the time and rhythm, play it with single bass notes on the piano. Then I think of the character (in the poem or book) who is singing it, and they, of themselves, begin to fling out words and ejaculations. I encourage that, because out of their feeling and broken words will come the whole lyric. But no rhymes yet—I don't bother with that at all. Just the stream of thought. Then comes the melody, and I begin to separate the stream of thought into verse. This all goes very fast. I scribble notes of music on a staff—scribble verses of the lyric on a big yellow pad. The rhymes happen of themselves. It is very seldom that I have to work over that at all. I don't consider them of much importance. In a few hours the whole thing is done. Then I polish, make the complete piano accompaniment.

We went to the Benzigers and I enjoyed every minute of the visit. They have a big beef-raising outfit on the border of Colorado a hundred miles from here.

They are a family very much like ourselves. They have lived

everywhere, have had many different chapters in their lives, adventures in Europe and also Korea as well as this country; and now this big cattle ranch. They are wondering if it is fair to their young daughters and sons to have them grow up here. Who will they marry? And their finances are always precarious—like ours.

"How are you really feeling, Martha?" I asked when we had a few moments alone together (it is a continual jamboree in that house).

She shrugged her shoulders and showed me the red rash on her arms, her neck and hands and said, laughing, "Nothing's the matter with me that a million dollars wouldn't cure."

But they are all worried about young Phil—such a handsome fellow. He contracted that strange fungus growth from the cattle —lump jaw.

Can it be cured? They don't know.

I would have been glad to stay several days at the Benzigers', but we had to get back for the milking.

Now the mink cap is ready.

The fur for this came from mink caught in Lone Tree Creek.

We have lots of fur-bearing animals on this ranch—mink and otter and muskrat and ermine and fox and coyote. We have seen, up on saddleback, a pair of black foxes—real silver-tips. Now and then when the ground is white, one sees the animals that have dark pelts; the rabbits and ermine turn white and are invisible.

Michael and I continue, after breakfast, to give our attention to the necessary letters, lists, plans. The portable sits on the kitchen table and Missy is on the cushion in my rocking chair keeping her eye on Poco.

He is trying to take in this new world and sits squatted, tiny head back and turning slowly, peering out of soft blue eyes that look as if they can't quite see. Now and then he waddles out onto the floor, collapsing every so often, then heads back for the blanket. He knows it is home, curls up in the corner with his back against the wall and lies quiet for hours, sometimes with his cheek pillowed on his paw. It looks as though he were sucking his thumb.

He knows me already—my hand, at least—and the other day when I kneeled down in front of him and waggled a finger, sure enough, up came two little paws batting at it, and then he rolled over for tickling.

A clear, zinging winter day . . .
Michael came boisterously in.
"We're going riding! Change your clothes! I want to show you a glorious sight!"

I ran to change while he saddled Pom and Juanita. Beautiful little Eitel, of course, came along, bucking, leaping like a trout in the air, doing quaint dance steps, bouncing sideways—

All these antics are natural gaits for horses. Going straight forward is the unnatural thing. They have to be trained for that.

One has never really seen a horse in action if one has seen him only toeing the line.

The glorious sight was the stunning fresh fall of snow on the mountains—Snowy Range, Neversummer Range. The long undulating rampart, the soaring peaks, and the vast hoods of clouds they had drawn down over their heads. Above those, the vivid, deep blue.

We pulled up our horses and sat silent. Within the joy of it was that strange ache that too much beauty brings. Almost despair.

We do errands in town . . . we wait for letters . . . Michael arranges the horses in the proper pastures for winter . . . Missy washes her baby.

Poco hates it. When she begins, there is a resumption of the ear-splitting shrieks—like a small boy having his ears washed. He tries to wiggle away; she clinches him around the neck and licks him unmercifully. Yesterday he hissed at her. She smacked him, he smacked back; she bit him, he bit back. And now, whenever he sees her red tongue out, he slaps it.

Missy, discouraged, and deciding that we spoil him, took him out to the rocks and shrubs to train him to hunt, and toughen him; but we missed him and went out looking for him and brought him back.

Michael gave him a box to live in with side walls about four

279

inches high. Poco spent ten minutes practicing, climbing in and out. He can barely get his round furry little body over the edge. Michael has hung a spool on a long string over it. Poco lies on his back, in the box, smacks the spool with a forepaw, then gives it a kick with a hind leg.

He suddenly falls asleep, spread-eagled on the disheveled blanket, the spool hanging against him, a saucer of milk nearby, for all the world like a human infant who, having been awake and playing since six o'clock, falls asleep in his unmade bed before his bath, clutching a toy in one hand and his milk bottle in the other.

Poco is very brave when he's in his box, not quite so brave out on the kitchen floor; apt to turn and flee when he suddenly meets the leg of the kitchen table. Back to the box, a scramble over the edge . . . safe inside again.

Yesterday he had one frightful moment when the dogs appeared.

Missy was down cellar, catching a mouse, Poco alone near the stove. Suddenly there were the two monsters, Bunny and Rachel, coming in with Michael.

I couldn't believe my eyes. Poco attacked. Made himself into an extraordinary shape, stiffened on four legs thrust out at all angles, ears flattened back, every hair up; and he opened his mouth wide, emitting ferocious hisses.

Rachel grinned, wagged her tail, stood over him admiringly, so Poco bounced closer to her sideways, with loud growls.

At this, Missy came rushing up. I expected fireworks. But with one glance she took in the situation, sat down lazily beside the box, and began washing herself. This had its effect. Poco sat down beside her, but continued to rumble.

Our letters have come, and we drove to town yesterday and bought my ticket and reservation for Los Angeles. Michael will not be leaving until after Thanksgiving, which he will spend with the Benzigers.

Only a week left. It is so cold we have to empty the radiator of the car every night. It stands on the gentle slope behind the house, just this side of the boys' cabins.

Before starting it, Michael pours water in the radiator. Then when the brake is released and the car moves down the incline, the engine catches. (Almost always . . .)

Winter makes everything more difficult.

The sun was shining yesterday when we began lunch.

So much to talk about these last days—Mr. Spencer and the lessons I will have with him, and whether I'll sell any stories in Hollywood (I'll certainly try), and of course the school and what boys we will have; there are a few tentative enrollees already.

"It's clouding over," Michael said, glancing out.

The light had gone out of the kitchen.

It grew darker. Michael looked again. "A fog," he said. "Coming from the east as usual. I hope this won't be bad."

Most of our bad storms come from the east and begin with a cold drifting fog.

I got up to put the things away in the pantry and this took me to the back of the house; and here too, from the window, I saw the fog blowing past.

It was in tatters and shreds. There was something queer about it. I stood looking.

I said, "The fog's awfully thick, Michael. It's funny looking. It looks like smoke."

And then I knew. Instantly knew it all. I ran back into the kitchen. "It *is* smoke, Michael. The barn!"

He shot out of the door, I, after him. We stood looking.

It was burning brightly all over. There was a wall of clear, bright orange flame all around it.

Why had we not heard the crackling? Here, it was loud—and now above the roar and crackling came the screams of horses—

"Fanny and Captain!" cried Michael and rushed for the barn. The work team was inside; outside, in the corral, Juanita, Eitel and Pom.

I ran after Michael, determined that not for all the horses in the world would I let him enter that inferno of burning hay.

The front wall was falling as we got there. The whole thing

281

must practically have exploded, as he always said it would. It was burning as if it had been soaked in gasoline.

He tore around the end of the shed into the corral, to see if perhaps the side wall of the barn was not yet aflame, but it was a sheet of fire. The door into the barn was in the middle of that wall but could not even be seen.

Juanita was in terror—prancing, rearing, facing the barn as if about to rush in.

Inside, Captain and Fanny were still screaming.

Michael ran at the wall where he knew the door was. I got him by the back of the belt and held on. "You're not going in!"

"Let go of me!"

"If you go, I'll follow you in—"

He tried to disengage me. "Let go!"

I said, "Look at Juanita!" She was advancing toward the barn.

Michael turned to her. We worked to quiet them. Michael stood between them and the barn, his arms out, talking quietly to them, while I flanked them and opened the gate into the next corral, then from that, drove them into the pasture and shut the gates so they could not return.

When we came back, all the walls of the barn were falling and, with a deepening roar as the fire ate into the hay, the flames all joined in a great tower that rose fifty feet in the air. Captain and Fanny screamed no more.

"Where can we get help?" I yelled.

"Take the car and go for the section gang on the railroad," Michael roared.

"There's no water in the radiator."

"I'll fill it." He ran to the kitchen.

"The hay's gone anyway," I said, running beside him.

"There's still the stack at the end of the shed—the fire's just beginning to creep along the shed—if I can save that I'll have something to feed the stock all winter."

The tower of flame rose higher, and suddenly there came a wind from the east and blew the tower down, as one blows down the flame of a candle, and laid it on the roof of the house.

And I thought of my piano. Waves of weak trembling shook me. I had no hope. Everything was doomed.

Michael had seen it too. He came running now with a bucket of water in each hand, threw the water up on the roof of the house. It steamed; the tower of flame straightened up. It was safe for a moment.

He ran for more water.

"Hold these buckets while I get up on the roof of the cow shed."

I passed the buckets up to him, and he drenched the roof of the shed, just in front of the advancing flames.

"Get me the ax."

I ran to the tool shed, brought the ax, and he started chopping a chasm in the roof of the shed. "If I can make a break here, I may save that stack of hay."

He had one eye on the house. The tower of flame lay down and licked it again, straightened up, bent down and licked again.

One or two shingle edges curled, burst into thin lines of orange flame.

Michael leaped down from the shed, ran for more buckets of water and threw them on the roof of the house and put out the flames.

The house, the little square stack of loose hay—these might perhaps be saved.

"Go for the section gang," he shouted at me, and I ran to the car. I had been waiting for him to put water in the radiator. It was in. When had he done it? I had not seen him.

I got into the driver's seat and prepared to release the brake. Would it start? It doesn't always. Oh, would it? Quite often I muff it.

The car moved, gathered a little speed; I let in the clutch; the engine sputtered, I gave it gas; it roared.

It is a mile and a half to the railroad tracks. I had only to cry, "Fire!" and the men dropped their tools and came running. I turned the car while they climbed in and onto the running boards.

They fought the fire for an hour. Michael had alternated pouring water on the roof of the house and chopping at the cow shed, but both were still in danger.

The very violence and intensity of the fire shortened its dura-

283

tion. Soon the fury was past. The barn was a hill of red-hot coals; half of the cow shed stood, and, at its far end, the little square tower of hay, intact.

It took the rest of the day, with the whole gang working, to extinguish the last of the flames.

When the milch cows came wandering home at milking time, they stood bewildered, looking at the smoking ruin, picked their way in and out, at last found a pile of wet grain where the bins had burned, and stood licking at it.

Another day.

Michael has fixed up a little lean-to in the corral, near the shed, where I can milk the cows.

It is not quite milking time yet, but the sun will set soon. I stand on the terrace, leaning against the wall of the house. I look at the dark pines on the cliff opposite, and the sharp slanting line their tops make against the sky.

I walk down on to the Green and turn and look to see what the sunset will be. It will be gorgeous. There was a line of gold outlining a billowing bank of cloud low over the horizon. Above it, and all over the western sky, were tatters of transparent cloud, frivolous, delicious. As I watched they began to turn pink.

I smelled snow.

I smelled ashes.

I smelled cooked meat.

On all the hedgerows were the scarlet hips of the winter-stripped wild rose bushes.

There's nothing restrained about nature. The sky is ablaze now. Bands of red-gold alternate with celestial blue, all festooned with curling wisps and puffs of tinted cloud. A beautiful day tomorrow, this promises; and day after tomorrow I leave.

Michael does not sleep. He does not speak. His face is heart-breaking. He thinks of Captain and Fanny. He thinks of the hay.

On the day of my departure we will go to town early enough for him to have a fitting of his suit at the tailor's. Then he will

284

put me on the train, have his dinner in town, and go to a show or to the Post.

George came out by bus today. Michael picked him up at Granite Canyon.

In a railroad town, all trains are known by number.

Number Twenty-seven, westward bound, leaves town at six-fifteen in the evening. An extra locomotive is coupled on to help pull it up the last stretch of "the big hill." That is the train I will take—will have my dinner on it . . . they usually have rainbow trout on the menu in these parts . . .

I've watched this very train pass scores of times when I've been out walking or riding on Section Eight.

It is fun to look into the lighted windows, see the passengers having dinner, sitting cosily vis-à-vis, with white-uniformed waiters serving. It is a scene taken out of the core of civilized life.

Sometimes they glance out, and if it is not too dark, they might see me standing there with the dogs; or perhaps on horseback; and they stare. I stare too, and watch until the rows of square bright windows have crawled past and the track is empty.

But now it is I myself sitting in that Pullman dining car, with the menu in my hand, waiting to order; and I am looking out the window as we pass the Goose Bar Ranch. I am wearing a pretty green suit.

I would hardly be surprised to see a woman on horseback there watching the train, two dogs squatted beside her, tongues hanging out; but the land is empty. It looks dreary and lifeless. There are no lights, no sign of life.

But it is not empty and lifeless.

I know old George is ensconced in the bunkhouse, tucked in for the winter. If he has not yet put Bunny and Rachel into the tool house, they are sitting on the hill watching the road that winds out to the highway, waiting for Michael to come home in the car. From that point, lights of passing trains can be seen. Perhaps at this moment their eyes are held by the lights of this train.

Perhaps Poco is lying in his box, kicking his spool with a

hind leg; Blazes is up there on the saddleback with all his mares and colts around him. And Trombone— Where is Trombone? Whatever shall we do with that stallion?

The waiter is asking for my order—rainbow trout, of course—perhaps it comes out of Lone Tree Creek.

As we grind up that grade to the top of the Rocky Mountain Divide—they call it the Summit—with the two locomotives laboring, my thoughts are split in a dozen directions. I think of Pat whom I shall so soon have in my arms; I think of Spencer and the smile that will be on his face when we discuss *Svenska*. I think, too, of my Hollywood agent, to whom I shall hand the short story about the little filly. I have named it, not just *Flicka*, but *My Friend Flicka*, because of my feeling that it is so fine a thing to make a real friend of a horse.

I have another short story in mind, but have only sketched it. This one will be about Pink's little goblin colt, who is a true oddity.

I think of Michael having his dinner in Cheyenne right now with one or two of the officers from the Post.

I think of the winter school in Connecticut, which after all is not to be this year, but some other. It is quite possible. It is really probable. When it comes about it will be without any difficulty at all.

Slowing up now, dropping that extra locomotive. . . . Over the big hill and picking up speed for the long, easy descent.